CATHEDRAL
OF THE
BLACK
MADONNA

CATHEDRAL
OF THE
BLACK
MADONNA

*The Druids and the
Mysteries of Chartres*

JEAN MARKALE

Translated by Jon Graham

Inner Traditions
Rochester, Vermont

Inner Traditions
One Park Street
Rochester, Vermont 05767
www.InnerTraditions.com

Originally published in French under the title *Chartres et l'énigme des Druides* by
Éditions Pygmalion/Gérard Watelet, Paris
First U.S. edition published by Inner Traditions in 2004

Library of Congress Cataloging-in-Publication Data
Markale, Jean.
  [Chartres et l'énigme des Druides. English]
  Cathedral of the Black Madonna : the Druids and the mysteries of Chartres /
Jean Markale ; translated by Jon Graham.— 1st U.S. ed.
      p. cm.
  Includes bibliographical references and index.
  ISBN 1-59477-020-4 (pbk.)
  1. Mary, Blessed Virgin, Saint—Devotion to—France. 2. Black Virgins. 3.
Christianity and other religions—Druidism. 4. Cathédrale de Chartres. I. Title.
  BT652.F7M37 2004
  282'.445124—dc22
                                                            2004018268

Printed and bound in the United States at Lake Book Manufacturing, Inc.

10 9 8 7 6 5 4 3 2 1

Text design and layout by Priscilla Baker
This book was typeset in Sabon, with Trajan as a display typeface

CONTENTS

PART 1

THE SITES

1

THE ENTRANCE TO THE LABYRINTH

All of us have our own view of things, especially when we first lay eyes upon something previously unknown to us. This is especially true for those famous old monuments whose legacies of the dim past are still endowed with an evocatively luminous power. The cathedral at Chartres is such a monument.

For me, odd as it sounds, the cathedral is associated with railroad trains. My generation first became acquainted with the world thanks to the train, which fueled many fantasies: Didn't it show me the entrance to a labyrinth in which I dreamed of losing myself, beyond all hope of ever finding my way out?

"Look! That's Chartres Cathedral!" From our third-class compartment (we rode third class only because there was not a fourth class), amid the din of wheels switching tracks, I spied through the window that bizarre silhouette suddenly looming from a mound rising out of a wooded valley. It was a sight many had seen long before me from a road through the appalling flatness of the Beauce. Yes, that was my first sight of Chartres, from the long trains burrowing into the West in search of an almost mythical Brittany, whose ghosts were already beginning to stir in my fertile imagination.

There is another curious circumstance, terribly charged with emotion and invoking incredible images, that dates from 1936, when I was eight and a half years old. It was a fairly sad period of my life, dominated by the absence—or, I should say, the flight—of my mother, whose shadow poisoned daily life for my grandmother and me, not to mention for my father, who struggled constantly to maintain his equilibrium. I never loved my mother. Nor did she love me. When I would throw myself into her arms, acting on my feelings of affection for her, she would roughly push me away under the pretext that I was wrinkling her dress. My mother was a stranger to me; although she was my creator, she behaved to me more like a foster mother. I was a lonely, introverted child confined in a closed environment. My sole resource was to imagine another world, one to which I had no right.

Around this time, without knowing what to call it, I began engaging in metaphysical speculation. Well educated in the best Catholic principles, respectful of the clergymen I would greet in the street whether I knew them or not (in those days they were recognizable by their cassocks)—no doubt in reaction against my maternal grandfather, who cawed like a crow every time he saw a priest—I asked myself weighty questions concerning the Beyond. Paradise had been described to me as an immense region where little angels played music and everyone wore white. But this image, which had been designed to reassure me, instead filled me with terror: What would I do *for eternity* in this bizarre place? Vertigo assailed me every time I pondered the notion, not because I had doubts about the reality of an eternal paradise, but because eternity, like infinity, was intolerable to the understanding—or misunderstanding—of a sad, distraught child. In any case, I firmly believe that this vertigo shaped my later behavior and largely explains the path I have chosen to attempt to discover a certain truth.

During this September in 1936, when strange rumors were flying about a figure named Adolf Hitler, when terrible things were said to be taking place in Spain, we had just spent some peaceful days in the Perche region, Mortagne to be precise, at the home of some family friends who have always been more than friends to me and with whom I always feel at home. My grandmother, my father, and I were heading back toward Paris. We had taken a bumpy ride in a train to Condé-sur-Huisne, where we got on another, faster train that would take us to Chartres, where we would catch the train to Paris. This is where the strange circumstance occurred.

Night had fallen, and it was foggy. I could see nothing outside the window but an opaque mass all around us. The train dived into the fog toward Chartres. It was an agonizingly long ride. I suddenly imagined that the only thing existing was the track on which the train was traveling, and there was *nothing around that track*. We were on a kind of dike or bridge extending across the universe, extending across infinity. This thought prompted the same vertigo that assailed me when I heard descriptions of heaven. When would we get to Chartres? I vividly remember my certainty that we would never reach Chartres, and that our journey through the fog would continue through eternity.

These were strange sensations that are difficult to capture in words. When I found myself on the Chartres train platform, stumbling because I was still half asleep, it was hard for me to believe the world really existed. Yet I was walking on the ground. There were lights. And the signs told us we were in Chartres. This name resonated magically inside my head as the sole awareness of my own reality.

I have never forgotten how Chartres represented deliverance from an unspeakable nightmare, Chartres, a peaceful haven, an island in a motionless sea—not in the middle of the "fertile glebe" so dear to Péguy, but among François Villon's "infernal marshes"— watched over by the reassuring image of Our Lady as if in response to the desperate appeals of those who have gone astray in the ruts of time and space. This is how the old city of Chartres appeared to me that foggy September evening, although it never occurred to me to raise my eyes to the contours of an unknown cathedral in the shadows. Our Lady the Virgin often rises over a mound to point out the road to travelers, and especially to prevent them from getting mired in the swamps of suffering.

I had no idea then of what a cathedral could be. Chartres was only a stop, one leg in a much longer journey along shores, over moors, and through forests, but the sense of deliverance I experienced that evening left an indelible imprint on my character. It was one name, simply a name, followed by the image of the Madonna and Child that can be found in other churches. Yet questions arose: What was the difference between Our Lady of Chartres and Our Lady of Paris, between Our Lady of Lourdes and Our Lady of Montligeon? Are they all the same person? Why does she have so many names? I hadn't reached the point of wondering about monotheism and polytheism, but all the same, there was material to intrigue a child. After all, there are numerous incarnations of Father Christmas, but they are all the same Father Christmas. So why not "Our Lady" in a never-ending variety?

Then war moved into my world, with all its accompanying anxieties, privations, and suffering. I can still clearly recall how cold I felt in the barely heated houses, the memory of doing my homework by smoky candlelight because the electricity had been cut. I remember the pangs of hunger that gripped my stomach. Yet this was also when I roamed in the shadows of the cathedrals. The architecture of Notre-Dame in Paris fascinated me. My imagination wandered through ancient cities that I had never seen. I walked down narrow streets past strange shops, beneath canopies that sheltered me from the rain, in dead cities that held in their centers vast edifices covered with flying buttresses and grotesque sculpture, topped by aggressive spires that soared into space. And the dull drone of airplanes, sinister messengers of sneaking death, often darkened this space. The noise of the bombs drowned out the music of the angels.

In this world of hatred and violence, I took refuge in the shadow of a past that I reconstructed with the great comfort of books. I discovered medieval literature: I reveled in the company of Tristan, Lancelot of the Lake, and Perceval; I wished to have all the powers of Merlin to transform with a single gesture the unwholesome world around me into a wonderful orchard filled with beautiful young girls with tormenting eyes. My image of heaven began to borrow elements that no longer had anything in common with the host of the blessed robed in white and singing praises to the Lord in an immutable eternity. I confess that the Isle of Avalon, its trees always full of ripe fruits, where Morgana and her sisters lived in a crystal palace, pleased me more than the sad, monotonous Christian paradise that inspired so much vertigo. In fact, when evoking the Isle of Avalon—or any other marvelous island from Celtic tradition, such as Emain Ablach, Insula Pomorum, the Land of Faery, or the Promised Isle—I never experienced any vertigo. I felt I was safe from everything there, including distress, given a sense of security by the presence of these beautiful and mysterious women who offered drafts of forgetfulness to the sailors wrecked upon their shores. Our Lady made way for Morgana, a queen of the night whom one yearns to love with a love that is absolute and *eternal*. The vertigo came then not from the duration, but from the instant of the fugitive encounter with the Queen of Faery. This was my first meeting with eroticism. But it was also a kind of adherence to the doctrines of courtly or rather *fine* love: salvation by the Woman, the merger with the Divine through the intermediary of woman.

Thinking about it now, I believe there is no difference between the desire for salvation through woman and trust in Our Lady the Virgin. Marian worship developed concurrently with the theme of *fine love*; they are two sides of the same reality. But this should probably not be repeated lest it be seen as evidence of a "sick mind." I already have enough of a reputation for being an unyielding agnostic. To dare compare Mary, mother of Jesus, with just any noble woman of the Courts of Love—some hussy!—is not even a sacrilege. It demonstrates the kind of antireligious belligerence whose just reward is excommunication.

And yet . . . the last time I attended a Christmas midnight Mass, which was not so long ago, at Vannes Cathedral, I was horrified at the reading of the Gospel. The priest coolly said that Joseph had traveled to Bethlehem for the census, *with Mary, his wife, who was pregnant.* Once I returned home, I opened my Jerusalem Bible and looked up the passage in the Gospel of Luke. It was quite edifying: " *. . . with Mary, his fiancée, who was pregnant.*" Until it has been proved otherwise, I believe that the Jerusalem Bible translation is a serious and objective work that closely matches the original text. Furthermore, one of the translators of this Bible, Father Auvray, is a former professor of mine, and I have always felt the greatest esteem for his expertise, honesty, and faith. So, at the risk of appearing an impenitent agnostic, I cannot refrain from denouncing the hypocrisy and dishonesty of a certain clergy, the very same that not only claims to deliver the divine word and the essential and unshakable Truth *ex cathedra,* but also asserts that it is the only one able to do so.

I am not an agnostic. When I was twelve years old I wished to join the priesthood. I was told that Renan and Stalin were seminarians, Fouché was Oratorian, and Talleyrand was a bishop. This did not stifle my ardent desire to become a Catholic priest. My desire was certainly fueled by my familial environment. The Oratorians, remarkable intellectuals who are devoted servants of the Faith, educated me. How much I owe these Oratorians! They were not satisfied with merely instilling in me the "catechism," nor in giving me the standard "brainwashing" treatment. They inspired me to reflect deeply about life, its meaning, the finality of the Creation, and finally God. They always welcomed warmly my requests and questions, responded to my anxieties, and helped put my stormy thoughts in order. I will never forget all the good they did for me. And many of them have become my friends.

For all that, I did not become a priest. I was too tormented by the image of Morgana the Fay to tranquilly content myself with the worship rendered to a Virgin Mary stripped of all sexuality. I know full well that some priests do not share my scruples and interpret not only canon law but also the fluctuations of their own minds as best suits their needs. One of my flaws is that I am as honest with myself as I am with others. I therefore elected the profane life. This does not mean I lost all sense of the sacred, which I continued to seek through all that crossed my path—in women, of course, but also in all the medieval cathedrals with whose magnetic aura I was permeated, as well as in those modest but mysterious country chapels and disused yet still-living sanctuaries that provide an incomparable testimony to the transcendence established between the human and the divine. Is this an agnostic attitude? You cannot be as passionately interested in the quest for the Grail as I am unless you *believe* in something. But in what? I have not leaned like Galahad over the sacred vessel and been blinded by the impossible light emanating from it, but I did realize one day that God could be present in the priest's chalice as well as in the Grail, and that the Virgin presided over church liturgies, even when they were botched by priests who no longer understood them.

It is easy to be disappointed and sometimes disconcerted by the attitudes of some representatives of the Church. We can repeat to our heart's content that the Church is a human institution, but it has aspects that are totally unacceptable, such as the fires of the Inquisition and the alliances contracted with totalitarian governments. And we can only condemn the hypocrisy of clerics who for centuries have compelled the poor to bow down before the great and powerful of this world ("You will get your reward in the Beyond!"), and currently "work in the social sphere," while at the same time forgetting the spiritual message they are supposed to share and spread. It smells a little like a betrayal, even if we risk being taken for "freethinkers" by remarking on it. It shows how my faith, beyond all doctrine and protected from any dogma, can be considered heretical.

And yet my abrupt realization that there was something real in these botched liturgies came about through a rather sordid experience. At the time I was madly in love with a woman who was involved in a relationship with a priest. I found myself with her at Mass one day, where I saw her putting on quite a show of faith. I remained like marble, content merely to witness the spectacle. During Communion, when she rushed up to receive the host, I could not help but imagine a different kind of communion, along the lines of that described by Rémy de Gourmont in his strange play about Lilith and Sammaël (Satan)—a blasphemy involving "communion" in both the holy and profane senses. Nor could I refrain from sending God a challenge similar to that of Saint Patrick in making a request of the Lord: "God, if you do not grant my prayer, I swear to take neither food nor drink before my prayer is granted, and if I die, it is you who will be responsible!" Legend claims that this always worked, not only for Saint Patrick but also for every other saint of the original Celtic Christian Church, individuals who knew what they wanted, who were heroes before they became statues. My opinions on such matters are well known, and it was not by chance that I wrote a book celebrating the merits of the different forms assumed by ancient Celtic Christianity, which were among the most ardent forms of worship existing.[1]

So I challenged God in the same way as did Saint Patrick. I had to have a *sign*. I had to know. I made this silent prayer: "God, if you are truly present in the host, in the appearance of bread, you cannot accept being ingested by this sacrilegious woman who has caused a priest to commit the same sacrilege; you cannot. Or else this is all just for show." A mute prayer, but a sincere one. I awaited a response. It arrived. During the night the woman became sick and vomited everything she had taken in. This was the *sign*. Since that time I have believed in the true presence of God in the host. The purest wind the dawn has to offer can sometimes emerge from the most sickening swamp.

How many times have I passed before the cathedral of Chartres without stopping, simply looking at it, intrigued by its strange architecture that raises so many questions for me and pushes me into an imaginary world. The Middle Ages was a time of faith and magnificence as well as a time of darkness and obscurity. As an adolescent, I assiduously frequented Notre-Dame in Paris as well as Notre-Dame de Montligeon in the Perche region, where I left behind some

---

1. Jean Markale, *Le Christianisme celtique* (Paris: Imago, 1984).

of my youthful fantasies. But what could Our Lady the Virgin have meant to me during those stormy times—she who was the mother not only of God, but of all humanity? I repeated to myself the words from the Gospel of John: "Jesus said to his mother, 'Woman, this is your son.' Then to the disciple he said 'This is your mother.'"

I had been taught that Jesus had given his mother to humanity. I did not understand. Certainly my grandmother, who had lost her eldest son during the First World War, repeatedly told me she felt like the *mater dolorosa,* the Virgin on whose knees lay the body of her dead son after he had been taken down from the cross. It was a touching image: My grandmother would have tears in her eyes when she said this. She was, for all intents and purposes, a "sorrowing mother" her entire life. But could I for a minute think of my own mother as a "sorrowing mother"?

I remember one of my teachers—not a priest—who thought it made good sense to give a course on the greatness of maternity (this was the middle of the Pétain era and its motto of "Work, family, country") that would extol the merits and sacrifices of every "mama." It made me feel sick. And in any case, what could Our Lady, Mary, the virgin mother of God, mean to me? Why should the various images of the *mater dolorosa* have any effect on me? And yet there was something tormenting me, something arising out of the depths of my entrails. It was, of course, the sense that something was missing. The litanies of the Virgin came back to my memory: "Consoler of ordeals . . ." A lot of good this did me, as the saying goes. But it did not prevent the image of the Pietà from permanently embedding itself in my mind.

Many years later I realized what was then really stirring inside and troubling me so. I was in a mountain village, Saugues, in the Velay region, not far from that mysterious Our Lady of Puy that haunts me the same way as Our Lady of Chartres. It was in September—it is always September!—and I was accompanied by a former student, in truth the best student I ever had during that long-ago era of 1968, when the most common philosophical activity was throwing paving stones at the representatives of Order. Don't worry, I was among them. But it did not keep me from having lively intellectual discussions with what may have been one of the most interesting classes of students I ever had the pleasure to teach.

So I found myself in Saugues with Dominique. She had led an eventful life over the twenty years since we had last seen each other. Her blue eyes expressed suffering and despair. She seemed no longer to be a part of this world, as if the forces of shadow had already snatched her. She had brought me to a desolate and deserted pond, where she told me strange voices spoke to her from beneath the water. She told me that their hands were reaching toward her to pull her down to their sunken city. She recounted legends, ones I have told many times myself, and threw out the name of Virginia Woolf as if by chance—but which I found a provocation, as if the dull blue-green waters would bring back the image of an Ophelia forever vanished. Dominique, so young and frail yet fierce and hard, showed the indelible traces of drug use. She spoke in beseeching tones, as if a drunken boat cast back by the storm . . .

She had me accompany her into the Saugues church, where she became lost in contemplation of a Pietà, which was quite beautiful and moving, by the way. We then left the building. She had said she wanted to sit beneath the porch on the stone benches that once served just this purpose but are now regarded as solely a decorative element. She snuggled up next to me, took my hand, and fell asleep on my chest. The rising wind stirred her hair like algae in a pond: another image of Ophelia. The people who passed by stared at us accusingly. One woman gave me a particularly scorching glare; if she had been able to strike me with lightning, she would have done so. I stared insolently back at her, asking myself how long it would take for the world to become warm and understanding.

And then I suddenly realized that the two of us, at that precise moment, were a reversed Pietà. We were not the sorrowful Mother holding her dead son against her, but rather the suffering Father holding his dead daughter and looking for any means to restore her to life. I then recalled to mind Breton Calvary depictions of this same scene, in which Christ's body never extends below Mary's knees. It is as if Mary, the universal Mother, wished to reintegrate her son and restore him to new life, eternal life, with a glorious body garbed in light. Yes, this was it. This was what Dominique was asking for, and the gesture she made by taking my hand spoke volumes about her deepest motivations. A strange scene that held a strange sensation. But I was not Mary, the Virgin of virgins. I was only a man. And yet I was aware of Dominique's terrifying desire: Restore me to life! This was when I finally grasped the meaning of the Pietà. But I also realized my own powerlessness. Dominique, her head stubbornly nestled against my chest, trying to live by the rhythm of my heart, was already dead, and I could do nothing more for her, nothing.

Several days later, when Dominique and I again went our separate ways, she pulled me close and whispered: "You know, when I die, the only name on my lips will be yours." She followed this a short while later with a question that was quite simple in its depth: "Can you promise me one thing? Die with me." And several minutes later: "When the time arrives, I will come looking for you; we will both leave together and never return." Like a coward, I left her. I knew there was nothing I could do. But there was some concern about my absence, and someone had telephoned Dominique. She told the caller that she had killed me, thus setting off an entire investigative inquiry. It was actually she who had "killed" herself. She had been saved *in extremis,* but I knew that this had merely postponed the inevitable. There was nothing more I could do for her. And the image of the Virgin Mary haunted me, because Mary is the only one capable of rescuing human beings from despair.

Why are there so many representations of the Virgin holding her child? Why are there so many representations of the *mater dolorosa*? It must correspond to something deep in human consciousness. Why would there be so many sanctuaries dedicated to Our Lady unless it is because the image of the mother haunts the memories of the sons and daughters of this world? When I began taking an interest in the Middle Ages and Gothic architecture, I eagerly read everything I could put my hands on that concerned the cathedral of Chartres. I learned that it was the most beautiful cathedral in the world. I learned that the most beautiful stained-glass windows from the thirteenth century could be found there. I also learned that the sanctuary had been built on the site of a pagan temple in which a mysterious well had been discovered along with a statue depicting a *virgo paritura,* a "Virgin on the threshold of giving birth." The Druids, it was said, were responsible for erecting the statue, for they had long foreseen the mystery of the Incarnation. I now know that this tradition must be taken with all the necessary reservations, particularly its claim that the *virgo paritura* is a premonition of the Christian Mary, but I must confess that to an adolescent haunted by the Middle Ages and utterly enthralled by the Celtic origins of Western civilization, the revelation was food for thought.

Chartres became for me a vital center of all the living forces I believed—and still believe—are essential to the development of Western spirituality. Here again I do not think such a conviction has anything to do with an agnostic attitude. But I also learned that a strange labyrinth had been laid down over the flagstones in the nave of the cathedral. This labyrinth prompted wildly varying conjectures as to its meaning. Some regarded it as a simple decorative element, others felt it contained the most arcane secrets of Hermetic philosophy. For my part, I know the labyrinth to be a feature of an old Cretan story, and I wondered what such a depiction was doing in a Christian sanctuary. I sensed that it had a purpose, however, and that it might be necessary to discover what this purpose was before entering it and finding the way out again.

I strove for many years to find the entrance to the labyrinth of Chartres. Although I continued to investigate the cathedral by devouring countless books about it, I did not visit it until I turned twenty-five. When I passed my *baccalauréat* [the French equivalent of receiving a high school diploma —*Translator*], my grandmother promised to make a pilgrimage to Our Lady of Chartres. Circumstances and the fragile state of her health did not allow her to fulfill this vow. I eventually did it for her, but at a much later date. I now think that I was not yet mature enough to handle such a confrontation, which ultimately took place in several stages, as if entrance to the famous labyrinth was forbidden to me. Initiation always takes place on deceptive and intentionally tortuous paths. My path was indeed tortuous, but I took it with no knowledge of what awaited me in the heart of the labyrinth. This touches on mysteries that lend their weight to the most unconscious human desire; to make our way to the holy of holies necessarily entails a certain period of apprenticeship.

But was this an apprenticeship in life or in what is called spirituality? Contemporary society has taken a definitive stand: We must live, therefore we must take part in a system that functions—more or less well—to protect the essentials. We must "have a job," and later we can spare time to think about the soul. This is the basic principle of what is falsely known as "secularism": It is all well and good to display our religious faith and concern ourselves with religious matters, but only on condition that we do so outside normal working hours—on Sunday, for example, the day of rest.

It reminds me of what my father used to tell me when I made too much of my desire to become a writer. He would invariably reply: "That's fine, but begin by studying seriously and getting a good job. Then you can *make literature* on Sunday, to amuse yourself." A fine program! It showed his real concern to see me find "my place" in a social hierarchy whose core value is security. I vainly remonstrated with him, retorting that humanity's progress had been achieved only because hooligans, marginal types, and troublemakers had broken through the "it goes without saying" mentality. He treated me like a dreamer. In any case, I never forgave him for considering literature a Sunday distraction, just like the obligatory Sunday promenade (what a bore!), the visits to Aunt Machin, the theater matinee, or the glass of beer on the terrace of a café. And when I spoke to him about going to hear a symphony, he answered that he would prefer attending an operetta: "At least it is relaxing and keeps me from thinking."

Here is the crux of the matter: *It* keeps us from thinking. I cannot resist proposing an analogy between this attitude—which my father was far from alone in promoting and defending—concerning so-called cultural phenomena and the behavior of those described as "good Christians" because they contribute regularly to the collection plate and attend eleven o'clock Mass every Sunday before returning home to carve the roast beef or lamb. The Lord was honored accordingly as a person was able. And Sunday is the Lord's day; therefore, it is a day unlike the others. It is possible and even obligatory to think about religion that day and also to relax. But the other days of the week are reserved for more serious matters: We earn our daily bread and work until the evening; once all financially remunerated activity is over, we can devote our efforts to doing "good works" for the parish. This was the kind of life proposed to me, with a completely straight face, as a model.

Obviously it was the same model I violently rejected. For even at that time, when I was only a dreamy adolescent, I could not for a second imagine that there was a ditch—what am I saying!? a *precipice*—between the profane life on the one hand and the spiritual and cultural life on the other. I had begun realizing that in so-called primitive societies, the sacred and the profane were two faces of but one reality, and I could not understand why the society I lived in would have flouted this basic rule. I had not yet read Pascal, so I was unaware of his deliberations on "amusement," but it seems I was already thinking along the same lines. Of course, the sermons I vaguely listened to on Sunday during that famous 11:15 Mass were loaded with pieces of good advice: "Be good Christians every day of the week! Live in Christ!" But no one really listened to them, and in any case we would have had to understand what they really meant. These same sermons always extolled the merits of the blessed Holy Virgin, the model for every mother—"And this is the reason, my children, that you should love your mother!" So I just swallowed my hostility.

I now think all this was what obstructed my approach to Our Lady of Chartres. My interest in the Middle Ages and Gothic art was not merely cultural; it was part of a greater whole. It would have been impossible for me to grasp the beauty of the architecture without being aware of the worship that took place in the sanctuary—in this instance, worship of the Virgin Mary. Other elements drew my attention. I had learned that some of the stained-glass windows illustrated the *Song of Roland,* which I had studied and appreciated in tenth grade under the guidance of the remarkable teacher and writer Jean Hani, the person truly responsible for giving me a taste for deep research. I knew that some of these windows had been crafted thanks to the generous donations of Pierre Mauclerc, count of Creux and duke of Brittany, through his wife, Duchess Alix. This association was, of course, a hook to my native region and did not leave me indifferent. I also knew that the statue of the philosopher Aristotle could be seen there, lost amid all the sages of Christendom. This struck me as bizarre at the time, for I was not yet aware that Thomism was simply a revival of Aristotelianism made relevant for that era. Most important, I knew there was a mysterious crypt where the shadows of the Druids lurked. At the time I still believed these legendary figures were capable of engaging in human sacrifices on dolmens. This dark pit attracted me.

But what was the Virgin Mary's role in this cathedral? It had been erected in her honor—and to preserve, it was said, a symbolic relic that was a silk cloth given by the Byzantine emperors to Charlemagne and was, according to legend, worn by the Virgin on either the Annunciation or the day of Christ's birth. But this was the real question concerning me then: In what way was the Virgin Mary, the exemplary mother, relevant to me when my own mother had rejected me? Under these circumstances, it is understandable that Chartres interested me much less than Saint-Julien-le-Pauvre in Paris or the Saint-Kornely church in Carnac.

Nonetheless, one day I did make my way to Chartres and entered the cathedral. But I was more concerned with fulfilling my grandmother's vow than determining what gave this sanctuary its intensity. Furthermore, it was in the context of a family outing—a Sunday excursion of the "something that should be seen" type. Nothing particularly striking remains in my memory of it, other than the dazzling light of the stained-glass windows and, a little more emphatically, the strange labyrinth that raised questions I was at the time in no position to address. It did not matter; it was a nice day. The next time we would go see the cathedral of Amiens or the one in Beauvais. These too were things that should be seen. And from the long-distance trains that carried me to the golden brown sunsets of Brittany, I would catch a quick glimpse of the two tall towers of Our Lady of Chartres flickering over the plain, sometimes illuminated by lightning flashes, like trees twisted by the wind over shores on which no ship will wreck.

It was almost twenty years before I returned to Chartres. This was a fairly dark period of my life. I anesthetized myself by driving at night on the small roads around Paris, through the deserted countryside, traversing dead towns in which the houses opened only on certain Sundays, losing myself in remote valleys that were still close to an agglomeration that I was beginning to find demoniacal. In fact I was running away from myself, but I did not know where I was going.

A woman who wanted to be called Françoise accompanied me. She loved to ride during the night. She intoxicated me with words and was good at making love. But her gaze never went beyond the crest of the hills; it was up to me to imagine what might lie on the other side. After all, this should have, if not delighted me, at least satisfied some of my fantasies and inspired delusions of which I was yet unaware. Sometimes the fog forced me to slow down to avoid tipping off a precipice of nothingness, whose existence I had sensed that night in September 1936 outside the railroad car rolling toward Chartres. But I knew now that the precipice was farther away, separate from the world—trickier, no doubt, but remote in time as well as in space. It was a way of forgetting something, perhaps even something essential. But the fact remains that it was always toward Chartres that I wandered during these nocturnal adventures. It is likely that I was haunted by a passage from Caesar's *Commentary on the Gallic Wars,* when he spoke of the land of the Carnutes, where he maintained that the largest sanctuary of the Gallic Druids was located.

I had passionately studied the history of Gaul for a long time, and I knew quite well the territories occupied by the different Gallic peoples, who had often left their names on a city or region. So I knew that the name Arras came from the Atrebates, that the name Auvergne derived from the Arvernes, and that the name Chartres reflected that of the Carnutes (although their domain extended much farther, to the very banks of the Loire, and encompassed Orléans, Saint-Benoît-sur-Loire, and even Blois). This was the site of the famous forest of the Carnutes where all the Druids of Gaul would gather once a year. It therefore represented a veritable central sanctuary of the Gallic religion, a kind of *omphalos* around which the vital forces of druidic spirituality radiated. It was perhaps to bury myself in this radiation that I made these nightly drives along the roads of the Beauce. In truth, the Beauce region is interesting only at night. The flatness of its countryside irritated me, and I certainly did not share the idiotic indulgence of Charles Peguy in his "Présentation de la Beauce à Notre-Dame de Chartres." I have always detested Peguy's poetry and have firmly placed him in my personal "hell" in company with Paul Claudel and André Gide (strange mixture!)—that is, among the twentieth-century writers of whose work reading but a single line inspires me to volcanic eruptions. We all have the right to love or reject whom we want to, and this is in no way a literary judgment.

On the other hand, I have never failed to mention Rabelais—in this instance, the famous episode from "Gargantua," in which the author shares a curious etymology with his readers. Gargantua is crossing through the great Carnute Forest on the back of an enormous mare. But it is quite hot, and horseflies are tormenting the mare. She swishes her tail ferociously to kill the flies, but as she is a gigantic animal, these blows from her tail tear up the trees, which start pulling down others with them until the entire forest is devastated. Not a single tree is left standing on the horizon, and Gargantua, contemplating this sight, utters these simple words, "Que beau ce!" [How beautiful!] Ever since, this region has been called the Beauce.

I can easily imagine that Rabelais was using this episode as an ironic commentary on the mania of medieval and ancient authors always to seek a historical or mythological reason for a place-name. But I also know that every joke by Rabelais hides something. During that time I was inclined to see in the name Beauce a derivative of the Gallo-Roman Belsa, which, in my opinion, contains the name, or cognomen rather, of the Gallic solar deity Bel or Belenos. This name means "brilliant" or "shining." Or Belsa could have been from Belisama, which means "very brilliant" and has given its name to the city of Bellême, not far from there, in the Perche region. Furthermore, this story of trees knocking each other down reminds me of a very ancient Celtic mythological theme, that of the "walking forest" or the Combat of the Trees, a historical version of which can be found in Titus Livy. Titus Livy portrays the Gauls as having sawed through a certain number of trees in a forest, then having allowed them to fall, knocking down others, ravaging the forest in the process but taking with it an entire Roman legion. Rabelais's anecdote therefore takes me back to the oldest Druidic tradition. So there was good reason for this fierce if unconscious desire to roam at night through an area that had once been a sacred enclosure, a *nemeton,* to use the Gallic expression—an ideal and symbolic projection of heaven on earth.

This was how I found myself one day back in Chartres. In truth, I had no desire to go there; it was solely that Françoise and I were tired and needed to find someplace to stay. Any other place would have served equally well, but Chartres was closest. Of course, the next day we wandered through the narrow streets near the cathedral.

Of course, we went into the sanctuary and descended into the crypt. I leaned over the edge of the well and evoked Our Lady of Under Ground. But this Madonna still bore the features of Morgana the Fay; I could more easily imagine her in the middle of an orchard on an island lost in the sea than in a dank, dark subterranean passage. After all, I knew that the Druids did not build temples and officiated in the open air. I did not know what to make of this sanctuary smothered in the center of the earth.

But what really held my interest was the labyrinth. I found it fascinating. But I could not find the entrance. The time was not yet right, and I was still but a blind man, like Maeterlinck's Golaud, who looks for his treasure at the bottom of the sea.

My first visit to the cathedral had been beneficial, but I had admired without understanding. This second visit was a setback: I neither admired nor felt nor understood. What I did gather, however, was that Françoise was a perverse Morgana, pulling me into the folds of a Vale of No Return, lighting the fires that blinded the knights who arrived from outside and ensnaring them with her spells. But when the story of this Vale of No Return is told, what is conveniently forgotten is that the knights are happy to be thus imprisoned; they view it as their due, and it is only when they have been reawakened by Lancelot of the Lake that their memories are restored. I was like one of these knights, aware that I had been blinded by Françoise, but perfectly at ease and asking for nothing more. And I was not even waiting for some Lancelot to open my eyes to behold the statue of Our Lady of Chartres.

This took place in 1971, when I was writing the most passionate pages of my book on the Celtic woman,[2] and this woman whom I could catch sight of in the night clearly had the appearance of Morgana. She was certainly just as beautiful and attractive, but she was also perverse and sensual, with an entire zone of shadows in the depths of her eyes that escaped me. Hadn't I used a Breton proverb,

---

2. Jean Markale, *Women of the Celts* (Rochester, Vt.: Inner Traditions, 1987).

"Woman is deeper than the deepest ocean," as the book's inscription? It was a vibrant homage to femininity, but also testimony to a certain fear, a certain vertigo: Being swallowed up completely would not be long in coming. There are exalted vertigos that prevent us from measuring the depth of the abyss. Sometimes, very strange fogs would issue from this abyss. The empress of the infernal marshes, as François Villon says, was watching me from the mists of twilight. But was it Françoise or Our Lady the Virgin?

Subsequently, I often wandered over the same Beauce roads, still at night, preferably, and no longer with Françoise. Other faces of Morgana haunted me, no doubt because I had yet to encounter the true Morgana, she who welcomes travelers and guides them over the tortuous paths of the Druidic forest, she who consoles, she who encourages and pulls back the veil hiding Somewhere Else—she who, in the final analysis, is not so different from the one called Our Lady the Virgin. Errantry has one valuable feature: It allows the elimination of roads where we risk getting bogged down—on condition, of course, that we take the time to observe what is going on around us. I cannot be made to stumble in the same ruts twice. The problem is that there are a lot of ruts on the paths of this vast world.

I then went into my "Romanesque" period. Having indulged in much fantasy during my youth and adolescence about the extravagance of the Gothic and the influence of the broken arch, I now rejected them for the semicircular vault and dreamed beneath the modest sanctuaries of the Romanesque era. I could see the Celtic tradition more clearly here, which is historically and artistically correct. The Romanesque capitals are the last flashings of Celtic spirituality, deeply rooted in the soil and taking the slightest opportunity to emerge in stone. The Romanesque vault, which is often said to be of Byzantine or at least Eastern origin, is the symbolic, *constructed* reconstitution of the "roof" of the Gallic *nemeton*—in other words, the starry sky that can be seen from a sacred clearing in the middle of a forest as yet untamed by human beings. Finally, the Romanesque sanctuary, solidly established on the ground, thickset and massive, protected from all indiscretion by its obscurity and mystery, is the ideal meeting place for cosmic and telluric forces, the vital core in which the invisible lights of the Other World are concentrated. So I haunted Romanesque buildings and would collect my thoughts there. I felt vibrations; I sensed images. So what could a Gothic cathedral like Chartres have to interest me?

But there was something much more subtle and complex at work. I had not yet found the entrance to the labyrinth because the "deceptive illusions" of which Pascal speaks forbade me access. But what were these deceptive illusions? Among them were my prejudices, of course, my refusal of any compromise, my distancing from any kind of religious dogmatism. And especially there was that impassioned search for Morgana the Fay, the erotic image (and how!) of the Goddess of the Beginnings, she who had presided over the birth of the world by ejecting from her belly humanity and all other living things, the Virgin of virgins, the *unique* yet *multiple* one, the demoness that haunted Chateaubriand, Isis-Venus-Astarte toward whom all Gérard de Nerval's yearnings aspired—especially when he spied, in the middle of his fog, sublimated beneath the features of Jenny Colon, the fictitious Aurélia, who was nevertheless present in every act of his life: "The thirteenth returns, it is still the first." Could it be that the image of Our Lady Mary, Itron Varia as she is called in Brittany, was hidden behind the shameless veils of this Morgana who is forever spied but never attained?

I strayed along nameless shores, over moors that led nowhere. I no longer had any concept of real time but instead the sense of an infinity to which I aspired without admitting it to myself, but which discouraged me every time an irregularity in the sky let me catch sight of some blinding glimmer. Furthermore, I now suffered through significant episodes of vertigo, similar to what I experienced as a child. I have never been able to look over the railing of a bridge or the slightest mountain precipice without distress. It is perhaps only when flying, when soaring through a layer of clouds that suddenly breaks apart for a dive toward a sea constellated by waves, that I manage to overcome this vertiginous feeling. And this sensation works in two directions: When I am standing motionless beneath a steeple and see its spire vanishing in the sky, I feel the same unease, the same desire to hide my face in my hands so as to not see where I am falling or what might be falling on me. In any event the result is the same, for it involves a sensation of being swallowed, a return to the bosom of the earth, the same earth of which I am a part and perhaps from which I should never have been born. This brings up again the problem of my birth, of my ambiguous relationship with my mother. Here, too, this "deceptive illusion" prevented me from gaining access to the statue of the Chartres Madonna, the triumphant image not of maternity, but of the love that unites mother and child.

It is this deceptive illusion that Môn endeavored to dissipate from my eyes and my mind. Môn had a bit of Morgana the Fay in her, but it was a purified Morgana, one who had been bruised by life and was aware of the higher reality beyond appearances that one should search for through the convulsive movements of life. Like Lancelot of the Lake, she had already helped to free me from the sleazy paradisiacal delights of the Vale of No Return by opening my eyes to the inanity of certain settings and the puerility of the phantasmagoria that had prevented me until that time from emerging from my imprisonment. She was also on a quest, and quite often our paths strayed to different sides of the straight line we still felt present in those large mysterious forests in which the Castle of Wonders lay. But the straight line, beyond the shadow of a doubt, is precisely the same one that does not exist in the world of appearances. It is an ideal and perfectly utopian line, invented by Euclid, that demolished the other geometrical systems. Who is right and who is wrong? No one and everyone, it seems, as no absolute truth can be drawn from scientific reasoning, no matter how rigorous.

Môn, in any case, clearly grasped that what was preventing my entrance into the labyrinth was the "quarrel" that I had not yet settled with my mother, who by then had been dead for a long time. It is difficult to find a harmonious balance with a living being; how can it be achieved with a being whose shadow lurked near me but could manifest itself only through resentment and silence? Despite belief in the survival of the spirit and even in the possibility of communication between those who are and those who are no longer, this dialogue proved to be quite difficult. I recalled the scene from Jean Cocteau's *La Machine infernale* in which Laius attempts to forewarn Jocasta of the imminent arrival of their son, Oedipus. He focuses all his energy on appearing in the mephitic vapors of a sewer, but each time he speaks, his form vanishes. And finally, he is constrained by invisible forces; he has no right to forestall Fate. Furthermore, not everyone is capable of grasping the mysterious messages sent from the Other World.

Nevertheless, Môn had taken a notion to reconcile me with my mother. According to her, to recover my peace of mind once and for all, I needed to make a gesture toward her and utter the fateful words I had never been able to speak: "Mama, I love you." This was hard, very hard. One morning we visited the cemetery where my mother is buried and remained there for a long time in meditation, as if something should happen. I was both very moved and very uneasy, all the more so because a photo of my mother—a vain and ridiculous photo—adorned her tombstone. It brought back some strange memories, or rather some strange past sensations. I did not manage to say the words of love, but I was overwhelmed: The image of the Mother rose before me like a light that could engulf me, that could regenerate and bestow upon me a new vitality and open my eyes to the essential realities.

Alas! Why did I then decide to show Môn my grandparents' house, a house that my mother had used some shrewd legal maneuvers to ensure that I would not inherit? Intentionally and systematically, she made certain that nothing would be left for me after her death. What fine proof of hatred. And there I was, trying to utter words of love! Now this house was abandoned and almost in ruins. The garden that my grandfather had cultivated with such love had become a no-man's land. It was a sad sight. If at least that house was still serving somebody . . . I had been disinherited for nothing, for the simple satisfaction of a mother's hatred for her son.

Following this painful experience, my resentment and bitterness grew. I could not have cared less about that house; I had no need of it. But it was the principle of the thing that gave it a symbolic value. Môn understood my confusion. She then told me that there was another image of maternity, and that perhaps I needed to get past the image of the physical mother—simply a womb, after all—to reach the concept of the universal Mother, the Virgin Mary. Môn was a Calvinist, prey herself to that fundamental search for essence, shaken by her own tempests and discovering in the image of Our Lady the exaltation of the universal love for beings and things that, normally, should be the engine of all human action.

It was in this state of mind that we went to Chartres one wet and windy day at the end of winter. We left from Paris, but instead of taking the highway, we wandered down winding roads that brought us into Chartres from an unusual direction, from the other side of the Eure River—that is to say, the right bank, whereas the cathedral stands on a rise on the left bank. This gave us a completely different view of the sanctuary from the one that appears on postcards and other tourist items. It was not the modern city of Chartres we saw before us, as is the case when leaving the station or getting off the highway toward clumps of houses and cement buildings. Instead it was a small town of the past that spread in terraces up the hill and was reflected in the churning waters of the river. I was driving Môn's car, looking for a bridge to take us across the Eure and having no luck. Then, once I did manage to get across, we got lost among stupefying dead ends. The streets kept shrinking away as far as the eye could see, as if under the spell of a magician who sought to test us to learn if we were capable of disentangling the skein he wove before us. It was still the unattainable entrance to the labyrinth, this time accompanied by gusts of wind that shook the trees in the small garden plots bordering the river.

I don't think I ever entered an ancient city with more difficulty and more respect. I recognized nothing, I did not know where I was going, although our goal, the cathedral, was constantly visible above the moss-covered tile roofs, mocking us with its two uneven spires and frenzied architecture, like something out of a medieval dream by Victor Hugo. I thought of other cities in which it was always necessary to wander before finding the square that sits in front of a cathedral—in Puy-en-Velay, of course, but also in Rouen, sleeping in its flamboyant nightmares that I once felt when in search of lost cities. It would not have taken much more for me to mistake the mound of Our Lady of Chartres for one of the last remnants of the town of Ys, the sunken city that slumbers somewhere in the tempest. And a tempest was precisely what was raging outside.

I eventually found a street that went up, but it twisted and turned, narrowed considerably in spots, and detoured from the desired direction while lingering on the side of the mound in places dominated by a conglomeration of roofs and gardens. A strange sensation, comparable to the one that we feel, according to the legends, when we pass from one world to the next, when we stray from the world of humans to enter the world of heroes and gods, the world that the Irish call the *sidh*, the world of the great megalithic mounds.

Then all at once, without warning, we emerged beneath the chevet of the cathedral. We had just a few yards to climb. We were now at the level of the sanctuary, on a large square whipped by the wind from every direction and pounded by the rain. This was how the cathedral appeared to me, in all its majesty and mystery. I had merely glimpsed it before, and knew that it was only now revealed by virtue of that initiatory route we had taken through the narrow streets of a city, similar to no other, whose shadows disappear in the convulsive movements of the earth.

We both felt the veritable materialization of the cathedral, a profound and intense shock however brief and spontaneous it was. Môn had never seen Chartres this way. As for me, I suddenly saw something that until then I had "pretended to myself" never to have seen. This impression of absolute discovery disconcerted me. It felt as though a tornado had just unfurled over my head, fully manifested by the wind spouts that enveloped us from everywhere, as if the sky had suddenly opened over the world. Truth to say, this very distinctive atmosphere was far from displeasing, and we felt a growing desire to let the sacred expedition that brought us there carry us to the center of the earth.

So we entered the cathedral by the southern portal and were immediately plunged into a blue radiance. Yet the dark sky was casting little light; we had to believe that the stained-glass windows of Chartres possessed their own illumination, strong enough on its own without needing sunlight, purely and simply an "inner sun," or a "black sun," although I have never been able to grasp what the difference between the two expressions is. If a "black sun" exists, it is because it is hidden and reveals itself only in certain places under certain conditions that are hard to predict. In any case, I can swear that on this damp winter day, the Chartres cathedral revealed an impossibly beautiful "black sun" that had the gift of making iridescent the smallest particles of stone or the tiniest glimmers of glass that shone overhead. And then somewhere, surrounded by the luminaries with flickering flames, the statue of Our Lady loomed out of the darkness on her pillar, like some ancient deity that humans had raised for blessing by the last playboys of the Western world, who dared venture into this already downgraded sanctuary as it is now, a "historical monument" rather than a temple of the Virgin.

I actually asked myself this question: Where was I—in a sanctuary or in a museum? The answer was easy: I was in both. It is a justification that eases the conscience of all our contemporaries. The churches would be empty if they were not the most appropriate exhibit halls for displaying the artwork of the past or for playing and listening to music. This is a sign of the times. Art supplants religion, and Christian sanctuaries are more often entered for the purpose of *admiring* than for praying. Where is the time when religion and art were so commingled that it was impossible to mention one without including the other? It is true that some late-nineteenth-century architecture in the style of Sacré-Coeur of Paris, Our Lady of Fourvière in Lyon, or the basilica of Sainte-Anne d'Auray have definitively dug a moat between art and religion by emphasizing triumphalism, self-sufficiency, and intimidation to the detriment of authentic faith and sincerity. Fortunately, we still have Chartres—and some other sanctuaries—to remind us that nothing can be divine or even sacred without being beautiful.

These thoughts that I mulled over in silence in no way affected my desire to enter the heart of what I considered to be the sanctuary. My intrusion here, not to mention my pilgrimage, corresponded to a deep need that in no way responded to a vague curiosity. The first time I entered Chartres was because it was something that had to be seen. And I saw nothing. The second time I was not there in search of Our Lady the Virgin but rather in quest of new sensations through the real and perfectly alive image of a woman. This third occasion, which would prove to be the decisive test, was the true discovery of the entrance to the labyrinth that allowed me access to the mysterious Black Madonna. And it was a woman who guided me, although she had never visited the sanctuary before, and showed me the entrance. I was sure that all I had to do was follow the path indicated to me and I would be able to discover what I had perhaps forgotten to look for. No doubt Môn had that flame in her eyes that does not burn but instead allows us to crawl slowly through underground corridors hidden from the gaze of the living. I have been able to grasp the world only through losing myself in the eyes of a woman, but never just any woman. I need signs, and few women are capable of helping me discover them. It requires a strange alchemy in which our slow metamorphosis occurs through the scorch marks we receive from a beloved being . . .

This is how I finally managed to enter the labyrinth. Now I needed to find the exit. But was finding this exit something I really wanted to do? Outside the wind continued to howl, and the rain squalls continued to batter the stone's grimacing faces. The feeling of security and the sensation of being sheltered from all the world's torments, the conviction that such a sanctuary could only be the supreme refuge, guided my eyes and prompted my questions. I was expecting no response; I simply wished for the stone to purr like a cat when I caressed it with my gaze. This is how we can feel at ease and stop fearing the relentless rages the universe inspires to test us.

I will long remember that strange day. Time had stopped engaging in the game of chess I gladly played with it each time I decided to define the world. There were few visitors and finally more faithful kneeling beneath Our Lady of the Pillar. I watched a woman emerge from prayer, walk toward the statue, and devotedly put her lips to the stone column. I could not refrain from snickering inside, as is my wont, for the phallic symbolism of the pillar was all too obvious. But this in no way denied the woman's sincerity, or her desire, through a perfectly natural gesture, to attain the exalting promise that Our Lady the Virgin wears on her face. The human being needs the concrete in order to reach the ineffable.

In the crypt around the Well of the Saints-Forts I could see that strange opening toward the world of darkness not far from the statue of Our Lady of Under Ground, that blaze of light that piety causes to spring out of shadow. I had a strong impression of being in the original sanctuary, not the one the Druids may have established on this site but the one their successors on this sacred mound began building in the Carolingian age, no doubt aware of their need to fulfill a mission, to encourage love for the Virgin who welcomes and protects her children scattered throughout the world. For this purpose they had conceived an extravagant plan: to raise above the ancient forest of the Carnutes a stone vessel that would sail eternally in the Beauce plain to bear witness to the proposition that what is beautiful is good and what is good is necessarily beautiful.

I knew that this was the center, the absolute starting point for this fantastic explosion of stone and luminous glass. I mused on the wonderment that seizes souls about which Julien Gracq speaks:

> The colors have simultaneously, for the blues and the reds, rather than the dry flame of carved gems, that of weakly sparkling cabochons that still bring the gangue to mind, and for the browns and yellows, some violet hues and others a gilded green, a stimulating succulence that I never recall seeing before: flowing honey, plums, raisins, the transparency of ripe grapes. It seems that if I lived in this city, I would come through here each day to satisfy an appetite for color that can awaken and be sated in this place alone, under two separate kinds, as different in nature as bread and wine.[3]

There are kinds of darkness that give birth to light, that give birth to color through the magic of *fiat lux!* In this maternal womb that is the crypt of Our Lady of Under Ground, I knew that everything was possible.

When we climbed from the crypt, the rain had stopped falling. But the wind continued to gust with that violence it takes from the dawn of time, through the narrow streets of an ancient town that seemed built to welcome it and sometimes put it to sleep in the embrasures of the doors and windows, or even in the mystery of enclosed gardens and high walls. The wind turned to the rhythm of the long breaths that could be felt emerging confusedly from the earth, for the earth was alive beneath our feet. And the stones vibrated, as if ready to burst, to show us, no doubt, that henceforth the entrance to the labyrinth was open to us so that we might calmly tread a path through the blue-tinged darkness of magnificence.

---

3. Julien Gracq, *En Lisant, en écrivant* (Paris: Corti, 1981).

2

The Vibrating Stones

At the mention of the name Chartres, the image of the cathedral looms on the horizon behind a modest screen of foliage on a vast spreading plain. In most people's minds, Chartres *is* its cathedral, and only its cathedral. No doubt we should see in this automatic reaction the implicit recognition that Notre-Dame of Chartres is the most beautiful cathedral in France, or at least the most gripping and the most complex. But this overlooks the fact that Chartres is first a town, and that this town holds other monuments, other churches. It does not acknowledge the fact that men and women have lived there for centuries on the top and sides of this mound around which the Eure River detours, between the houses with their subtly moss-worn tile roofs, to flow north along that axis of the world that generates the wind that breaks against the towers of the cathedral. Water flows tranquilly through the town of Chartres. There is a wind that grows calm. Flame-bright flowers appear in the gardens in both spring and fall, when the sun splashes its light against the walls. And then there is stone, the eternal stone torn from the earth and built into the sky not as a challenge but as an appeal to the infinite number of invisible worlds. Chartres is a town, with everything that goes into making a town.

Certainly the modern neighborhoods resemble those in any modern city—the triumph of concrete, the squared-off insipidity of a rational and so-called functional urbanization. But there is also the old city, nestled on the northeast sides of the mound and spilling over the summit itself around the prodigious mass of the sanctuary. Seen from the square in front of the church, the town is somewhat English in appearance. To a native it can seem almost like an unfamiliar country. The atmosphere of Chartres is most distinctive. There is nothing reminiscent of the area around the Parisian metropolitan complex. Nothing serves as a reminder of the vast west that opens to the sea. There is, of course, nothing reminiscent of the south. It is easy there to lose sight of where you are. You are in Chartres, that is all, in a city with a long history that reaches back to the time when the Gallic Carnutes built a fortress-sanctuary in the middle of what was then a vast sacred forest. This forest has now disappeared, but the sanctuary, although not in the original clearing, is still there, flanked by homes where stone and tile have replaced cob and thatch. This is how we can measure the perennial nature of a place that does not escape transformation by the colors of time.

A good many streets in Chartres are still bordered by ancient houses, some of which have been beautifully restored. Visitors can see the corbeled gables, like those in the rue du Cheval blanc close to the cathedral, or latticework and brick constructions. The upper town connects to the lower city, which sits on the banks of the Eure by stairs called *tertres,* and by narrow, winding streets. When strolling on one of these—the rue Chantault—we can see an impressive number of doors and windows from different periods. There is even a twelfth-century Romanesque house—one of the oldest in France—whose tympanum holds some curious carvings. Below here, near the Massacre Bridge, stands Our Lady of the Breach Chapel, which houses the ancient statue of the Virgin that once stood above the Drouaise Gate.

In the rue des Écuyers, a turret stair with sculpted half-timbers stands just beneath the old castle. Its name, Staircase of Queen Berthe, preserves the memory of the widow of the count of Chartres, Eudes I, she who wed the king of France, Robert II. In the rue de la

Poissonnerie sits one of the strangest homes in the city, the Salmon House, built during the fifteenth century. The façade is richly decorated: On the consoles are an enormous salmon, an Annunciation, and snails on a grapevine. On the second story is the depiction, fairly common in the Middle Ages, of the Sow Who Spins, with the sow here greatly hindered by its spindle and distaff. In the rue Noel-Bellay, the Huvé House offers a rich Renaissance façade with pediments, columns, and caryatids. It was built around 1550 by the doctor Claude Huvé, a humanist and enthusiast of all that was beautiful. On the Place Jean Moulin, the Hôtel de Champrond has a portal with a basket-handle arch. In the rue de Grenets there is a late-Gothic-style mansion, and near l'Étape-au-Vin, the Hotel Montescot is an ancient Henry IV–style dwelling that became the town hall in 1792.

The neighborhood of the cathedral includes the canons' quarter, known as Cloître Notre-Dame (Our Lady's Cloister). This is a vast complex that was once sealed by nine portals, of which two survive, including the one on the rue Saint-Yves facing the northern gate. On it we can still see the hinges and those places where the chains that closed it were embedded. This quarter has a wealth of old homes, of which the most beautiful, those facing the Royal Portal, date from the thirteenth century. They have admirably carved tympanums, including arabesques of leaves and images of winged griffons and a battle scene. Farther south, on the corner of the rue des Changes, stands another carefully restored thirteenth-century house, which displays tympanums decorated with depictions of heads covered with leaves instead of hair. These remnants provide a fairly good picture of the wealth of the ancient Episcopal city.

The same could be said about the former bishops' residence in Chartres. Near the north porch of the cathedral an eighteenth-century grillwork gate gives access to the honor garden of the Episcopal palace, today the Museum of Fine Arts. The façade is typical of the Louis XIII era. But some sixteenth-century arcades of the ancient commons remain, beyond which, where the Orangery once stood, extends a terrace that looks over the lower city and the Eure Valley.

From here we can see that the old city of Chartres held an impressive number of churches. Some are still standing, but others are either in ruins or have been redeployed to serve other than cultural purposes. For example, the Saint-Martin-au-Val Church today serves as a chapel for the Saint-Brice retirement home. In spite of a restoration job in dubious taste, the building has retained its original Romanesque unity, with an exceptional opulence and a curiously elevated choir. Four of the capitals sculpted in round point with Irish-style interlacing composition seem to have retained their authenticity.

But the crypt is beyond doubt the most interesting remnant here. It is located beneath the choir and can be reached by its south side. A fragment of the Gallo-Roman wall measured out in fishbone can be clearly distinguished over the door. It is thought that this crypt was rebuilt during the late tenth century, using materials taken from an older sanctuary—curved column shafts and monoliths, bases adorned with cable molding, and capitals of various manufacture. One of these capitals, to the right of the altar, has some similarities to certain capitals in the Jouarre Crypt (Seine-et-Marne), whose construction is a typical example of pre-Roman Irish style transposed onto the Continent. The very unusual capital next to it could date from the Merovingian era.

The two capitals on the western wall are quite striking because of their primitive appearance; they are also akin to Irish Celtic art. This is important insofar as Saint-Martin-au-Val, or at least its crypt, could well be a much older sanctuary than is the cathedral itself. A Gallo-Roman cemetery once occupied the immediate side of the building, and amid the first Christian sepulchers an oratory dedicated to Saint Martin de Tours was built, which was the origin of the monastery that until 1663 belonged to the Marmoutier Abbey. During the entire Merovingian era Irish monks, including the famous Saint Colomban, contributed greatly to reconverting a country that had in large part abandoned Christianity. Juxtaposing this historical and archaeological observation with the tradition concerning the Druids' *virgo paritura* raises certain questions. By all evidence there was a Celtic contribution to Chartres the exact scope of which is unknown. And what of the custom, still observed today, in which every new bishop of Chartres, before being solemnly enthroned in his cathedral, spends the preceding night in a prayer vigil at Saint-Martin-au-Val? Could this be reminiscent of an ancient initiation that early Christianity borrowed from the Druids?

The foundation of Saint-Aignan Church is also quite ancient, and it is thought that originally it must have been located within the nearby castle of the counts of Chartres. But the current building dates from the sixteenth century. Some recent renovations have robbed it of a little of its character, although we can still see a four-teenth-century portal recessed in the Renaissance façade, a flamboy-antly styled crypt, and the vault of the Saint-Michel Chapel on the south side, which is richly decorated and dates from 1543. Several sixteenth-century stained-glass windows have survived various catastrophes, particularly those depicting the Dormition, the Funeral, and the Crowning of Our Lady, as well as a curious stained glass from 1547 credited to the famous glassworker Jean Jouan; its subject is Saint Michel, and it inspired both Raphael and Dürer. The main entrance to the church is through a lateral door, dated 1541, which has been decorated with great care.

Saint-André Church, a former collegiate church, contains signif-icant eleventh-century remnants. Following the fire of 1134 that ravaged part of the city, it was rebuilt, but it suffered considerable damage in both 1861 and 1944. The choir, which was built out over the Eure on an arch that spanned the river, was destroyed. The façade dates from the twelfth century and offers capitals in the purest Romanesque style, with colorful figures and plant motifs. The height of the nave is most impressive. A tower once topped by a framework spire overlooks the enclosed area that was once the Cemetery of the Innocents. On the north side, the Saint-Ignatius

Chapel presents a blend of Renaissance and Flamboyant[1] architecture. Lower doors lead to stairways that go through the side aisles and end in a crypt dating from before the twelfth century, whose floor is almost level with the Eure River. It seems that this church was originally built for the purpose of incorporating an ancient water cult into the new Christian faith. This is not surprising if we refer back to the Druidic traditions associated with the founding of the sanctuaries in Chartres.

But it is the Saint-Pierre Church that is most worthy of interest. It is one of the most remarkable monuments of Chartres and in many respects can hold its own in comparison with the cathedral. It is the ancient Benedictine abbey of Saint-Père-en-Vallée. Fallen into disuse during the tenth century, it was inhabited anew and restored by the monks from the abbey of Saint-Benoît de Fleury, now known as Saint-Benoît-sur-Loire. But its origins lie in the Merovingian era. In the seventh century, Saint-Père Abbey received a large donation from Sainte Bathilde, wife of King Clovis II.

In the tenth century, the abbey was still located outside the city walls, and its position in the valley was particularly vulnerable. The count and the bishop asked Hugh Capet for permission to allow the abbey to construct its own defenses, which it did, and the church's bell tower keep dates from this time. The 1134 fire caused significant damage to the abbey. The monk Hiduard, from 1151 to 1165, directed the construction of a new choir whose lower story remains with the ambulatory and chapels. At this time the tomb of Gilduin, a twenty-four-year-old deacon who died at Saint-Père-en-Vallée while on pilgrimage to Chartres, was discovered in the foundations. This odd figure came from Rome, where he had obtained from the pope permission to turn down the post of archbishop of Dol-de-Bretagne, to which he had been elected against his wishes. At that

---

1. [This refers to a specifically French-Flemish architectural style of the fifteenth and sixteenth centuries. Flamelike tracery is one of the salient characteristics of this rather florid style, hence the flam(e)boyant name. —*Trans.*]

time the Breton church, still officially dependent on the metropolis of Tours, attempted, under the impetus of the Breton kings, to free itself from foreign tutelage. Gilduin left behind a reputation for saintliness, and the faithful again crowded around his tomb in 1165, leaving offerings that allowed the grandiose reconstruction of the abbey to proceed.

Its general appearance is Radiant Gothic. The nave was erected in the first half of the thirteenth century, and on the thick supports of the choir an extraordinarily light stone armature was erected, permitting the placement of a large number of windows. This is all against a vast overall design that addresses the issue of light. The bays of grisaille glass with color figures alternate with the historiated stained-glass windows in the nave, which allows for an extraordinary harmony of tints and tones while avoiding even the slightest symmetry. Movement and expression are reduced to their essentials; the same "cartoon" has even been used for two of the important figures, the artists being satisfied with merely reversing the colors. The stained-glass windows on the north are reserved for Saint John the Baptist and the apostles. Those of the south are dedicated to the saints, respecting a scholarly hierarchy that goes from monks to bishops to popes. The Virgin and Christ are located in the last bay of the nave. Saint Gilduin, clad as a deacon, wards off with his hand a cross that is discreetly depicted running down the length of the border. Generally speaking, the windows of what is now Saint-Pierre Church are among the most beautiful in France. They are equal to those of the cathedral; their only "flaw" is that they are less known and less visited.

The cathedral crowns the mound of Chartres and overshadows everything that is spread about the surrounding area with its great power of enchantment. This is because this mass of vibrating stone and glass is complete beneath a sky that often unleashes torrents, all the better to flood with light the hearts of the men and women who take shelter in its guardian shadow. Our Lady of Chartres, the Virgin crowned with towers—as once Cybele, mother of the gods, was crowned—in her perpetual labor of giving birth: The cathedral is truly the exaltation of this image, both divine and maternal, a sublime arch that holds the world in gestation.

The appearance of the cathedral is most gripping when the structure is approached from the lower city because of the sudden transition from narrowness and the horizontal to something that rises up and challenges all the laws of gravity and balance. This is the mystery of the sacred: It transforms all that it touches.

Emerging from a bend in the street, we find ourselves just beneath the Saint-Piat Chapel, which adjoins the building on the east side. This chapel was not part of the original cathedral; it is merely an artificial extension achieved in the fourteenth century, just above a capitulary hall, and is connected to the rest of the building by an elegant openwork staircase. This is where the treasury of the cathedral is now housed, and also where the bishops of Chartres are buried. There are no tombs in the cathedral itself; it is dedicated to the Majestic Virgin and has therefore triumphed over death.

The Saint-Piat Chapel, sitting on the side, is probably the ideal spot for grasping the cathedral in all its architectural complexity. The apse develops an extraordinary fan of flying buttresses; because the choir is skirted by a double ambulatory, each of these buttresses has two spring points and altogether they extend toward the nave like a kind of impenetrable forest. Their shapes are reminiscent of wheel quarters, braced as they are by small columns that bring to mind the spokes of a wheel. Each of these small columns is formed from a single monolithic block, base and capital included, to ensure greater stability. It is generally agreed that these are the first trial pieces of a fairly bold style, and that these flying buttresses are the oldest still in existence. Added, no doubt soon after, is an upper flight supported by the pedestals that had been intended for the pinnacles. This is the beginning of the Gothic style, and Romanesque elements also remain. This is why the projecting buttresses suggest the strong cascades—the lateral pressure of the nave walls—that they channel so harmoniously.

Romanesque technique is also visible around the chevet. The chapels in the apse have semicircular vaults and are themselves supported by the crypt. The three oldest chapels (dating from 1020) were surrounded by a second wall around 1200, and new, narrower chapels were inserted between. As a result, the flying buttresses have uneven openings. In fact, all of this shows the triumph of the disparate and the unequal, all hanging together somehow and forming a particularly fortunate whole—a synthesis of rather odd elements that, without the genius of the architects, could have been a graceless and heteroclite jumble. But here resides the miracle of Chartres: Time has found no grip on the deliberate will of its constructors to build an eternal work.

This brings us to the south portal, a creation of the Gothic era. Following the 1194 fire that almost destroyed the Romanesque building (of which only the crypt and western portal remain), the desire was to make the new building even more beautiful and grandiose. Instead of having only one portal, as is the case in many cathedrals, Chartres was graced with two more that were worthy of the old one that had survived, and these became the doors to the transepts. The Chartres cathedral is unique in the world in that it is the only one to boast three portals of such importance. The south portal was inspired by the principal façade of Laon, which had just been built, and in turn inspired the builders of Amiens several years later.

The central image of this southern portal is the Christ accompanied by his apostles and the martyrs and those commonly called the Confessors, who relieved the apostles on their evangelical mission. It is the symbolic depiction of the Church on its march toward eternity, leading humanity to the Last Judgment. The tympanum of the middle porch shows Christ surrounded by angels. To the left (on Christ's right) is Heaven; to the right is Hell. Mary and John are beneath Christ, and immediately below them is a depiction of the Judgment. Charity is also present on the portal: Christ here is giving a blessing and is surrounded by statues of the apostles. The tympanum on the left porch depicts Christ above the martyrdom of Saint

Étienne. The statues are those of different martyrs, in particular Saint Laurent, Saint Clement, perhaps Saint Piat and Saint Denis.

But some may be surprised to find Roland, Charlemagne's nephew from the *chansons de geste*. The legend of Charlemagne is portrayed in the stained-glass windows, but it seems that the intention in Chartres was to give this heroic and, in the final analysis, much more mythical than real hero a meaning quite in harmony with the idea of the Crusades. Roland is fighting single-handedly against a Saracen army—that is to say, Muslims in the properly historical context of the time, but also pagans—relentlessly striving to destroy the Christian message. In this sense Roland is one of the ramparts of the Christian faith, and his glorious death is one with the sacrifice of the greatest martyrs. The porch on the right seems to demonstrate that faith is defended not only by blood and sacrificing one's life but also by knowledge. This explains the presence on the tympanum of the Confessors around Christ, who is above Saint Martin the Evangelist and Saint Nicholas the "Resuscitator." The porch therefore highlights the church fathers, such as Saint Sylvester, Saint Ambrose, Saint Jerome, and Saint Gregory, in the company of local saints such as Laumer (or Lomer) and Avit.

The western façade is the most famous and familiar. It is the oldest and also the one that can be seen from the other side of the church square at the greatest distance. This is the site of the well-known Royal Portal, without which Chartres would not be quite what it is. The central figure is Christ in Majesty, who is above the twelve apostles and surrounded by the twenty-four old men from the Apocalypse. At either end of the lintel on which the twelve apostles are depicted stand statues of two inspired prophets from the Hebrew scriptures, Eli and Enoch. On the tympanum of the left porch (again at Christ's right), the Ascension of Jesus is depicted above angels and apostles. This representation of the Ascension is surrounded by a calendar that depicts the signs of the zodiac and the labors of each month. The tympanum of the porch on the right is dedicated to Christ's childhood and includes the Virgin Mother presenting the Child. Surrounding her are angels and the masters of antiquity who taught the liberal arts, such as grammar and music. The capitals are dedicated to several episodes in Christ's life, notably the Last Supper and the Pilgrims of Emmaus. The statue columns depict great figures from the Hebrew Scriptures such as Moses, David, Solomon, and the Queen of Sheba.

This western façade shows hardly any architectural or artistic unity. It was constructed during several different eras and is asymmetrical. Three and a half centuries separate the construction of the two spires. The lower part of the porch belonged to the building that was destroyed in 1194. But it does not matter. A sober and perfectly harmonious beauty emanates from this complexity, which has no equivalent in medieval art. The two bell towers are not the same height. That on the right, called the Old Bell Tower, was constructed in one go starting in 1145, and it survived the 1194 fire. Toward 1200, work continued anew on the New Bell Tower to the north, whose base had also survived, and the whole was completed with the addition of the level with its rose window, for this opportunity was taken to elevate the nave, which was already an impressive height and held the record for the time. The height was extended to 115 feet above the ground, which means that a modern ten-story building would not touch the top of the vault. Above the rose story the Gallery of the Kings, consisting of an admirable parade of figures, was built after 1250.

The Old Bell Tower is remarkable in both concept and achievement. The spire itself holds a record for height, soaring straight up some 160 feet, unfettered by superfluous ornamentation. This spire has the distinction of being hollow and not supported on any framework. The walls gradually shrink the higher one gets. Each stone is carved in the shape of a scale and slightly spills over the joint in such a way as to prevent rainwater from penetrating to the inside. The bell tower easily supported the tons of bells once housed there, notably at the time of the great fire, demonstrating the incomparable stability that Viollet-le-Duc recognized when he declared that to his knowledge there was no other medieval construction as cleverly built as this spire. At the base of the bell tower stands a large statue similar in style to those of the Royal Portal. This is the Angel of the Meridian, so named because he offers a sundial oriented to noon. An odd representation of a donkey playing a hurdy-gurdy can be found on the neighboring buttress.

As for the New Bell Tower, while its base is Romanesque, it was finally completed in 1513 following a delay caused by a fire started by lightning. Its stone spire is the highest in France after the cathedral of Strasbourg. It would take a modern building of thirty-two stories to reach the top. More complex than the Old Bell Tower, it offers an abundance of Flamboyant decoration, notably statues of the apostles accompanying a standing Christ on the west façade.

But let's examine more closely the Royal Portal. Its strangest feature is its mix of styles, which in no way affects the profound unity that emerges when one studies this incomparable group. The statuary is still Romanesque but already foreshadows classic Gothic sculpture. The portal's unity resides primarily in the desire of the artists to illustrate the central figure of Christ in Majesty. The result is an image of the Kingdom of God as it was envisioned symbolically in the twelfth century. According to Villette, "The vertical rhythm asserted in the long and motionless forms of the large statues gives to all this hedge of honor a nobility that has no equivalent elsewhere. . . . The geometrical decor of the columns is varied, and the subject of the small columns is that of an exuberant fantasy."[2] Also visible are precise references to classical antiquity that bring us to the history of Chartres and the fact that in the cathedral's shadow, the School of Chartres was one of the most brilliant universities of Europe from the eleventh to the thirteenth century. Thus there should be no surprise at finding among these statues the figure of Aristotle, the great inspirer of Scholasticism, holding a writing desk on his knees and wearing a furrowed brow. This memorial recog-

---

2. Jean Villette, *Chartres et sa cathédrale* (Paris: Arthaud, 1979), 61–62.

nizes the role of this late disciple of Plato as creator of a certain form of dialectic in which the Middle Ages gladly thought to recognize itself. Similarly, Cicero represents rhetoric, Ptolemy grammar, and Pythagoras music, or rather the universal rhythm, what is sometimes called the "music of the angels."

We must not overlook the left tympanum, where the Virgin presents the Infant Jesus. Here the presence of the philosophers and thinkers of antiquity shows that the Virgin Mary, through her maternal function, is also the Throne of Wisdom, the word *wisdom* designating in medieval terminology both knowledge and technical intelligence used in the service of God and humanity. But what would the works of the mind be without the labors of every day? On the arch of the left tympanum the signs of the zodiac alternate with peasant occupations, reinfusing knowledge into ordinary life. It is never forgotten that humanity is incarnated, and that all reside in the balance of matter and spirit.

The north façade of Our Lady of Chartres is probably the least renowned, yet it is the most meaningful part of the cathedral's exterior and the most revealing of the cathedral's constructors' intentions. Traditionally, the north part of medieval churches is dedicated to a more secret, or at least a more discreet, teaching. The north is in shadow and cold, which explains why, on the north side of many buildings, scenes are depicted that, if not infernal, are at least connected with the Prince of Darkness. This is the case with Notre-Dame in Paris, where the legend of the cleric Theophilus, who made a pact with the devil and was eventually saved by the intervention of the Virgin Mary, dominates the ornamentation.

Furthermore, following the traditional orientation, which is much older than Christianity, the observer is always pointed toward the east and the rising sun. North, consequently, is to the left, the *sinister* side etymologically (in Latin, *sinistra manu*, "at the left hand"), which term subsequently became burdened with a very vexing connotation. In ancient days, during services, men were arranged on the right and the women on the left facing the altar, which automatically suggested a lesser position for women, who were suspected of maintaining privileged relations with the devil and were thus lowered to the sinister side. But paradoxically, the left side of the sanctuary—when it was not the chevet chapel—was generally dedicated to Mary, the Virgin Mother, the woman who crushes the head of the serpent or dragon of the depths. The desire to make the left side of the cathedral the privileged location consecrated to Mary, mother of God, was never made more manifest than in Chartres.

The north façade was begun at the same time as the southern, but was finished last. Villette writes:

> The porch was planned from the very onset, and its foundations were laid at the same time as those of the portals. Deprived of the gallery they should have crowned, the gables retain a sober appearance. The towers, conceived during the course of the construction, are supported—as in the south, incidentally—on the abutment piers that had been prepared for the flying buttresses. Here the buttresses are adorned with small edifices with pediments, in accordance with the part that connects to the abutment piers of the choir and chevet. Finally there are the greatly protruding statues that accompany the rose.[3]

Equally worthy of note is the very handsome clock pavilion at the foot of the New Bell Tower. It was built in 1520 in Renaissance style, with a face that has retained its gilding and polychromy. Beneath the first buttress of the nave, there is a well with a notch to allow the buckets to be drawn up. The presence of this well cannot help but bring to mind the Well of the Saints-Forts in the crypt. In any case, it is food for thought that in Chartres, as in many other places, the worship of the Virgin Mary was always connected in one way or another

---

3. Villette, *Chartres et sa cathédrale,* 59.

with the presence of a well or fountain, a more or less unconscious legacy of ancient traditions going far back before Christianity.

The north portal is therefore consecrated to Our Lady. The tympanum in the middle depicts the Crowning of the Virgin, and immediately beneath it is a representation of the death and the Assumption of Mary. The branches of a Tree of Jesse extend around it, and higher up there are the historied depictions of the Creation. The left tympanum (to the Virgin's right) is dedicated to the childhood of Christ, encircled by the parable of the Ten Virgins, the whole surmounted by a series of sculptures giving concrete form to both the active and the contemplative life. The right tympanum has Job as its chief figure, above a Solomon's Judgment, the whole encircled by biblical figures such as Solomon, Tobias, Esther, and Judith, and topped with a magnificent "calendar of the peasant."

The statue columns below concern the Annunciation and the Visitation on the left; Balaam, Solomon, the Architect of the Temple, the Queen of Sheba, and the Sibyl on the right. In the middle a superb grouping of Saint Anne and the Virgin surrounded by statues of Melchizedek, the priest king; Jeremiah, the prophet; Moses, the legislator; David, the supreme king; Isaiah, the visionary; Jeremiah, the "lucid one"; John the Baptist, the precursor; and finally Peter, the theoretical builder of the Roman Church. This grouping is consistent with the story of the Creation and Original Sin to end with the triumph of Mary, the new Eve, who, by her acceptance of the divine mission, contributes to the total redemption of suffering and laboring humanity.

But though the Virgin is triumphant, as is fully expressed in the central tympanum by the Assumption and Crowning of Mary, her triumph remains profoundly human. Mary is a *woman,* and as such she is subject to the same laws as all other humans, even if she is accorded such an exceptional place. The Royal Portal highlights the Virgin as Throne of Wisdom, though Wisdom is equally present on the north portal, mainly on the right-hand side. The theme is that human wisdom is a direct derivative of divine wisdom. This is shown by the young Queen of Sheba (a "pagan"), who is irresistibly drawn to the wise King Solomon, inspired by the Spirit of God. He turns majestically to welcome her, while the mad Marcoulf, who is sculpted on the pedestal, clearly illustrates his antithesis.

If there is such emphasis on the rebuilding of the Temple of Jerusalem, it is to show not only that the construction of such a temple was a human labor, but that it had been necessary to erect a monument allowing, under certain very precise conditions, the establishment of a privileged link between heaven and earth. Throughout the entire Middle Ages, Solomon was regarded as the initiated architect who knew God's secrets. We know how heavily the shadow of this king has weighed on the brotherhoods of builders before becoming the embodied symbol of both operative and contemplative Freemasonry. This is why the left side of the portal is also dedicated to the activities that flow from this divine wisdom: animal husbandry and farming, music and industry. Depicted next to the doctor are the architect with his square, the painter with his palette, the philosopher, and the alchemist.

The purpose of traditional alchemy, of course, was not to transform lead into gold but to discover the great secrets of life that remain hidden to common mortals. Commoners are those who are not inspired by the fire of the alchemists. They are not inspired by the divine breath that is the elemental cause and indispensable mediator between primal matter, or original Chaos, and the philosopher's stone, which is the result of the slow crafting of this matter that is then purified and given life by the mind. The contemplative life and the active life are two sides of the same reality. This is the lesson of the south portal of the cathedral, and it comes through the triumphant image of the Virgin Mary, she who is crowned eternally by the angels under the eyes of God and humanity.

It would take days and days to grasp the great wealth of art and knowledge sculpted on the outer walls of the cathedral of Chartres. During the Middle Ages, every visit to a sanctuary was a long initiatory journey. There was no expectation that it would be possible to abruptly enter a church, fall to one's knees, and start to pray. It was first necessary *to reach this stage.* Our contemporaries who can casually enter a cathedral either to admire the masterpieces it houses or to indulge in banal cultural practices seem to have forgotten this. But a cathedral like Chartres does not allow itself to be entered so easily. It is necessary that we remain long on the outside to become imbued with the message left by its builders before we dare to bury ourselves in what could be called the "holy of holies"—the interior, where the second part of the message is engraved and which cannot be deciphered until we have deciphered the first.

It is thus appropriate to enter the cathedral through its western portal. The traditional orientation of churches intends the choir to be located on the east, supposedly because it was necessary to turn toward Jerusalem. This explanation is quite simplistic and rests on a coincidence that is valid only in Western Europe and North Africa. The eastern orientation is clearly pre-Christian; the Celts practiced it themselves, facing the rising sun. This was how the four fundamental directions were defined and their meanings were derived: In front was life; to the right, or the south, was light, the movement of life; and behind, the west, was death and disappearance into the night. This left only the north, on the left or "sinister" side. Here was "nonbeing," immobility, *l'ifern yên*—in other words, the *frozen hell* of Armorican Breton tradition—characterized by the absence of light. In the Christian viewpoint, the merit of such an orientation was its reinforcement of the theme of the Resurrection. The light dies in the west but is perpetually reborn in the east. Life, then, following a stay in a transitory Other World, reappears in triumph at the dawn, like Christ on the morning of the third day. Because each of us can hope to be reborn as Jesus was, we must make the symbolic gesture of entering the divine sanctuary from the west and turning around to the east, therefore benefiting from the material and spiritual light that emanates from behind the altar, from the back of the choir. Thus death is vanquished.

In Chartres, everything is constructed to permit this symbolic advance inside the cathedral. There are first the baptismal fonts, which, as in all Christian sanctuaries, are located near the western entrance, signifying that baptism is the absolute initiation for entering the sanctuary. But there is also the enormous space that opens up like the mirror of the Other World mentioned in the scriptures. The nave, which bears a close resemblance to a capsized vessel, allows visitors to sail within it. The nave of Chartres is one of the most impressive because of the colors the light produces as it comes through the countless stained-glass windows.

In fact, there we can feel something beyond measure, something that inspires respect. Is it the spiritual aura of the site or the builders' technique that causes this sensation? It is definitely one or the other, but we should not overlook the constraints of 1194 architecture, which bear responsibility for the entire effect. The cathedral was heir to a Romanesque design and was obliged to use the crypt dating from 1020 for its foundations, which explains the exceptional width of the nave, some fifty feet (compared to only thirty-eight feet in Notre-Dame in Paris). The nave of Chartres is the largest of this type—that is, flanked by flying buttresses. Thanks to these, the architect was able to eliminate the galleries that were formerly needed to balance the pressures of the high vaults. Galleries, beautiful as they may be, always block some of the light. They are replaced here by a kind of triforium that serves as a circulation gallery, which furthermore allows the aisles to be greater in height, which in turn considerably expands the surface available for the windows: "Henceforth the problem of the light is resolved," says Villette, "and, starting from this experiment, the entire history of Gothic architecture will consist of the preeminence of empty spaces over full spaces."[4]

The drama of the edifice stems from how the massive architectural features of the lower part of the construction are combined with its higher masses. The forms shooting skyward grow lighter as they ascend, but toward the ground the foundational courses are

---

4. Villette, *Chartres et sa cathédrale*, 60.

exceptionally heavy and thick. The pillars are alternately cylindrical and octagonal, which both breaks the monotony and distributes the weight more evenly, partially on weaker but highly elegant supports and partially on blocks of a density that can withstand any weight. A choir that is the largest in all France and flanked by a double ambulatory naturally extends the nave. The sixteenth-century construction of the choir enclosure by the architect and restorer Jean de Beauce in Flamboyant style and the installation (at the end of Louis XV's reign) of the monumental group of the Assumption sculpted by Bridan above the high altar have somewhat amended the original building plan. But the wide scope of the choir almost supports this sculpted group, which is neither in the best of taste nor in harmony with medieval style.

The transept of Chartres, along with the one in Laon, is also the most important in France. It measures almost 212 feet, which is the entire length of the church of Saint-Germain-des-Prés in Paris. Here the architect was not obliged to respect the Romanesque blueprint or to use the crypt and generally allowed his construction to run over the original building on all sides. He took advantage of this to install aisles, which are relatively rare. The width of the transept is somewhat reduced, however, in comparison with that of the principal axis, the nave of the choir. But such as it is, this transept emphasizes the two lateral rosace windows, which, seen from the transept crosses, form an amazing display of colors that is intensified by the light added through the western rose window located farther away. Everywhere we look on this crossing, we see only discrete or blinding rays of pure color, gushing lines of force rocketing toward the sky. And when we transfer our gaze to the floor, it is to see how it too has been as intensely worked as the rest of the construction.

The floor inside the cathedral is composed of paving stones that have not been changed since the beginning of the thirteenth century. It is slightly sloped to allow for easier washing, an important feature at a time when pilgrims were still allowed to camp inside the sanctuary. The flagstone surface is uniform rather than interrupted by tombstones as in the majority of cathedrals. There is not a single tomb in Our Lady of Chartres, but both surprising and intriguing is the famous labyrinth located almost at the very center of the nave. At times this labyrinth can be found obscured by chairs and benches, motivated perhaps by the numerous studies written about its meaning.

Chartres was not the sole example of this symbolic, and obviously initiatory, decoration; there were labyrinths on the floors of various cathedrals and churches, but it is the only one that has been preserved in its entirety. It is the flat depiction of a labyrinth forty feet in diameter that creates a "path" some nine hundred feet in length. Sometimes it is called the Jerusalem Way, because the pilgrims could not travel east until they had symbolically fulfilled their pilgrimage here. The official explanation provided by the clergy is simultaneously simple, logical, and reassuring: It is a representation that reminds the faithful that paradise lies at the end of a difficult road full of snares. But this explanation appears simplistic, to say the least, and contradicts the very myth of the labyrinth.

There can be no doubt that this labyrinth was intended for pilgrims who, having entered by the western door, prepared to make a precise circuit inside the cathedral. It was initially a way for them to familiarize themselves with the site and especially to discover the path closest to the spiritual reality of which they had come in search. But the theme of the labyrinth inherited from earliest antiquity, illustrated by the Minoan legend of Minos, Pasiphaë, Ariadne, Theseus, and the Minotaur, is much more complex and ambiguous than some would have us believe. Certainly, on a psychological level it can be considered the wanderings and gropings of the human mind in search of the light—that is to say, of a truth that can always be seen sketched against the horizon but which escapes our grasp when we attempt to possess it. Certainly, on a religious level it is the image of the soul's wandering during terrestrial existence, or as a depiction of it as prey to temptation, blindness, and lack of knowledge, which should one day or another find its way to the divine Light represented by the triumphant Christ.

But the story of Theseus going to kill the Minotaur in the heart of the labyrinth and then finding the exit thanks to the thread given him by Ariadne fails to convey that finding the exit was one goal but that *finding the entrance* was quite another, perhaps even more important goal—especially considering that the dialectic of Heraclitus, in corroborating the legend, says the exit is exactly the same opening as the entrance by virtue of the fact that the paths that climb are also those that descend. And it is Ariadne who guides Theseus *not only to rediscover the exit but also first to find the entrance.* Now who would Ariadne be if not one of the archaic Cretan depictions of the Mother Goddess? Is there some relationship, then, however unconscious, between the presence of this labyrinth in a sanctuary dedicated to the worship of Mary, mother of God, and the strange palace of Knossos, in which figures like Pasiphaë and Ariadne incontestably evoke the fertility cults connected to the Goddess of the Beginnings? The labyrinth of Crete was not only a "prison" for the Minotaur; it was also a "temple." The only ones who could enter were those who had some kind of knowledge of the path to travel. It seems that it was the same in the Middle Ages in the majority of the large sanctuaries, Chartres in particular, where each sculpture, every architectural element, each stained-glass image presents all the characteristics of a double language, the exoteric within the grasp of everyone and the esoteric reserved to a few.

Without going further in what is purely and simply an observation, it should be emphasized that this labyrinth is integrated into the overall plan of the cathedral. It therefore has a role to play that, given its place and its development, is not negligible. Before making their way to the heart of this sanctuary, all pilgrims and visitors to Chartres should experience this labyrinth, first to learn to concentrate, the better to profit from the artistic and spiritual riches offered to both sight and awareness, then to allow themselves to be guided as they meander through the cathedral (which is much more shadowy than the labyrinth itself), and finally to recognize exactly where the *heart of the sanctuary* is located. This is not necessarily the geometric center of the structure or the perspective from the high altar. Pilgrims can note in any case that all paths *lead to the left,* the sinister side where the supreme feminine is exalted, in this instance the Virgin Mary, the incontestable mistress of this millennium-old sanctuary.

One of the essential elements of Our Lady of Chartres, at least on the ground level, is quite obviously the famous statue of Our Lady of the Pillar, which is placed not far from the transept in the outermost part of the double ambulatory to the left of the choir. Furthermore, the Virgin of the Assumption that clutters the high altar indicates with an eloquent gesture of her hand the appropriate direction to take to the heart of the sanctuary, which is, as if by chance, above the place where the chapel of Our Lady of Under Ground is located in the crypt—along with quite a few other things that archaeologists, although at work for some time, are hesitant to unearth—in the very entrails of what formed the original *nemeton* of the Druids in the land of the Carnutes.

It is only relatively recently that the statue of Our Lady of the Pillar was placed in this spot. As her name indicates, she is elevated on a pillar that seems to reveal and symbolize the telluric forces that spring from under the ground. She is a Virgin with Child, clad in sumptuous garb, which is appropriate given that one of the treasures of Chartres—which escaped the fire and the ravages of the Revolution—is a piece of a veil that the Virgin Mary is said to have worn and which had been offered to the sanctuary by Charles the Bald. The authenticity of this relic is suspect, as is the way it was brought into the West, but it contributed to the prodigious development of Chartres as a site of pilgrimage, so it is right for Our Lady of the Pillar to be attired so richly. She should also be crowned, as the whole monument is, to the glory of the triumphant Virgin, she who after her sleep and her Assumption was crowned Queen of the Angels. Particularly remarkable, and enigmatic in many respects, Our Lady of the Pillar is a Black Madonna.

This statue raises certain issues. It is a polychrome work whose colors have almost totally disappeared; it currently shows only the dark tint of the wood. Some say the wood is walnut; others declare it is pear. It does not matter; the statue clearly falls in the category of what are called Black Virgins or Black Madonnas. Mary is represented sitting, holding Jesus on her left knee. She is looking straight ahead and holds a pear in her right hand, while the child, who is holding the globe of the world in his left hand, is making the gesture of benediction with his right.

What is often unremarked is that the statue is not very old, relatively speaking. Certainly by its general appearance and attitude it is irresistibly evocative of thirteenth-century Virgins. But all the compositional details, as well as the inscription carved on it in capital letters, indicate that it was created in the Renaissance. Concurring testimonies specify that it was donated by a canon named Wastin des Feugerets, who died in 1521. Thus it can be dated from the sixteenth century. But these same testimonies explicitly state that following some fairly mysterious circumstances, the statue had replaced an older figure "in gilded vermeil" that had been donated "in the month of May 1220, by Pierre de Bordeaux, Archdeacon of Vendôme." That this ancient statue was gilded in no way invalidates its character as a Black Madonna. It was common to cover statues with paint and gilding.

But there is no proof that this first statue was in fact a Black Madonna. Comparative studies on the different representations of the Virgin with Child on the cathedral's windows can give only an idea of the general appearance of the statue of 1220. According to Delaporte, Mary was "seated, the head erect, looking straight ahead; with her left hand she held the Infant Jesus on her left knee; with the other hand she raised an object that was either a scepter or a fruit."[5] It would seem that the current statue of Our Lady of the Pillar was a kind of copy or adaptation of the 1220 statue. But we

5. Y. Delaporte, *Les Trois Notre-Dame de la cathédrale de Chartres* (Chartres: E. Houvet, 1965), 42. This is a small but thoroughly documented study on the problems posed by the statue, with references and citations concerning the origin and successive relocations of the statues of Our Lady of Chartres.

do not know whether the statue of 1220 was carved in that same era or if it was a very ancient statue donated by the archdeacon of Vendôme. In any case, it is Our Lady of the Pillar and the Virgin preceding her that Chartrian tradition identifies as the Black Madonna. The no less mysterious Our Lady of Under Ground that was destroyed during the Revolution—although two imitations remain, as well as the recent statue now housed in the crypt (probably at the very spot that once held the original statue)—is not the Black Madonna of Chartres.

Thanks to these descriptions and even some engravings, we know the original placement of the Black Madonna: She was fastened to the rood screen that closed the choir, on a stone column to the left of its entrance. "Around her, copper columns supported crossbeams of the same metal on which lamps were hung." But the rood screen was demolished in 1763, and it was necessary to relocate the statue. Its new home was on the northwest pillar of the square of the transept, facing the nave, but this was only until 1791. There was a curious desire on the part of the Church to restore worship of Our Lady of Under Ground, who was in the now inaccessible crypt. The statues were thus exchanged; Our Lady of Under Ground took the place of the Black Madonna and the latter was relegated who knows where. In any case, no further attention was given to the Black Madonna, and it was the statue of Our Lady of Under Ground that was burned by revolutionaries when worship was banned in the cathedral, which had become the Temple of Reason during the Revolution. After 1795, when worship had been reauthorized, the Black Madonna was removed from obscurity and placed in its current location, on a pillar that is only one of the columns of the former rood screen. And this Black Madonna, spared from vandalism, under its name of Our Lady of the Pillar, is the most venerated of all representations of the Virgin in the Chartres cathedral, as is clear from the abundant candles permanently lit in this enclosure that is now a veritable chapel.

The interior of the cathedral is not lacking for statues. In this regard the perimeter of the choir is furnished as best as it possibly could be. Begun in 1514 in the Flamboyant style, the construction of the choir enclosure required many years before it was finally finished in 1529 in the purest Renaissance style. But the sculptures were far from being completed. According to a plan that seems to have been set since work began, principal scenes from the life of Christ and the Virgin were sculpted on the choir's perimeter. This lengthy construction lasted until almost the end of the ancien régime. Thus, it is not the work of a single sculptor or school properly speaking, nor is it of a single style. It could easily have turned out as a bizarre assemblage of heteroclite compositions, but an amazing continuity exists in these forty scenes that have been developed in a space of more than 250 square feet. The ornamentation, characteristic of the styles of different eras, is particularly rich, although some may feel that its presence is regrettable in a monument that nevertheless manages to retain the specific nature of Radiant Gothic.

The now vanished rood screen belonged to this style. It had been erected during the time of Saint Louis. Its tribune was held up by columns, and it consisted of seven vaulted bays that offered arcades topped by gables on the nave side. It was wantonly destroyed in 1763 because it obstructed the view. The sculptures that adorned it were mutilated and buried on the spot, where they were found when the renovation work was undertaken. They are currently on display in the Saint-Piat Chapel, which extends the cathedral's chevet. Notable among them is a very remarkable Nativity and a no less handsome Sleep of the Magi, in which the sages lie side by side with their feet resting against the stable wall from which horses are emerging, already harnessed for their departure.

The Saint-Piat Chapel houses the cathedral's treasury, including everything that was saved from the former building and everything that excavations and restoration work have recovered. This is where the remnants of the famous Tunic of the Virgin are on display, not in a reliquary but in a "monstrance." The veil was donated to the sanctuary by Charles the Bald around the year 876. The gift did not mark the origin of Chartres as a pilgrimage site (it seems that devotion to Our Lady of Chartres began much earlier), but it was the reason for its success as such throughout the rest of Europe. When French queens were pregnant, the Chartres chapter house gave them a shirt that had touched the reliquary containing the Virgin's veil to facilitate an easy pregnancy. Also notable in this treasury, among the most diverse collection of objects, are a sumptuous sixteenth-century cloak donated for the Black Madonna and a small piece of damask cloth cut to fit the former statue of Our Lady of Under Ground.

The building itself dates from the fourteenth century, with stained glass from the same era that is not lacking in interest. These windows can hardly compete with the stained-glass windows of the cathedral itself, however, which are so extraordinary and of such consummate craftsmanship that they have come to eclipse all the twelfth- and thirteenth-century stained glass that can still be seen in France.

The art of making stained glass was born in France around the tenth century. Various testimonies confirm that "windows with colored glass and subjects" existed at that time in Reims and in Dijon. Other documents specify, with respect to the Abbey of Fleury (Saint-Benoît-sur-Loire), that a lead setting was used to hold together the different pieces. It was a phenomenal invention that allowed great flexibility in the crafting of subject matter, for until that time, glass panes were mounted on wooden frames or even, if we are to believe the chronicler Gregory of Tours, on flagstones that had been perforated beforehand. In Muslim lands, glass panes were affixed to plaster armatures reinforced with plant fiber.

The new process spread beyond France quite quickly, and at the end of the eleventh century the monastery of Monte-Cassino was noted for possessing stained-glass windows consisting of panes that were assembled with the help of pieces of lead, the panel thus formed being affixed to an iron armature. Stained glass, then, had come within the reach of the cathedral builders. Romanesque architecture lent itself poorly to this technique, however, because the thickness of the walls considerably reduced the space that was open to the light. Conversely, once Gothic architecture was perfected and walls had become both lighter and less compact, the time had certainly come to invest more thought to using the spaces of light, and stained-glass windows became customary. This explains the inordinate number of stained-glass windows in a cathedral like Chartres, which is centered on the play of light and shadow. All the windows of the Chartres cathedral added together equal more than 6,500 square feet of surface space, a considerable area.

The windows are not all from the same era. Some are remnants of the former building, destroyed in 1194. The largest number are from the thirteenth century, when the existing cathedral was built. Others are of later provenance. Obviously we must also take into account the different restorations that have been undertaken since the art of stained-glass windows, which was virtually abandoned during the classical period, began to inspire unusual interest on both artistic and religious planes, not to mention the mystical one. After all, when entering the cathedral of Chartres, the visitor is gripped not only by the architectural breadth of the site, but also by the strange lights emanating from the windows, especially the blue tones.

The "blue of Chartres" is famous. It is not very precisely defined, though, and the stained glass of Bourges came from the same studio utilizing the same methods. Villette observes:

> But stained glass takes on its full value only if it is given a neighborhood of raw light; now the cathedral of Chartres, alone or almost—with Sainte-Chapelle of Paris—fulfills the best conditions. The tinted glass as a whole retains all the potency of its colors even after centuries. The lead settings strongly emphasize the colors. Only some of the flesh tones have turned brown. Atmospheric agents have attacked the outer face of the stained glass—the thickness of which varies from two to six millimeters—which adds even more quality to the effects of refraction that were obtained formerly

by a variety of "defects" achieved through blowing. The stained glass windows that are striated, buckled, and riddled with bubbles are the richest.[6]

In fact, everything here obeys a master plan, as well as a perfect knowledge of the variations of outside light. Whatever the time of day, whatever the atmospheric conditions—full sunlight, dull gray, or black cloud—all is organized to maintain a contrast among the different tonalities. While direct sunlight ignites the reds and yellows, it is during the shadows of twilight that the blues stir to life and reach their maximum intensity. It is on this that the legendary reputation of "Chartres blue" rests.

The oldest stained-glass windows are those of the western portal, three windows that were created around 1150 and survived the 1194 fire thanks to the narthex tribune that protected them from the flames. These are venerable and wholly admirable compositions. To the left we see the Easter mystery, the death and resurrection of Jesus Christ. In the middle are the principal episodes of the life of Jesus. On the right there is an amazing Tree of Jesse. The height of these windows (the central one is more than thirty-three feet tall), the delicate nature of the drawing, and the perfection of the assemblage make these three windows a group without peer in the entire world, and probably the most beautiful example of the art of stained glass that it is possible to see.

Tangibly belonging to this same era, but surrounded by more recent elements, the stained-glass window known as Notre-Dame de la Belle Verrière, which occupies the second window of the southern ambulatory, thus acting as a counterweight to the statue of Our Lady of the Pillar, is also one of the masterworks of the cathedral. This depiction of the Virgin is almost as venerated as is the statue of the Black Madonna. The Virgin Mother, wearing luminous blue robes, stands out against a magnificent red background. Émile Mâle

---

6. Villette, *Chartres et sa cathédrale*, 83.

said of this Virgin that it was "the most beautiful stained-glass window in existence." He also viewed it as reminiscent of the depiction of the ancient mother goddesses of the Celtic tradition. Mary is seated on a throne looking straight ahead, with her back quite straight and her feet resting on a footstool covered by a carpet. Her head is encircled by a blue halo bordered with pearls and topped by a rich crown. Her hands are resting on the Infant Jesus, who is sitting on her lap. Jesus is also facing forward, clad in an uncolored robe and a blackish brown cloak, his head surrounded by a cross-shaped halo. He is giving a blessing with his right hand and holds an open book in his left. Above them three rays pour from the beak of the dove of the Holy Ghost and end at the Virgin's halo. At the bottom of the window, two episodes of the life of Jesus are depicted, his three temptations and the first miracle at the wedding in Cana.

This Blue Virgin has generated much discussion. Certain details of its composition, the blue alone, the archaic nature of its design, all combine to give it an obvious impression of great age. But could it be the representation of an even older model? Could it be a piece of stained glass that escaped the fire and was reinstalled after completion of the renovation? We know from an 1137 text that during that time, the cathedral did contain a stained-glass window depicting the Virgin that was the object of specific devotion. It was then customary to maintain a lit lamp before her, which itself is rather odd because such a ritual is usually reserved for statues or icons, not stained glass. It is quite probable that this Virgin mentioned by the charter of 1134 was the Blue Virgin, for she has for centuries enjoyed a popular enthusiasm that has never ebbed and is still denoted by a wall blackened by the flames of the candles burned in her honor. In any event, she formed part of the glasswork of the original Romanesque cathedral, which is known to have possessed at least eighteen windows, three of which date to the latter years of the eleventh century.

A large number of the other windows date from the twelfth century and were installed during the construction of the current

Radiant Gothic cathedral. This is the case with the rose windows, whose size and subject matter make such a huge impression. The large rose window of the western façade is devoted to the Last Judgment and has Christ in its center—a standard for beauty. A triumphant Christ of the Apocalypse occupies the center of the rose window of the southern portal. Around him crowd the eighty old men of the Apocalypse as well as the angels and the four companions. The meaning is quite clear, involving the mystical and eternal union after the end of time between God and God's creatures, who have finally been freed from sin and transcended to their glorious status. Below are five stained-glass images that set the stage for this victory. In the middle is the one who made transcendence possible: Mary depicted as Queen and Mother. Around her, in a very charged symbolism, range the prophet Jeremiah carrying the Evangelist Luke, Isaiah carrying Matthew, Ezekiel carrying John, and Daniel carrying Mark. Also visible toward the bottom is the coat of arms of the donor, Pierre de Dreux, known as Pierre Mauclerc, who had married the heiress to the duchy of Brittany, Alix de Thouars.

The large rose window of the north façade is obviously devoted to the Virgin. She is represented as Queen and Mother in the center, receiving the gifts of the Holy Ghost. Here she is the Throne of Wisdom, she who knows the mysterious designs of God. She is the mistress of all knowledge and all bounty, bounty and knowledge not being viewed as separate in the Marian tradition. There are angels all around her, and lower down are Christ's ancestors, the kings of Judah, and the minor prophets of the Hebrew scriptures. The five lower stained-glass windows emphasize yet further the Throne of Wisdom aspect. The middle window is dedicated to Saint Anne, who is holding Mary on her knees. This was intended to show, without even referring to the idea of the Immaculate Conception (which would not become dogma until the nineteenth century), that the Virgin was predestined at birth to a certain extent for the divine mission she would fulfill. Below this window is the French coat of arms, a reminder that the donor was Blanche de Castille, the mother of

Saint Louis. To the left, one window depicts Melchizedek above the enemy king Nebuchadnezzar, and another window shows David above Saul. To the right is the wise king and builder Solomon (to whom the face of Saint Louis has most likely been given) above Jeroboam, and Aaron above the pharaoh of Egypt. This is how the subtle relations existing between the Hebrew people and their neighbors were suggested, relations Christianity inevitably inherited.

The richness and variety of the other stained-glass windows defy description. Everything can be found here, from the noblest scene to the most banal, even the most informal, episode. Bustling through them are kings and queens and princes wearing richly embroidered magnificent silken robes; bishops, priests, and monks in distinctively colored liturgical clothing; and mail-clad knights engaged in battles. And from all this, which could be baroque with its wealth of detail, emerge peasants wearing coarse homespun, heads covered with hoods to keep out the wind as they engage in the works of the field, or else working shirtless to bring in the harvest under a burning sun. Artisans hold the tools of their trade. Some sculpt stone and some carve wood; others weave in their workshops. Fishmongers beneath colored parasols, along with bakers and butchers, offer customers their wares. Drapers and furriers display their merchandise with great pride. A blacksmith shoes a horse caged in a wooden frame, a shoemaker laces boots, and a vintner trims his vines.

This reminds us that a good number of stained-glass windows were offered by the faithful, and their donors enjoyed seeing themselves depicted in them. It also allows us to leaf through an admirable book of documentary images of daily life in the thirteenth century. How many times these stained-glass windows of Chartres have been used to illustrate literary tales on life in the Middle Ages!

But this extraordinary book of images—which could even be compared to a comic strip—contains many elements besides these evocations of everyday life. Legends are teeming there, both those pulled from the Golden Legend, meaning the legendary lives of the saints, and from traditions that were viewed as profane and even diabolic. The devil is not absent from the windows of Chartres, no more than he is from the exterior sculptures. The same holds true for the majority of medieval religious buildings, as if it had been deemed necessary to present the enemy to the view of the faithful so that they might crystallize upon him all their evil impulses, thus to get rid of them in a veritable exorcism. This diabolical image is particularly terrifying in the depiction of the "weighing of souls" in the western rose window. Facing a radiant Saint Michael, who is serene and full of benevolence, the devil with his horned head and animal-like face is putting forth his obvious counterweight, and it is clear that he is attempting to seduce the Archangel of Light. In another medallion a laughing and very carnivalesque devil, armed with a pitchfork and an expression that can only be labeled sadistic, is pushing before him a group of terrified damned souls.

Elsewhere another very serious but nonetheless horrible devil clutches the throat of a sick person as if to strangle him. And in the window of Sainte Marguerite de Cortone, he has taken on the appearance of a dragon with a head as red as the fires of hell. All this is connected with the numerous sculpted scenes visible on the cathedral's exterior, mainly where the jaws of hell gape on the south portal and on the arches of this portal, such as those notable groups in which the devil can be seen dragging a woman who has succumbed to temptation, a courtesan, and a miser. In the window of Saint John, a devil takes possession of the soul of a dying person, which resembles a tiny human body.

As for the depiction of hell itself, it is fully within the realm of folk imagery, with monstrous demons who seem to take enormous pleasure from torturing the damned. On the window of Saint Nicholas a devil tries to drag to the bottom of the sea a child who has fallen from the boat carrying him on a pilgrimage. On another window dedicated to the same saint, this same devil is found in the company of magicians preparing a mysterious elixir meant to burn down the church dedicated to Saint Nicholas. Sometimes he appears as an imp whispering ambiguous suggestions in people's ears. For example, he is shown suggesting to Emperor Maxence that he first burn alive the fifty Alexandrian doctors converted by the preaching of Saint Catherine and then decapitate the saint herself. He is also shown inspiring Maxence to condemn Pantaleon to be executed. He hovers near the left shoulder of the English king Henry II Plantagenet as the monarch discusses the respective rights of civil power and the Church with Thomas à Becket. Elsewhere he reproaches a king, who is lying on a bed, for not having burned the ship that carried the relics of Saint Etienne to Constantinople.

Diabolic imagery is particularly abundant and effective in Chartres. It was not solely out of a taste for colorful subject matter that the artists provided so many depictions of the face of the Enemy. It was to assert again that evil was present everywhere, that it lurked in the shadow of every believer, and that in order to be exorcised it had to be *actually seen*. One of the roles played by the cathedral was to provide exorcism for the largest number of people. How would it be possible to envision Chartres as a temple of the triumphant Virgin without practicing this kind of necessary ritual for the profound purification and "reduction to nothing" of the dark and evil impulses of the human being?

The stained-glass windows of Chartres also reveal many hagiographic as well as simply historic or epic legends. Particularly surprising are the numerous depictions of the legendary history of Roland. In the lower circle of the beautiful stained glass of Charlemagne, the king of the Franks commands the construction of a church in honor of Saint Jacques of Pampelune. Farther up is the flowering of the spears carried by those going to die at Roncevaux, and next to it is an overall view of the battle itself. In the lozenge, the battle between Roland and the pagan Ferragut is depicted. We can also see Charlemagne's return to France, Roland blowing a horn, and Roland attempting to break his sword, Durandal. All this is obviously an illustration of *The Song of Roland*, a text that was enormously popular during the twelfth and thirteenth centuries.

On the south porch, the statue of Roland himself, the pedestal of which carries a strange scene, extends these depictions of the legend of Roland. In the center is a column supporting a grimacing idol. To its left is a crowned king holding a sword (now broken) while lifting his right hand toward the idol and bending a knee to the ground. On the other side, a knight in a coat of mail kneels and extends his right arm toward the idol. This is clearly the episode of Ganelon's betrayal. Roland's "stepfather" swears an oath to the pagan king Marsilla to deliver the hero into his power, while the king swears to kill him, an evident attempt to establish a parallel between Ganelon's betrayal and that of Judas Iscariot.

In medieval imagery, as well as in the traditions, Roland became a kind of martyr who saved Christianity from the threat of the Saracens. A similar example can be seen at the cathedral of Verona, in Italy. The windows of Chartres accord Roland a distinctive importance, while oddly alluding to the allegedly irregular nature of the hero's birth. In fact, the stained-glass window of Charlemagne is dominated by the Mass of Saint Gilles, a legendary episode in which Charlemagne does not have the courage to confess a grave sin, the incest he has committed with his sister Gisele that has resulted in the birth of Roland. The death of Roland in Roncevaux and the suffering of Charlemagne thus take on a redemptive value. In any case, the motif of the Mass of Saint Gilles reappears three times in the cathedral—on a window, in a painted mural in the crypt, and in a sculpture on the south portal. In emphasizing the sin that presided over the birth of Roland, there appears to have been an intent to show the spiritual journey of the hero, who became, according to the *Chronicle of the Pseudo-Turpin,* a "martyr of Christ" at the time of his death. Moreover, this was the time of the Crusades, and Pope Alexander II had in 1063 promised remission of sins for all who went to Spain to fight the Saracens.

There are many other historicized tales in the windows of Chartres whose subjects are as likely to have been pulled from folk hagiography as from the Bible. The parable of the Good Samaritan is placed parallel to the story of Adam and Eve, as if to establish a connection between the wounded man who received charitable assistance and the cursed human race that was redeemed by the love of Jesus Christ. One could just as easily follow the veritable adventure novel that is the life of Saint Eustache, the story of Joseph with all its ups and downs, the caravan of the aged Jacob on the road to Egypt, the episodes of Noah's life against the backdrop of the Flood, and the delightful images from the life of Saint Lubin, not to mention the sober tragedy of Thomas à Becket. The reading of all the stained-glass windows of Chartres would require week upon patient week. All are worthy of interest, and all are exceptionally beautiful.

All these religious and artistic riches form part of the thirteenth-century cathedral, even if the building inherited a few remnants from its predecessor. It is beneath the current sanctuary where we find, if not the archaic edifice, then the most evocative and moving remains of what was once there upon the sacred mound of Chartres: the crypt that set the conditions for the definitive construction of the monument and the broad lines of its architecture.

This crypt, named after Saint Fulbert—which is open for worship only in the morning and accessible to visitors only at certain times, and then under the watchful eye of a guide—is extremely complex. It raises issues that have never been resolved or whose resolution has been actively avoided. The crypt's general design is that of an immense horseshoe, two galleries connected by a curved corridor beneath the chevet of the cathedral. Saint Fulbert's crypt is the largest in the world after that of Saint Peter's Basilica in Rome and Canterbury Cathedral, but it offers its own peculiarities. It was built from 1120 to 1130 under the direction of Fulbert, bishop of Chartres, following the burning and destruction of the ancient Carolingian cathedral, built after 858, of which nothing currently remains but the crypt of Saint Lubin, on a level yet lower (and hardly explored) just beneath the site of the high altar. The intention was to make it into an underground sanctuary above which the Romanesque cathedral was built. But to do this, the builders used what remained of the Carolingian cathedral's walls. The crypt of

Saint Fulbert wraps around the cathedral that was destroyed by fire, hence its horseshoe shape. It follows that the Carolingian cathedral was situated exactly at the actual level of the crypt, which was then the ground floor on the top of the mound.

This in no way resolves the questions surrounding the Saint Lubin crypt, which is at a lower level. Was it built at the same time as the Carolingian sanctuary or is it a remnant of a yet lower monument? From the composition of the walls (a blend of stones and Gallo-Roman substrata), it seems that the Saint Lubin crypt is even older. Furthermore, before 858 another church existed on this site that had long served as a cathedral church. But the crypt of Saint Fulbert played a very important role in the religious life of the cathedral. The baptismal fonts were in its southern gallery, which leads to the assumption that it was necessary to go through the crypt before entering the upper level. This is reminiscent of the ancient initiation demanded of the catechumens, in which they had to trace a spiritual and sometimes material journey before being accepted into the mysteries of the Eucharistic celebration.

Most important, the strange Well of the Saints-Forts is located in the crypt on the north side. An object of veneration for centuries, it was subsequently filled in by the clergy to avoid displays of piety that sank a little too deeply into paganism, and was later restored. This extremely ancient well was located *outside the Carolingian cathedral,* and of course outside the original building on this site. Chartrian tradition is not very clear about this well and the worship that surrounds it. According to the chronicle of the monk Paul, it was in this well that the bodies of two Christian victims of Danish pirates were cast by Norsemen during the 858 siege of Chartres, hence the veneration that surrounds this site and its name of *Saints-Forts* (strong saints). All this is subject to caution, because the old *Chronicle of Chartres* recounts that during Saint Peter's lifetime, Saints Altin and Eodald, whom he sent to Gaul with Saints Savinien and Potentien (more specifically charged with spreading the Gospel through the land of Sens, where the religious metropolis was), had discovered a church already founded in Chartres that needed only their consecration. But in doing this they incurred the wrath of the Roman governor Quirinus, persecutor of Christians, including his own daughter Modeste. He ordered the missionaries slain and their corpses tossed in a well located close to the local church.

There is no way to sort out this confusion in the accounts, especially because the medieval clergy spared no effort to connect the founding of a diocese, or even a famous parish, to the apostolic era; it was thought that such a connection provided absolute proof of the authenticity of the foundation. But Altin and Eodald vanish from the later chronicles, leaving only the names of Savinien and Potentien. These two saints have their own chapels not far from the well and the chapel of Our Lady of Under Ground. The chronicler Rouillard, who wrote during the time of Henri IV, even reported that behind the Virgin's altar "there was a small hiding place." This was all that was needed for imagination to begin embroidering. The "small hiding place" was made into the prison of Savinien and Potentien and, according to the *Old Chronicle,* Altin and Eodald were able to flee.

In fact, this famous hiding place is merely a closet, which was rediscovered during excavations in 1976. And whatever the truth might be about the well and its very likely ancient origin (in connection with pre-Christian cults), it has solidly retained its reputation as the Well of the Saints-Forts, thereby emphasizing the connection between Savinien and Potentien, whose chapels, dating from the eleventh century, still open onto the crypt, like the one reserved for Our Lady of Under Ground. At the beginning of the thirteenth century, four other chapels were added, characterized by their rudimentary ogival vaults and larger windows.

During the course of the different renovation and excavation efforts, murals were discovered that had been concealed beneath several layers of coatings. One, in the southern gallery, is a fresco that is strangely reminiscent of the famed Bayeux tapestry. Not far from the Saint-Savinien Chapel is a depiction of the Virgin. The characteristics of this painting date its creation to around the end of the twelfth century:

> The Virgin and Child display the frontal posture that characterizes the Majestic Virgins of the Romanesque period. The Virgin is crowned but with a flat and flowerless diadem. . . . Her facial features bear a serious expression. . . . Christ's face is no longer that of a child, it is the face of God made man of eternal Wisdom; for Romanesque artists, this face would have had to possess adult features. The Child is blessing with an expansive gesture of his right hand, whereas his left hand is probably holding a scepter.[7]

This type of representation is fairly similar to that of the ancient statue of Our Lady of Under Ground, but it is definitely not a reproduction. The Virgin is seated on a throne, the upper portion of which extends quite high, revealing the painting's kinship with Byzantine depictions. It is incontestably a Virgin of the Throne of Wisdom type, which conforms to the general signification of the Chartres sanctuary. But the discovery of frescoes in the crypt of Saint Fulbert gives the impression that in the Romanesque construction the cultural displays extended on both levels, with the crypt then playing a very important role, not only through its decoration but also by the link it established with the past, for it was closer to what had been the original sanctuary. What remain to be determined are just what this original sanctuary was, what there may be left of it between the two galleries of the current crypt, and especially what still might remain beneath this level, in addition to the crypt dedicated to Saint Lubin. Our understanding of this whole complex would be facilitated greatly thereby.

The Saint Fulbert crypt is remarkably interesting for its use in worshipping the famous Our Lady of Under Ground. Currently, there is a statue that goes by this name in one of the chapels of the

---

7. *Notre-Dames de Chartres* 26 (March 1976): 20.

crypt, but this is not the ancient statue, which, as mentioned previously, was destroyed during the Revolution. Nevertheless, we know what it looked like thanks to numerous drawings and engravings, as well as to the two copies that are currently housed in the Carmelite Order of Chartres. One of these copies, which is smaller than the original, was carved from oak in the seventeenth century. It was oddly covered with black paint, no doubt from a desire to establish a parallel between it and the Black Madonna who is Our Lady of the Pillar. The second and more elegant copy is a "transposition," in early-eighteenth-century style, of the ancient representation of Our Lady. The anonymous sculptor did take it upon himself to alter anything that appeared too crude or barbaric to him, but overall this work can provide a fairly exact idea of the appearance of the statue in the crypt worshipped for so many centuries.[8]

The crypt does hold a statue of Our Lady of Under Ground, a work by the Parisian sculptor Fontenelle that was put in place on September 15, 1857. The artist had access to all the documents concerning the original statue, but he made something entirely different. First, the original statue was no more than 31.5 inches tall (80 cm). The new one measures 36.2 inches (92 cm), not counting the base. Next, the face of the Virgin, instead of being majestic, even without its archaic features, is truly sweet and characterless. Finally, the embellishments of the chair and the gilding of the risers are not necessarily in the best taste. This lends supports to what the Chartrian archaeologist Paul Durand said even as early as 1869:

> It is regrettable that the artist who executed this work did not conform with scrupulous exactitude to the original sculpture. What is still most irritating is the mediocrity of this sculpture. When one is accustomed to the serious and elevated nature of the ancient works, one cannot look without bitterness at all these figures

---

8. These two copies housed at the Carmelite Order of Chartres are not on view to the public.

depicted with these contrived and insignificant physiognomies that
the bad taste of our day is accumulating in our churches.[9]

And this unfortunate Paul Durand did not even have the leisure of
contemplating the horrors to be found in the sanctuaries of Lourdes
and Fourvière!

Whatever the case may be, Our Lady of Under Ground is there,
in her place, to remind us of the tradition according to which it was
here, long before the birth of Mary, that the Druids worshipped a
virgo paritura. Furthermore, an inscription on the pedestal of the
statue, with the dative *Virgini pariturae,* informs those pilgrims and
tourists who find their way here of this Druidic tradition.

Of course, the former statue was definitely not the same one that
the Druids worshipped; it dates no further back than the twelfth century. Moreover, the tradition that maintains the Druids would have
foreseen the Virgin Mary appeared only in the fourteenth century
and without mentioning the Druids by name. They were identified as
such only in the *Chronicle of Rouillard,* the title character of which
was a contemporary of Henri IV. The story of a statue dedicated to
a "Virgin about to give birth" that would have foreshadowed Mary,
mother of Jesus, is merely a fable invented after the fact by the
Chartrian clergy, who wished to establish the great antiquity of the
worship and pilgrimage of Our Lady of Chartres. But this fable does
have an origin; there was no lack of faces of mother goddesses in the
Celtic Druidic tradition. It is probable that during the Middle Ages,
the inhabitants of the region had a vague recollection of the Druids'
worship of some mother goddess. It was necessary, then, to revive
and channel this tradition, which was managed successfully thanks
to Our Lady of Under Ground. This gave everyone an easy conscience.

But we should not underestimate the profound value of the presence of Our Lady of Under Ground in the immediate proximity of the
Well of the Saints-Forts, inside this somewhat enigmatic crypt at a site

---

9. Paul Durand, Archaeological Society of Eure-et-Loir, *Procès-Verbaux* 4: 235.

that could well be the telluric center of the cathedral. It is certainly not by chance that a statue of the Virgin was situated here throughout this site's entire history. Nor would it be by chance that the statue of a Black Madonna was placed on an upper level, on a pillar, which, above all, symbolizes the world's axis and which, on a practical scale, connects in some way the sanctuary below with the one above.

And the cellar of Our Lady of Chartres is far from having been systematically explored. There has been much talk about a cave located far beneath the crypt of Saint Fulbert, even farther down than the crypt of Saint Lubin. The opinions of archaeologists and researchers diverge on this point. The fact that it has not yet been found does not mean that it does not exist. But if the existence of this cave is accepted, what is it? Surely it was not a Druidic grotto; the Celtic priests officiated only in the open air in clearings or on the top of the mounds. It could have been a Gallo-Roman cellar, because once Gaul had been Romanized, the Celts began building temples, which they had never done previously. Given the succession of religions and civilizations, it could also certainly have been a dolmen or covered alley dating from Neolithic times, which is to say anywhere from 2000 to 4000 B.C.E. Numerous megalithic monuments reveal on their interior supports depictions of a goddess mother,[10] mainly in Armorican Brittany and Ireland. The region of Chartres was once rich in monuments of this kind, and there still exists, not far from here in the Eure Valley at Changé-Saint-Piat, a covered alley that includes a representation of what archaeologists call a bud- or pot-shaped idol in which it is not difficult to recognize the ancient Goddess of the Beginnings. So just what is it exactly? We do not know. But it cannot be by chance that the worship of the Virgin Mary is so magnified at Chartres on the sacred mound from which the Carnute people may have taken their name, and the city as well.[11]

---

10. See Jean Markale, *Carnac et l'énigme de l'Atlantide* (Paris: Pygmalion, 1987).
11. The etymology of the name of the Carnutes is still disputed, but it may have been derived from a pre–Indo-European word, *car* or *carn,* meaning "sacred mound."

Whatever the truth may be concerning all these problems posed by the Saint Fulbert crypt, there currently exists in Chartres a cathedral dedicated to the worship of the Virgin Mary, who is presented in her triumph and in her role as the Throne of Wisdom on a place that has been since time unrecorded a sacred site, one of those places where the delicate exchanges between the divine world and the human world are achieved. Furthermore, this cathedral of Chartres is one of the most beautiful and most complete monuments bequeathed us by the medieval past. If the Virgin Mary can be considered the very embodiment of perfection and completeness, then the cathedral of Chartres is the symbol of this perfection and completeness inscribed eternally in stone.

3

CHARTRES OVER THE
COURSE OF HISTORY

Chartres owes its name to the Gallic people of the Carnutes, who, during the time of the Gallic War, occupied a vast territory consisting of the Beauce, Orléanais, and Blésois. It was bordered on the north by the Dreux Forest, which separated it from the domain of the Aulerci Eburovices; on the east by the Rambouillet Massif, which separated it from the Parisii; on the southeast, beyond Saint-Benoît-sur-Loire, by now vanished forests that separated it from the Senones; on the south, beyond the Loire and encompassing the Sologne, by the Cher River, which separated it from the Bituriges; and on the east by the Vibraye Massif and the first hills of the Maine, which separated it from the Turones and the Aulerci Cenomani. According to Caesar, this Carnute territory was considered the center of Gaul, and it was home to the great sanctuary where all the Druids of Gaul would gather once a year.

During this time Chartres was called Autricum, which means "ford on the Eure," the river's earlier name having been the pre–Indo-European Altura.[1] Caesar makes no mention of Autricum, and the

---

1. The name Adour was also derived from this term. It should mean "running water" and was incorporated into Gallic as *dubro,* which can be recognized in Dore and Dordogne (deep water), and then became *dour* (the Vannetais *deur*) in Armorican Brittany.

name does not appear until the second century B.C.E., in Ptolemy's *Geography,* then on the famous Peutinger Table,[2] created during the third century, in which it can be seen that the town is connected on one side to Dreux and the Seine estuary and on the other to Mans and the Aquitaine. During the time of the Gallic wars, Autricum is not supposed to have played a major role. Cenabum (or Genabum), however, which is now Orléans (or Gien; opinions vary), seems to have been the most important center of the Carnutes, which is logical given its position on the banks of a large river that allowed for more intensive sailing than did the Eure.

Everything indicates that Cenabum was the political and military center of the Carnutes, which reinforces the hypothesis that Autricum was a sanctuary rather than a fortified town. Among the Gauls, furthermore, outside the southern zones influenced by Mediterranean urbanism, there were never actually towns and cities in the sense that those terms are understood today. When Caesar, in his *Commentaries,* speaks of Gallic towns, he is actually referring to fortresses that were occupied only in times of war or for markets and gatherings, or fortress sanctuaries (such as Alesia). But this does not imply that the Carnutes had no other important centers. While place-names of Gallic origin are rare in the Beauce region itself, there is a wealth of them along its perimeter, as shown by the names Dreux (from the Durocassi, a subject people of the Carnutes), Châteaudun ("castle-castle"; the French *château* and the Gallic *duno* have the same meaning), Vendôme (a superlative meaning "the very white"), Blois (literally "the wolves"; see the Breton *bleizh*), the Beuvron ("river of beavers," like the Parisian Bièvre), and Salbris ("bridge over the Sauldre"), not to mention the numerous Nogents (Novientum, "new village"), mainly in the Eure Valley, to which most of the waters in this region flow.

The importance and extent of the Carnutes should not obscure

---

2. [The Peutinger Table is the medieval copy of a Roman map. Historians find it to be a rich source of information. —*Trans.*]

the fact that this valley was inhabited long before the arrival of the Celts. In the vicinity of Chartres, mainly in the Eure Valley, numerous dolmens have been found, evidence that the megalith builders settled this area between 4000 and 2000 B.C.E. These settlements must have existed throughout the Bronze Age. But it is likely that all valleys carved by rivers were inhabited. The rest should have been an immense forest that can hardly be imagined today, and of which only fragments remain on the perimeters. All traditions, including Caesar's historical testimony, agree that the land of the Carnutes was a huge forest.

This is where the problem of the name Beauce comes in. The name incontestably comes from a Gallic term that moved into Latin in the form of Belsa, and it is claimed that *belsa* meant "clearing." The Beauce around Chartres would have been a vast clearing surrounded by impenetrable forests, which provides ample justification for the "clue" about this site dropped by Caesar about the great central sanctuary of Gaul, because we know that Druidic worship was celebrated in the *nemeton,* meaning a clearing in the middle of the forest. Chartres would then have occupied the midway point in this kind of sacred geography, and it could well have been an *omphalos,* a symbolic center of the world. But *belsa* also contains the term *bel,* which is the generic root of the names of the Celtic deity of light, Belenos (the Shining One) and Belisama (the Very Shining One), who was Beli in Welsh mythology. We could then consider the Beauce as the "clearing" or "sanctuary" (which amounts to the same thing for the Gauls) of Bel or Belenos. This epithet most often designated Lugh, the Master of All the Arts, the god not assigned any one function. Caesar, who identified Lugh with Mercury, indicated that he was the most honored of Gallic deities. Whatever the etymology of Belsa, we should bow to the evidence. The idea of sanctuary is connected to the idea of the clearing, and there can be no clearing or sanctuary unless there is a forest. Thus we find ourselves back in the sacred forest of the Carnutes mentioned by Caesar.

No decisive archaeological traces of the Celtic period have been found in Chartres or its surrounding area. All that can be established is that long before the Roman occupation, the site of Chartres, Autricum, was if not a town at least a fortress sanctuary of the Carnutes. Data brought to light in the nineteenth century but disputed today, however, might offer some new elements concerning Autricum's exact role. They concern traces of significant ground undulation that followed the contours of the city of Chartres from northeast to southeast for more than a mile and which was still quite visible during the nineteenth century before the growth of Chartres's urban area:

> This ground displacement, definitely achieved by artificial means, appeared like a ditch bordered by slopes whose parallel crests appear to have been more than 125 feet apart. It could be followed from the rue de Fresnaye to the borders of the hospital. Today it is no longer visible, except at a place called the Citadelle, immediately to the south of the rue de Rechèvres, where this work was most abrupt at the time it was mapped.[3]

Nineteenth-century archaeologists viewed the undulation as remnants of a Roman camp, which is impossible given the surface area involved. According to Joly,

> The examination of this map shows that this work could extend in both directions to meet the Eure in the north at a point called the Barre-des-Près (denoting an ancient defense work) and to the south by following the rue de Reverdy, which gives way to an ancient street in the sector of Saint-Martin-en-Val. It would thereby have described an arc of more than 25 miles containing a space of more than 250 hectares.[4]

---

3. Roger Joly, *Histoire de Chartres* (Roanne, France: Horvath, 1982).
4. Ibid., 9–10.

This is both significant and intriguing. Never was this construction mentioned in ancient times, but in 1438, when Chartres was threatened by the English, it was said that "the trenches of Nicochet, Mautrou, and Saint Lubin" were repaired. These three names designate the places where the circumvallation in question cuts the roads from Mans and Châteaudun and the ancient way known as the Countesses Road.

It was clearly, then, an encircling wall that had fallen into disuse and which the French tried to make operative again when confronted by English troops. But it could have been only an advance fortification and not the actual city defenses; given the population, it would have been impossible to defend a perimeter that extended so far. Could this circumvallation really have been a defensive military construction? Joly speculates,

> In the light of theories recently formed based on numerous obser-
> vations made throughout Western Europe, couldn't this be seen as
> one of those proto-historical enceintes whose role seems to have
> been more symbolic than defensive and would therefore denote the
> antiquity and importance of the site of Chartres? Only an archae-
> ological excavation, a particularly delicate endeavor, would allow
> this hypothesis to be verified.[5]

But it is a very attractive hypothesis, especially with respect to the great Druidic sanctuary of the land of the Carnutes. Wouldn't this site have had a sacred enclosure wall?

Once the Roman conquest was ensured, Autricum gradually became a Gallo-Roman town and took on the name of its inhabitants. In three centuries the settlement developed on a surface that hardly varied until the eve of the Second World War. And for this, archaeological testimonies are not lacking. The most important remnants were found on the borders of the cathedral, whose crypt

---

5. Joly, *Histoire de Chartres*, 11.

reveals clearly Roman structures. Saint-André Church rises on the site of a theater or amphitheater whose curved remains influenced the topography of the quarter. And the remains of significant construction on the Faubourg Saint-Brice have been unearthed near the spot where the roads out of Blois and Orléans join in order to cross the Eure. The study of Roman roads has further shown that Chartres was an important crossroads; privileged relations had been established with Orléans and Blois, but there were also roads toward Rouen by way of Dreux and toward the Armorican peninsula by way of Le Mans, as well as toward Cotentin (and Mont-Saint-Michel) by way of Mortagne and Domfront. Relations with Paris, however, did not seem at all ensured, at least directly. Chartres during the empire was subordinate to Lyon (Lugdunum), but by the intermediary of Sens, the capital of the Gallic Senones, which during the Christian era would be the metropolitan archbishopric on whom the bishopric of Chartres depended. In the middle of the third century, Chartres had the reputation of being the second city of the Fourth Lyonnais [the Fourth District of the Lyonnais province], after Sens.

But a period of decline began around 270, prompted, it seems, by the first German invasions. The city suffered great destruction, and entire quarters appear to have been abandoned. Only the summit of the plateau, for strategic reasons, and the banks of the Eure, for economic reasons, maintained their activity. At the same time, Christianity began invading the empire, considerably influencing lifestyles and behaviors.

Local hagiography pushes back Chartres's conversion to Christianity to apostolic times, toward the middle of the first century. The Chartrian clergy deliberately promoted this belief, no doubt better to incorporate what remained of ancient pagan traditions that were particularly vital and spiritually prominent. The medieval clergy saw no hiatus between Druidism and Christianity; the transition occurred as a matter of course at the time the evangelical message arrived to confirm historically what Celtic myths had been teaching over the long centuries, starting with the theme of the Virgin about to give birth. We know now for certain that all this is only legend. But pay heed: A legend never exists without a hidden reality. The Chartrian clergy, as we shall see, were not totally in error in asserting a continuity between the Christianity they knew and a Druidism they imagined through oral traditions, not all of which were necessarily dubious.

Certainly, as in all the other towns of Roman Gaul, there were most likely small communities of Christians who maintained a discreet, clandestine existence. Bear in mind that Christianity began in the West as a grouping of small sects more or less outside the law and more or less persecuted by imperial authority. But we have to wait for the year 340 for Chartres to be endowed with a bishop, in the person of Aventin. Before this, there was no reason to have a church there, much less a cathedral. It can be presumed that Christians met in private homes, mainly in the suburb where stands Saint-Martin-au-Val, one of the places housing the sepulchers of the first bishops; or even in the Saint-Chéron quarter, the supposed residence of a mythical Saint Chéron. (The name is derived from the term *sanctus caraunus,* meaning a sacred pagan mound, which was subsequently mistaken for a proper name.) Greatly revered throughout the Beauce, Saint Chéron, like Saint George and Saint Christopher (neither of whom exists, according to the contemporary Roman Catholic Church), performed numerous miracles for those who beseeched him.

Thus, starting with Aventin, the Church had an official existence in Chartres. It may have dated from the edict of Constantine, who in 313 gave Christians the right to worship, but only that right. Christianity then coexisted with other religions, including matriarchal religion (the worship of Cybele more or less blended with that of Mithra). Soon, however, the edict of Theodosius suppressed these other religions and instituted Christianity as the empire's one religion, at which point Chartres became an active center of a campaign to convert the countryside, in conjunction with the preaching of Saint Martin de Tours.

As in many other towns, there were different sanctuaries independent of one another in Chartres, but they were united under the bishop's authority, forming what is called a cathedral group. The different intentional or chance excavations performed during urban construction have revealed an impressive number of now vanished churches. West of the current cathedral square there was even a Sainte-Même Chapel, which is believed to have been the oldest sanctuary in the city. It was demolished in 1790 after having been used to store grain for a long time. And it is possible that Saint-Aignan was older than the first cathedral edifice, but all we can do is hypothesize about this until some intensive excavations have been made beneath the former Carolingian cathedral.

Chartres itself was not initially dedicated to the Virgin Mary. It was not until the second half of the sixth century that it became customary to name a sanctuary after a saint. Nevertheless, the use of such names certainly became fashionable early on. The feast day of the dedication of the cathedral is September 8, the Nativity of Our Lady. This is quite revealing of the Chartres community's intention to highlight the Virgin about to give birth, and it explains the subsequent diffusion of the legend of the *virgo paritura*. Was this based on a desire to ensure the Chartrian church a certain preeminence in the devotion to Mary? Or was it instead seeking to incorporate the worship that a mother goddess had received for centuries on this site? The question remains open.

Starting with the reign of Julian the Apostate, however, Gaul began receiving large infusions of Germanic immigrants, both as federated communities that lived under their own laws and as *lètes*, which meant they were given a special status that obliged them to contribute to regional defense. The town of Allaines, for example, was created near Orléans and populated by Alains. Chartres, meanwhile, became the residence of a prefect of the Teuton *lètes*. Then in 486, Chartres, one of the last towns under Roman administration, was made part of the new kingdom of Clovis. The bishop of Chartres, Saint Solennus, was one of the three clerics chosen by the king of the Franks to instruct him in the faith of Christ.

Following the death of Clovis, his sons fought bitterly over the succession of power, and Chartres changed masters often for close to a century. In the year 600, Thierry, son of Childebert, lay siege to the city. Chroniclers have recorded how he captured Bishop Béthaire by ruse, but the bishop, through his strength of character, earned the respect of his opponent and therefore obtained the safety of the city. This shows the importance of the Chartrian church from both a political and a religious perspective. When Clothaire II managed to reunify the Frankish kingdom following the death of Thierry, he made Béthaire his chaplain.

At this time, efforts were begun to found numerous ecclesiastical establishments, particularly Saint-Martin-au-Val, Saint-Chéron, Saint-Maurice Abbey, and Saint-Pierre-en-Vallée Abbey, which benefited from the generosity of Queen Bathilde, wife of Clovis II, as well as the priory of Saint-Lubin-des-Vignes. It can also be presumed that parish churches such as Saint-Michel, Saint-Saturnin, Holy Faith, and Magdalene of Saint-John were built outside the city walls at this same time. At the close of the Merovingian era, Chartres was both a powerful fortress and a kind of "holy city" in which religious life was considerably evolved.

In 743, Hunald of Aquitaine, in revolt against Carloman and Pippin the Short, son of Charles Martel, burned down Chartres "without sparing the church consecrated to the Mother of God," as declared in the *Annales de Metz*. It was perhaps in reparations that Pippin the Short donated part of the Forest of Yvelines to the church of Chartres, a donation confirmed in 768 when Pippin became king. According to the chronicle of the monk Paul, Chartres was then "a city of many inhabitants and the richest of all the cities of Neustria, renowned for the height of its walls, the beauty of its buildings, and the culture of the fine arts." But the son of Charlemagne, contesting the succession of power, very nearly destroyed it.

Finally, Chartres was allotted to Charles the Bald. But at this time of the Carolingian Renaissance, another peril was looming on the horizon: the Normans. When the Beauce was directly threatened, Bishop Hélie received the mission to reinforce the troops he was already charged with maintaining on a permanent basis. Nevertheless, the Norsemen, after ravaging the Perche, managed to take possession of Chartres on June 12, 858, under the leadership of their chieftain, Hasting. The city was pillaged and burned and part of the populace massacred. Bishop Frotbold was murdered in his church, or perhaps thrown in the Eure River when caught trying to flee. According to the chronicle of the monk Paul, the survivors, after gathering the scorched remains of the victims, once again cast them down a well that tradition says was inside the cathedral and which was called from then on the Lieu-Fort ["strong place"] because "the merits of their ashes produced many miracles." This seems to have been the origin of the Well of the Saints-Fort, which was actually located outside the Carolingian cathedral.

In any case, nine years after Hasting's strike, Charles the Bald convened a general tribunal in 867 to determine what measures to take against Salaün, king of Brittany. In 876 he solemnly offered Chartres the precious relic known as the Virgin's Tunic, which was allegedly given to Charlemagne by the emperor of Constantinople.[6] The treasure was entrusted to Bishop Gislebert, who, as imperial notary for thirty years, was an intimate of Charles the Bald. It was under these circumstances that Gislebert undertook the restoration of the cathedral, and it was probably he who worked out the crypt named Saint-Lubin.

---

6. According to Joly, "Two appraisals, one performed in 1793 following the vandalism of the reliquary, the other in 1927 at the time of the Marian festivals, have concluded that the embroidered cloth was a Muslim work from the eighth or ninth century" (*Histoire de Chartres*, 220). This tells us what degree of importance we should attach to the "relics" that were miraculously rediscovered during the Middle Ages. With all the many pieces of the "True Cross" that are spread throughout the world, a several-story dwelling could be built, as it could with the relics of certain saints (which include three tibias and several skulls each).

In the spring of 911, the Viking chieftain Rollon laid siege to Chartres with a large army equipped with siege machines. This was not a campaign for plunder but an actual war. Rollon sought to put an end to a hub of resistance that threatened his communication and supply lines on his expeditions toward the Loire. Defense of the city was again ensured by its bishop, a certain Gaucelin or Ganselme. The resistance held on for several months, allowing the reinforcements to arrive that had been requested from Francia, Burgundy, and even Poitiers. In July of that same year, 911, the bishop decided to mount a sortie. To inspire his troops, he had the Virgin's Tunic displayed as a standard. The Normans were routed. But at the end of the same year, Rollon married Gisèle, daughter of the king of France, Charles the Simple, and with the signing of the Saint-Clair-sur-Epte treaty obtained the territories that would become Normandy.

This shows how important the battle of Chartres was in the course of French history. None failed to attribute the Frankish victory to the presence of the venerable relic. There is nothing novel about such an event, but it further fueled the fervor of the Marian cult in Chartres, as well as the devotion to the holy relic. Now more than ever Chartres was the city of the Virgin who protected her children, the Christians. Politics and religion were closely aligned in the exercise of a worship whose origins appeared to be spontaneous, inherited from the earliest antiquity, and clearly founded among the people. The consequences of the Christian victory at Chartres are incalculable. It changed the destiny of France and of Europe. Henceforth the Norsemen, converted to Christ, would become the most faithful supporters of a triumphant Christianity.

This failed to prevent one of Rollon's descendants, Richard of Normandy, from sacking and burning a large portion of the city of Chartres in 962. The situation at this time was rather muddled. For one thing, the count of Chartres, known as Thibaud the Deceiver, was a somewhat restless and bizarre individual.

Yes, there were counts of Chartres. The institution of the office dates from the time of Charlemagne. Originally, the count (from the Latin *comitem,* "companion") was a faithful ally of the king or emperor, appointed to administer in his name one of the territories of his empire. In Chartres itself there is no evidence of the existence of this institution until 806, at which time there is mention of a count named Gunfridas. Only after 877 did the office of the count become hereditary. The documents concerning this period are confused and contradictory. They claim, for example, that Hasting himself would have been count of Chartres, but there was confusion among individuals sharing the same name, all of Danish origin.

The fact is that in 886, Eudes, count of Dunois (Châteaudun), vigorously and successfully opposed an attempt made by the Danes, then besieging Paris, to pillage the Chartres countryside. Was Eudes also count of Chartres? Another document, the *Vieille Chronique,* declares that it was Bishop Hardouin, sole holder of Gallo-Frankish power over the city, who first instituted the role of count as a way to establish a separation between the temporal and the spiritual. It is true that Charlemagne had in mind that the count and bishop would jointly administer the territory under their charge, thereby implementing the old Indo-European rule symbolized by the Indian mythological duo Mithra-Varuna and in Celtic society by the Druid-king pair (of which the Arthur-Merlin pairing is the romanticized personification). But this *Vieille Chronique* also claims that even before the birth of the Virgin, the prince of the city and territory of Chartres had given these two to the Virgin and Jesus, and because of that the bishops would have originally been the counts and lords of the city and its land. All this, of course, belongs to the tradition of the *virgo paritura* and should not be given any credibility.

Thibaud the Deceiver left his mark on the earldom of Chartres, however. He was the son of a viscount of Tours, who was a loyal vassal of the Robertians in their struggle against the Carolingian dynasty. Thibaud owned a tower in Chartres as a symbol of his authority, which extended over not only the Chartrian territory but also that of Dunois, Blésois, Tours, and Saumur, with several fiefs scattered along the borders. He was a figure of boundless ambition who vainly attempted to establish his power in Brittany and then turned against Richard of Normandy. The latter, with the help of Danish pagans, made Thibaud pay dearly for this, and the inhabitants of Chartres suffered the consequences in 962. These were so extensive that, as the chronicle said, "not even a dog could be heard barking in the earldom." Thibaud the Deceiver died around 977. His youngest son, Eudes, succeeded him, followed by his son Thibaud, who died on pilgrimage, leaving the earldom to his brother Eudes II, already count of Blois, Tours, and Châteaudun.

This did nothing to solve the problems that had arisen. In fact, the mother of Eudes and Thibaud had wed in a second marriage, to Robert the Pious, son of Hugh Capet, and had been repudiated for consanguinity. Queen Berthe retired to live near her sons but managed to inspire them with a certain amount of bitterness. Seeking to avenge his mother, Eudes II attacked the royal domain and captured Melun. Then his wife, Mahaut, sister of the duke of Normandy, died before leaving a child, and he refused to return Dreux, which was her dowry. Richard of Normandy, supported by Robert the Pious and assisted by the Danes, attacked Eudes's domains. But the Danes ravaged the royal property as well as the lands of the count of Chartres. A compromise was clearly necessary. Eudes would be able to retain Dreux if he returned Melun. Definitely quite impatient, he also attacked the count of Anjou, Foulques Nerra, but he was defeated and lost Saumur. By the play of inheritances, however, Eudes came into possession of the powerful earldom of Champagne in 1019. From then on he lived in Troyes and left the city of Chartres in the care of his viscount, Gilduin.

At this time the bishop was Fulbert, who had been a student of Gerbert d'Aurillac, the pope in the year 1000, when he was a doctor in Reims. Fulbert was a remarkable scholar and a famous teacher; many compared him to Socrates. Under his aegis the schools of Chartres became famous and went on to play a significant role in the diffusion of scholastic philosophy for at least two centuries, until the founding of the University of Paris in 1215 brought about their decline. It was during Fulbert's episcopacy that the Carolingian cathedral was burned down, and it was Fulbert who directed the reconstruction, which resulted in the building of the crypt and the Romanesque cathedral. Thanks to the friendly feelings and interest he had inspired throughout Europe, Fulbert obtained significant funds for the reconstruction from a number of monarchs, including the king of France, Robert; the king of England, Canut; the duke of Aquitaine, William IV; and the duke of Normandy, Richard; not to mention the counts of Chartres and Champagne. The new cathedral was almost completed at the time of Fulbert's death in 1028, but another fire delayed its consecration, which did not take place until 1037. But it is beyond question that Fulbert, through his wisdom, his influence, and his talents as an organizer, left an undying memory in Chartres and its cathedral sanctuary.

Fulbert's successors, such as Bernard de Chartres and his brother Yves (who died in 1117 and was known as Saint Yves de Chartres), and Gilbert de la Porrée, who died in 1141, were all eminent intellectuals. But the most illustrious, who occupied the seat for only four years, was John of Salisbury, who was born in 1110 and died in 1180, a brilliant theoretician, a great mystic, and the faithful secretary of Thomas à Becket, who was assassinated on the orders of King Henry II. Why was Chartres given an "English" bishop (even though England in that era, under the tutelage of the Plantagenets, was more French than English), especially given that prelates of French origin often held British Episcopal seats?

It has been claimed that during his youth, John of Salisbury had finished some of his studies in France and had spent three years in Chartres, retaining afterward very pleasant memories of that time. When he arrived on the Continent, he went to the school where Pierre Abélard taught in Paris and there learned the rudiments of dialectics. But Abélard, as we know, was forced into exile, and John of Salisbury changed disciplines, learning grammar from Guillaume de Conches, a true philologist. It is possible that Guillaume de Conches taught in Chartres, where John of Salisbury would have met him and benefited from his teachings. Whatever the truth of the matter, John of Salisbury acquired an extensive and multidisciplinary education, becoming a fourteenth-century humanist who was very much ahead of his time. He was never a teacher. He lived among the high and mighty of this world, such as the pope, the kings of England, and the archbishops of Canterbury. This is how he was first servant, then secretary, to Thomas à Becket. He traveled widely and wrote several books, including the *Historia Pontificalis;* the *Metalogicon,* in which he touched on the problem of dialectics; and most important, the famous *Policraticus,* a political treatise of a range and audacity not previously achieved.

John of Salisbury did not conceive of philosophy as abstract learning, but rather as wisdom and a discipline of life. Purely speculative problems seemed a waste of time and energy to him; he preferred the Delphic maxim "Know thyself." He was a man of wisdom in the sense that he sought to describe real, material structures in relation to a divine plan in which he firmly believed. The true philosophy for him was "love of God" and to know the divine plan: "The measure prescribed of charity is that it is necessary to love God with a love beyond measure." John of Salisbury was certainly friends with Bernard de Clairvaux, and his works give off a certain monastic aroma. To define his works with a single expression, we might say that they reflect an intellectual asceticism. The views he lays out in his *Policraticus,* however, are quite amazing; although they smack of the purest orthodoxy, they are nonetheless innovative.

The *Policraticus* is an extensive, theologically based meditation on the institutions of the early Middle Ages, from which John draws his own conclusions. It is independent from the Continental schools of thought from which Thomism would later arise, and is a return to original sources—the Bible and the works of the Church fathers—but is also a resurgence of what the Celtic Christian Church, a church that was heavily influenced by Druidism, was saying and thinking at the time.[7] It is a feudal approach to the topic, which is entirely normal given the time in which it was written. John defines the relationship that should exist between a ruler and his subjects. It should involve not merely an oath that is a formality but also a total commitment on the parts of both parties. John of Salisbury's preference was for a form of government similar to that of the Hebrews under the leadership of the Judges, before the throne of Israel was established.

His basic postulate is the existence of some prior, higher, transcendental law. The first logical consequence of this postulate is that any people who follow this law and submit to its demands have no need of a king. It may be surprising to find here the same mentality that inspired the libertarian theories of the end of the nineteenth century, but this is indeed the case. It also explains this philosophy's kinship with Rousseau's *Social Contract,* for John of Salisbury also asserted that if human beings are fundamentally good, they cannot help but obey the higher law: "The first patriarchs followed nature, the best guide in life. They were succeeded by a line of leaders beginning with Moses, who followed the Law, then by Judges, who ruled the people through the authority of the Law. And we see that the more recent of them were priests. In the end, because of the wrath of the Lord, they had kings, some of whom were good but most of whom were wicked" *(Policraticus).* If we understand him correctly, this rule by the throne was a punishment. This agrees with Saint Augustine's thought (*De Civitate Dei,* XIX, 15) that "the just men of earlier ages were more like shepherds of their flocks than kings of men."

John of Salisbury is not too far from Diderot when he asserts that there is no need for the subordination of one human being to another: "Men will only find harmony and connection with each

---

7. See Jean Markale, *Le Christianisme primitif et ses survivances populaires.* There is also an analysis of the theories of John of Salisbury in the chapter "The Political Background" in Jean Markale, *King of the Celts* (Rochester, Vt.: Inner Traditions, 1994), 59–64.

other if they group or have been grouped together under the dispassionate reasoning of divine law. And it is better to form a group by oneself, than to be organized by the authority of a government" *(Policraticus)*. It is undoubtedly not by chance that John of Salisbury became the bishop of Chartres. Is not Chartres the glorification of the Virgin as the Throne of Wisdom, the absolute keeper of knowledge of the divine law?

But all this was mere theory. The fact remains that kings existed. John had to define the role of the king. First and foremost, he is only the *princeps* (Latin for the "first head"). As such he is the representative of the community and minister of the common interest. He bears the "public persona" and must look upon himself as the servant of the people. The king is an officer, which means his role is to act, but his actions are never his own; they are those of the *Universitas,* the organized community that he heads: "The prince is the servant of the Lord, but he fulfills his duty by faithfully serving his fellow servants (of God or the Law), in other words those called his subjects" *(Policraticus* IV, 7). But how should the king be chosen?

John of Salisbury rejects the notion of hereditary power, and his work already intimates the Thomist prescription *a Deo per populum* (from God through the people), which assumes the acceptance, if not selection, of the king by his people. "Whereas public offices may be passed down to the heir of the current holder, the government of the people does not pass down in the same way as a matter of right. It is accorded to the individual who has in him the spirit of God, and a knowledge of the Law" *(Policraticus* V, 6). Thus, the king is confronted with a series of obligations that he is compelled to respect because they represent a force higher than his own. And if he no longer obeys his duties, he becomes a "tyrant"—so it is "better to remove the crown from the king's head than allow him to destroy the order and the best part of the community at his good pleasure" *(Policraticus* VII, 30).

Popes certainly always reserved for themselves the right to

depose kings, but in the thought of John of Salisbury, even revolution and tyrannicide can be legitimate: "It is as legal to kill a tyrant as it is to kill a sworn enemy" (*Policraticus* VIII, 20). But tyrannicide should not be considered an act of private vengeance; it is an act of collective responsibility. This easily explains John of Salisbury's attitude following Thomas à Becket's murder. He ceaselessly denounced the "tyranny" of Henry Plantagenet and did all he could to magnify the memory of the holy archbishop of Canterbury. He introduced the worship of Saint Thomas to Chartres itself, presenting him as a model not only of holiness but also of civic duty, insofar as the archbishop had stood up against all the abuses of the English king.

The wisdom, honesty, and insight of John of Salisbury make him one of the most appealing figures of the twelfth century, and it is to Chartres's honor that he was chosen bishop. This, more than any previous act, gave homage to the Holy Ghost descended into the womb of the Virgin Mary: It was acknowledgment that if wisdom was nothing without love, love was nothing without wisdom. Who can still honestly claim that this was the Dark Ages? In any case, Chartres gleamed with a light all its own. There is good reason that the cathedral is filled with depictions of philosophers and inspired prophets.

Accordingly, the city of Chartres enjoyed considerable growth during the eleventh and twelfth centuries, as much for the power and renown of its counts as for the supremacy of its schools. Toward 1060, the upper city was encircled by an imposing fortified enceinte that on its most vulnerable side could be passed through only at the Perchéronne Gate. On the rim of the plateau facing north and east, the Evrière Gate, as its name indicates, gave access to the river, the Cendreuse Gate, and the Foucher-Nivelon postern, which was protected by the Count's Tower. Beneath the cathedral there were also at one time a gate called Saint-Jean-de-la-Vallée and, on the right bank of the Eure, the Morard and Aimbard Gates, as well as the Tireveau postern. The defense of the city seems to have been quite well organized. In addition, a prodigious expansion of Church properties also took place at this time. All the different abbeys were growing richer and expanding. Of course, as was true everywhere that monastic establishments were located during the Middle Ages, there were a large number of vineyards, especially on the sun-drenched hillsides of Champhol and Saint-Chéron and around Saint-Lubin. The surface area of vineyards sometimes reached as much as four hectares for a single landholder, a considerable figure that attests to the demand for wine, both for worship and for everyday drinking.

Inside the city, numerous merchants and artisans were established and working, it seems, under the best possible conditions. Large fairs took place, namely during the four Marian feast days: the Nativity, the Annunciation, the Purification, and the Assumption. Some merchants enjoyed special privileges and the protection of the cathedral enceinte, which would later be called Notre-Dame Cloister. A veritable city inside a city, it escaped the count's jurisdiction and was under the authority of the bishop alone. It so happens that ecclesiastical authority was less demanding than that of the civil powers. The "sworn" of Notre-Dame Cloister were by and large beneficiaries of this juridical status, which also increased the prestige of the chapter. Certainly, in the case of a conflict or quarrel, the sworn of the chapter would seek refuge in the homes of the canons, but these latter welcomed them gladly; and if the count's officers forced their way into the chapter house, there was always recourse to excommunication to persuade the representatives of the count's power to back off. It would sometimes happen, however, that quarrels of this nature degenerated into battles, even all-out sieges. Cohabitation was not always easy, even during this period when the Church and the state seemed to be able to get along for better or for worse.

It was in the midst of this highly prosperous time that the great fire of 1194 broke out on June 10, lasting into the morning of June 11. Fulbert's cathedral was heavily damaged. Only the Royal Portal, the crypts, and the recently built West Towers were spared. The chronicles of the time describe how the populace fell into deep despair upon seeing their magnificent sanctuary in a state of almost total destruction and believing that the precious relic of the Tunic of Mary had been lost to the flames. The third day after the fire the pope's legate, Cardinal Melchior of Pisa, gathered everyone in front of the ruins of the cathedral and exhorted the people to make every effort to rebuild the sanctuary. At this very moment a procession appeared, carrying with it the intact relic. The clerics had brought it inside the crypt, where they waited out the fire underground. The legate immediately proclaimed this a sign from Mary to build a church that would be even more magnificent than the old one.

This wish was carried out. With delirious enthusiasm, the local men gathered in the quarries of Berchères-les-Pierres, some six miles away, to help extract blocks of stone, then transport them on carts to the worksite that had sprung up in the heart of the city. Donations flooded in from all over—from the various barons of the kingdom, the king of France, Philip Augustus, and then Louis VIII. Even Richard the Lion Heart, although a prisoner in Germany, authorized the priests of his domains to gather offerings to send to Chartres. Among the generous donors were Blanche de Castille, Pierre Mauclerc, and Alix of Brittany; the king of Castille, Ferdinand III; and the count of Champagne, Thibaud VI, whose gift was some of the stained glass in the choir. In 1220 the cathedral that we know today was virtually completed. But the festival of the dedication did not take place until 1260.

As an earldom, however, Chartres was enjoying its final days of independence. In 1234 Thibaud of Champagne, the trouvère [troubadour] prince, ceded his right to sovereignty to the king of France. By inheritance the earldom came into the possession of Jeanne de Châtillin, wife of the third son of Saint Louis, Pierre de France. Upon becoming a widow, she sold all her rights to her brother-in-law, Philip the Bold, in 1286. Seven years later Philip the Fair gave the earldom of Chartres to his brother Charles of Valois, but when the latter's son, Philip, became king of France, the earldom was for all intents and purposes part of the royal domain.

The Hundred Years' War destroyed the splendor of Chartres. The Beauce was located on a very strategic site: It guarded the approaches to Paris from the west and sat on the road leading from Normandy to the banks of the Loire. It was even the most direct route connecting the English territories on the Channel to those in the southwest. This position would bring great suffering to the entire Chartrian region.

In 1358, Chartres was practically blockaded for six months by a large company bivouacked in Épernon. On May 8, 1360, the famous Anglo-French treaty ratifying the defeat of John the Good in Poitiers, which also strove to end the war of succession in Brittany, was signed in a small hamlet right outside the gates of Chartres, Brétigny. In 1367, a company of archers was established in service of the king of France and under the direct orders of the *vidame,* who had originally been the leader of the bishop's men at arms. It was again in Chartres, in 1392, that King Charles VI gathered an army to invade Brittany. During this expedition, he went mad while in the forest of Mans. In 1409 the cathedral was the theater (a perfect word in this instance!) for the reconciliation between the duke of Orléans, Louis, and the duke of Burgundy, John the Fearless.

This was a false peace, however, and civil war broke out again the following year between the Armagnacs and the Burgundians. The notables of Chartres had sided with the duke of Orléans, but in 1417 they surrendered to the Burgundian leader Hélion de Jacqueville. Then, following the treaty of Troyes in 1420, the city of Chartres recognized the king of England as heir to the crown of France. But the dauphin Charles, after a futile attempt to gain possession of Chartres, finally recovered it thanks to Dunois, the Bastard of Orléans. The Chartres economy, which had suffered greatly from all the wars, was rapidly restored to health with the help of Charles VII and Louis XI, who saw in this Beauce center both a strategic site and a commercial crossroads of the utmost importance.

A charter was granted Chartres in 1296, but this was not the basis for its becoming a commune. To the contrary, everything was put into place for municipal administration to originate solely from royal authority. Nothing could be done without the assent of the bailiff, representative of the count, then the king. In 1562 a governor was installed who performed the same duties concurrently with the bailiff. The former earldom of Chartres, which had been connected to the crown for two centuries, was elevated into a duchy and given to Hercule d'Este, duke of Ferrara, son of Lucrezia Borgia and husband of the second daughter of Louis XII and Anne of Brittany, Renée of France (in fact, heiress of Brittany). But the title was an honorific at best, because the revenues from this domain were mediocre. In any event, the duke and duchess of Chartres never lived in this Beauce city. This was the beginning of the decline of the wealthy bourgeois class composed of merchants and artisans. The bourgeoisie found its way to the vocations of the robe and the liberal professions but did not ignore literature and the fine arts. The old Chartrian mentality was not dead, and still fresh was the memory of the time when the cathedral schools attracted intellectuals from all over Europe.

New sources of turmoil made their presence felt, this time over religious issues. In 1523, a heretic was burned alive in Chartres for having overturned a statue of the Virgin in the cathedral. The bishop was then the formidable Louis Guillard, who held the poet Clément Marot in prison for having written—and published—poems that were hardly orthodox. The Reformation made considerable headway in the Chartrian bourgeois milieu, but despite everything, the population remained divided into two camps, Catholic and Protestant, although Rouen and Orléans were held by the Protestants. Condé[8] was fighting in the nearby countryside but

---

8. [Louis I de Bourbon, prince of Condé (1530–1569), was a Protestant leader and general. Although he enjoyed the favor of the regent, Catherine de Medici, he had little support in the French court. He took command of the Huguenots in the Wars of Religion and was captured at Dreux (1562). Following his release in 1563, he again took up arms in 1567 against the Catholics and was killed at the battle of Jarnac. —*Trans.*]

failed to capture Chartres. He ultimately collided with the duke of Guise near Dreux and was captured.

A fragile peace was established during which Catherine de Medici and Charles IX stayed in Chartres, endeavoring to reach a compromise with Condé, who was being held at that time in the Abbey of Saint-Père. But the Huguenots regained the upper hand in 1567, and during the following year Condé laid siege to the city with a massive force. The city was not taken, and Condé was forced to lift his siege, but the suburbs and surrounding settlements had suffered greatly from this action. The Abbey of Saint-John, the Cordeliers Convent, and the Hospital of the Six-Vingt aveugles had been destroyed. All the outlying areas of Chartres had been put to the torch, by both Catholics and Protestants. This did not prevent the Catholics from claiming victory against the heretics, a victory they attributed to the intercession of the city's guardian, the Virgin Mary.

This did not end the troubles; Chartres was doomed to suffer similar privations from the disorder sparked by the League [the Holy League, which refused to accept the rule of a Protestant king —*Translator*] and its battles against the royal troops and against Henri of Bourbon, the nonbeliever who was still the sole legitimate heir to the throne of France. In 1588, Henry III met in Chartres with Henry of Guise, whom he rightly suspected of having designs on the throne. Henry of Valois, seething with rage, had been compelled under threat to invite the Chartrians to declare their support for the duke of Guise and the league. But stricken by the news of the assassination of the duke of Guise on order of the king, the Chartrians declared themselves body and soul for the duke of Mayenne, the new leader of the league.

The year 1590 saw the Chartres countryside transformed into a permanent battlefield. Henry of Navarre besieged Dreux and fought Mayenne's army at Ivry, while league troops took Nogent-le-Roi, then lost and recaptured Courville and Illiers. But on February 10, 1591, Biron, commander of the Navarre troops, laid siege to Chartres. There was a long series of skirmishes, various maneuvers, and heavy destruction. Henry of Navarre joined Biron on the field and personally organized the siege. On April 10, Chartres capitulated, and the royal army took occupation of the city nine days later. Henri of Navarre made his solemn entrance into the city on April 20 and was welcomed at Saint Michael's Gate by the residents and the clergy, who led him to the cathedral. But he did not enter the building. Instead, he attended a Calvinist sermon the next day, while 40,000 people followed a procession to Saint-Père to give thanks for the restoration of peace. The city was taxed 36,000 *écus* for having put up resistance to the king of France. But soon, to calm spirits, the Navarrais pardoned those who were most compromised and made efforts to ensure that the city's inhabitants did not suffer too greatly from the situation.

Chartres then became a kind of capital of a torn French kingdom in which the legitimate king was striving to conquer the hearts of his subjects. Visits from the greatest leaders followed one after the other, and negotiations were pursued more or less openly, especially between Henry of Navarre and representatives of the Catholic Church. On July 25, 1593, Henry renounced Calvinism, and on February 25, 1594, he was crowned king of France in the cathedral of Chartres by Bishop Nicolas de Thou, because Reims was still in the hands of the Holy League and thus unavailable. The coronation and the vow taken by Henry IV to support the Catholic religion would open the gates of Paris to him three weeks later. The civil war was finally over.

This does not mean that all disorder came to an end. Despite the Edict of Nantes, cohabitation between Protestants and Catholics was delicate. The Huguenots made several attempts to take possession of Chartres, but the vast majority of the city remained Catholic. In 1607, Henry of Savoy inherited the duchy of Chartres from his mother, but in 1623 he sold it for 250,000 *écus* in gold to King Louis XIII. The king gave it as prerogative to his brother, Gaston of Orléans. Of course, Gaston's rebellion would have serious repercussions on Chartres and its region. This was equally true at the time of the Fronde, in which the same Gaston played a leading role.[9] In 1651, extensive rioting took place in Chartres. This was followed by an attempt by an army supporting the Fronde to capture the city; the army abandoned its plans only after being paid an indemnity of 16,000 pounds. Peace was restored, but Chartres fell into the hands of a central authority and could no longer claim any municipal freedom. Gaston of Orléans died in 1660, leaving no male heir, and the duchy of Chartres reverted to the throne. But Louis XIV placed it in the hands of his brother Philip, and it remained in the Orléans lineage until the Revolution.

Although civil autonomy was practically nonexistent in Chartres during the final years of the ancien régime, this was not true of the Church, which continued to evolve, even if it led to conflicts with civil authorities. The chief concern of the Chartres bishops was defending the faithful of the diocese from both poverty and ignorance, thereby renewing the old tradition of the medieval schools of the city. The Daughters of Providence was established in 1643 with the chief intention of preventing poor women from turning to prostitution. In 1692, members of the Daughters of Saint Paul devoted themselves to educating women and training them in their household duties. In 1659, a large seminary was installed on the site of the ancient hospice of the Madeleine du Grand-Beaulieu. But in 1695, the diocese of Chartres, heir to the ancient city of the Carnutes, lost a large part of its territory after the creation of the new diocese of Blois.

During the eighteenth century, the population of Chartres dwindled. From 20,000 inhabitants at the end of the sixteenth century, the population had fallen to 15,000, then to 13,000 due to the attraction of the nearby capital as well as in response to the decline of economic activity. The great property owners were the monasteries and the bishopric, and their holdings consisted of large green spaces inside the city walls. The Place des Halles, where an important

---

9. [The Fronde (1648–1653) was a civil war in France that led to war with Spain (1653–59). *Fronde* means "sling" and refers to how Parisian mobs threw stones at windows (belonging to supporters of Cardinal Mazarin). The revolt originated in an attempt to impose limitations on the king's authority. —*Trans*].

market in grains was located, was the center of interurban activity. There were eleven parishes, seven of which were inside the city walls. Now more than ever, Notre-Dame Cloister formed a city within a city.

The suburbs meanwhile re-formed as small, drab villages of poor thatched cottages. Even the leisure classes, outside of a few privileged families, no longer had fine mansions at their disposal. The nobility of the Beauce did not have a reputation for wealth, and it was often said that "the Beauce gentleman would remain in bed when his breeches were being mended." Although the populace was unevenly distributed among the different parishes, it was clear that those of the upper city were more numerous and wealthier. The cathedral, for its part, had weathered every storm. It remained the perfect symbol of this profoundly Catholic city. Yet it was also here that on September 11, 1788, the first meeting of the Masonic Lodge known as the Franchise took place in a modest house on the rue de Beauvais, an association that would last until 1840.

The Revolution unfolded in Chartres just as it did elsewhere in France, although with fewer exactions and less disorder than in some other cities. There were some pillaging, some brawls, some reversals of fortune, and some executions, but the biggest difficulties lay in the acquisition of fresh supplies and in the high cost of living, unemployment, and brigandage (particularly the misdeeds of the sinister Orgères Band).

Chartres emerged from the tempest considerably impoverished. Its religious movements had meanwhile suffered a sad fate. Saint-Foy Church and Saint-Aignan Church were sold to a private citizen who sought to demolish them. But the owner wanted to turn Saint-Aignan into a performance site, which allowed it to escape destruction. Eventually the Saint-Foy would become a theater. Saint-Saturnien was demolished, and the space was used to create a square dedicated to the memory of the heroes of Chartres, such as General Marceau. The churches of Saint-Maurice, Saint-Michel, Saint-Bartholomew, Saint-Chéron, and Saint-Brice were demolished, and residential housing was built on their former sites. Upon the destruction of Saint-Martin-le-Viandier, a square was created in the space it had occupied. Saint-Hilaire served to house the local chapter of the Folk Society before it too was demolished. But Saint-André was turned into storage for fodder and was spared despite various degradations. The Carmelite Convent, as well as that of the Jacobins, became a prison. Saint-Père Abbey was turned into a plant for manufacturing saltpeter, and the convent buildings were turned to other uses. Saint-Martin-au-Val was converted into a hospice, and the Episcopal palace served as a prefecture until 1821.

The cathedral itself barely escaped demolition: It was deemed that the congestion caused by the handling and transport of the building's materials through the city would cause more problems than benefits. The municipal authorities were content with removing the lead from the covers and grilles of the chapels to make into bullets and picks. This is how the magnificent cathedral we see today emerged from these dark times—if not unscathed, at least generally protected.

During the consulate and the empire, but also during the restoration, Chartres fell into the hands of one of the families who had acquired wealth and influence through the purchase of national properties, the Billard de Saint-Laumer family. They were members of the bourgeois class, who turned everything to its profit and did not hesitate to swear loyalty to every regime, empire or royal, when it was not a foreign occupation, as was the case in 1814. The disruptions of the traditional hierarchy caused by the Revolution had benefited some but not the majority of the Chartres population.

Generally speaking, the time of the empire was a period of stagnation for Chartres. The local tanning and textile industries hardly developed. Certainly Chartres remained one of the most active wheat markets in the Beauce, but that was all. There was no longer any dynamism and no opening to the Industrial Revolution, which had just breasted the horizon. The change of regime in 1830 only emphasized the anticlerical components of municipal life. The mayor of Chartres, Adolphe Chasles, was the nephew of the former curé of the cathedral. He was an Orléans supporter but quite modest in his convictions. Once elected deputy from Eure-et-Loir, he presided over the inauguration ceremony of the chapel for the Aligre Asylum in Lèves, which replaced the Sainte-Marie de Josaphat Abbey, which had been bought and demolished by his grandfather and father and from which they had realized a substantial profit. And yet to be elected, Chasles had to run a resolutely anticlerical campaign.

On the other side, the Church was getting its head back up. The Concordat of 1802 had attached the Eure-et-Loir Département to the diocese of Versailles, created specifically for this purpose on this occasion. The government had then decided that Chartres would be divided into two parishes, the cathedral and the ancient Saint-Père Abbey, renamed Saint-Pierre, which would be ample for the needs of a populace that was slowly becoming de-Christianized. The restoration of the Episcopal seat of Chartres was decided in 1817 but did not take effect until 1821. In this year, Monsignor de Latil, a former chaplain of the earldom of Artois, became bishop of Chartres and strove to reorganize the local clergy, often with much clumsiness and regrettable displays of open bias.

His successor, Claudel de Montals, a man of the ancien régime but of clearly Gallican tendencies, held this position for thirty years, but he spent his time fighting against all sides without any benefit to the religious life of his diocese. In 1833 he was even confronted by a serious riot sparked by his refusal to authorize a priest, Abbé Ledru, in Lèves, to celebrate the Mass in French, as all his parishioners wanted. Vatican II was still far from the horizon, and the bishop barely had time to take refuge in the cathedral while his bishopric was plundered by the populace. In 1836, a fire destroyed the timbered framework of the cathedral, which was called the Forest. The framework was rebuilt in iron, which is quite contrary not only to custom but also to the energetic value of the sanctuary.[10]

---

10. The first churches built by the Celts contained no nails or iron fittings, as iron has the property of diverting so-called telluric currents.

Academic quarrels began poisoning life in Chartres, and the line was already appearing that would eventually expand into the moat separating the proponents of the so-called school of the devil from those of the so-called school of the Good Lord. During this time the city continued to live—or at least to survive—thanks to its grain market. April 9, 1848, saw the first elections by universal suffrage. The mayor-elect, confirmed by the prefect, Charles Rémond, declared as a Republican, just like the future Cardinal Pius, who represented the bishop at the planting of the Freedom Tree on April 11 that same year.

The Second Empire, despite a fairly strong opposition to the plebiscite, inspired the local legitimist or Orléans bourgeoisie to rally. It was only in 1865 that the Republicans managed to return in force to the Chartres city hall. That said, Chartres did become more prosperous during this period. A theater was built in 1861, followed by a hospital several years later. Old-fashioned houses were razed, and an urbanization scheme along the broad lines of what Baron Haussmann had planned for Paris was implemented. In 1869 an exposition that provided a veritable panorama of local activity took place; even the emperor paid a visit. The head of the foundry, Alexandre Brault, and Mayor Billard de Saint-Laumer (of the same family mentioned earlier) were awarded medals of the Legion of Honor. A traditional tannery continued to persevere, while printing and window-making industries took on new life. Meanwhile, the vineyards continued to be quite prosperous, curiously enough, until the phylloxera epidemic in 1881.

During the Franco-Prussian War in 1870, the Prussians occupied the city, where they would remain until March 18, 1871. The beginnings of the Third Republic passed without causing too many clashes, but soon the academic quarrel would rekindle the hotheadedness of the different parties. At first there was a semblance of balance between the lay schools and the confessional schools, but the Jules Ferry laws [which mandated public education —*Trans.*] took a long time to be applied. A state school for girls was opened in 1880 on the rue Sainte-Même to remove some of the load from the teachers training college, but it would not be until 1891 that the Saint-André and Saint-Ferdinand schools would become state-run institutions.

Debate was endless on the transformation of the *collège* [private secondary school] into a *lycée* [high school], and the new *lycée* would not be inaugurated until 1887. Discussion continued for much of this time over the opening of a secondary *collège* for young girls. This *collège* would be established in 1885 in the former teachers training school. Saint-Père Abbey, meanwhile, had become a military barracks. Water conveyance had become a major concern, and an ozonization process was applied starting in 1906. The central train station was rebuilt on the site of the former Notre-Dame cemetery. Various urbanization construction projects were implemented. But Chartres continued to stagnate under the influence of a smug conservatism that only a few newspapers, such as *La Dépêche*, founded in 1899 by Georges Fessard, managed to disturb. Eventually, however, the Chartres area would become radical-socialist, Freemason, and somewhat anticlerical.

But the approach of World War I in 1914 brought about the establishment of a military presence in Chartres, which was aided by a popular desire to avenge the former defeats suffered at the hands of the Germans. The garrison consisted of a cavalry regiment, an infantry battalion, a squadron of train crews, and an artillery regiment. Above all, a large drill ground between the roads to Sours and to Nogent-le-Phaye was reserved for testing airplanes. This would be the origin of the Chartres Air Base.

Spared during the First World War, the Beauceron capital sank back into its torpor between 1918 and 1939. Chartres was no longer anything but a small provincial city, a farm-product market of diminished activity. The animal auctions were in a state of collapse. Sheep were no longer being raised on the plains. Meanwhile, the rich Beauce landowners were gradually abandoning the countryside to move into the city, which sparked the construction of new apartment buildings and houses. Neglected sections of the city began to be repopulated. The train station was modernized when the Paris–Le Mans line was electrified, which coincided with the disappearance of the old Ouest-État network and the creation of the S.N.C.F. [Société Nationale des Chemins de Fer, the state-run railroad system in France —*Trans.*]. The Chartres station, with its branch lines and shunting capacity, became quite important, and construction began on a new line from Montparnasse that would pass through Limours and Gallardon. This line was never completed. It was around this time that rumors of war began to alarm the local leaders. Precautionary measures were planned for the populace, primarily because of the nearby air base. One of the most important safeguards was the removal of the stained glass from the cathedral. We owe our ability to admire these windows today to these precautions.

The Second World War left its mark on the city of Chartres; it was bombed several times by the Germans as well as the Americans. Fortunately, the cathedral suffered very little from these perils, despite the burdensome presence of the neighboring station, which was an important communication hub at that time. The primary damage suffered was in June 1940, in the Aviation Quarter, then again between September 1943 and August 1944. On August 16, 17, and 18, 1944, a handful of resistance fighters managed to capture Chartres and contain German efforts to retake the city until American troops could arrive and bring a successful conclusion to the battle for freedom.

Chartres has grown nonstop since the end of the war. The first task immediately following the Liberation was to rebuild everything that had been destroyed, but the requirements of industrial society shattered the traditional city limits. The population, which was 26,000 inhabitants in 1946, rose to more than 42,000 in 1951. New city neighborhoods were laid out, first in Bel-Air and in Rechèvres, then in Beaulieu, Saint-Chéron, and Puits-Drouet, and finally in the Madeleine. Three new parishes were added: Saint-Jean-Baptiste de

Rechèvres, Saint-Paul de Beaulieu, and the Madeleine. Urban problems of Chartres were those of all old cities. Renovation was needed, automobile traffic had to be regularized, and commercial and trade zones had to be laid out. An industrial zone that grouped together nonpolluting industries (perfumeries, electronics, printing, and small mechanics) was accordingly established in the south along the Paris-Rennes highway. But Chartres offered few real prospects, and the inhabitants, taking advantage of the rail connections and direct roads, most often found employment in the Parisian region, with the effect that the old Beauceron city has become a kind of bedroom community.

Chartres has lost none of its artistic and touristic value, however. After 1964, in the context of the Malraux Law, a plan was created (and made official in 1971) to protect the old city. It concerns a section of sixty-four hectares, which is equivalent to three fourths of the space inside the walls. The state, the region, and the commune have participated jointly in the renovation of the old dwellings as well as the enhancement of the environment. In this regard, the work undertaken has been crowned with success, and a very sure hand has restored the old quarters. Furthermore, the old artistic professions such as stained-glass making have been restored to honor. In fact, the International Stained Glass Center is located in the old wheat-storage buildings in the medieval neighborhood of Loëns. The center was inaugurated in 1980, and since that time has spread the prestige of this medieval French art far and wide.

The choice of Chartres for this international center is perfectly logical. The cathedral incontestably constitutes the richest collection of twelfth- and thirteenth-century stained glass in existence, and these windows are, for the most part, although carefully restored, intact. They have traveled through the centuries without having been deformed or destroyed by wars, revolutions, or even the negative effects of bad weather. Chartres figures among the fifty-seven sites chosen for inclusion in the first World Cultural Heritage list, published by UNESCO in 1980. This is a marvelous honor for

Chartres. Art lovers, tourists, historians of the Middle Ages, musicians, and music lovers drawn by the renovation of the Great Organs, all join with the crowds of pilgrims who come to meditate in the crypt, near the Well of the Saints-Forts, before the statue of Our Lady of Under Ground, or in the cathedral itself, in front of the Black Madonna on her pillar. More than ever, beauty and faith are indissolubly linked in Chartres for the greatest exaltation of the spirit. The Cathedral of Our Lady of Chartres, like an immutable beacon in the center of storms that emerge from every direction, remains what it once was and what it was ever intended to be: the Throne of Wisdom.

PART 2

THE VIRGIN'S GREAT SHADOW

4

THE MOTHER OF GOD

genetrix?

In 431 the Council of Ephesus definitively proclaimed as Christian doctrine the concept of Theotokos, meaning "mother" or rather "genetrix" of God, applied to Mary of the Gospels, she who gave birth to Jesus. Before this date, numerous controversies swirled around the figure of Mary among the various Christian theoreticians now known as the church fathers. It is obvious that the incarnation of God cannot be accepted without reference to a physical birth. In this domain, pre-Christian religious traditions have always vacillated between incarnation properly speaking and epiphany (or theophany), meaning the manifestation of a higher being in human form by his own power in a pure and simple materialization. Accordingly, in the *Iliad* and in the *Odyssey,* divine figures appear to humans in an almost natural fashion, although at times they use disguises better to test those they want to guide or provoke. Athena, Aphrodite, and Circe are personified deities whom it is normal, so to speak, to meet at a bend in the road, but who disappear into the invisible world once their intervention has been achieved.

The same holds true in Celtic tradition, at least what we know of it. The gods take part on certain occasions in the life of humans and bear the exact same appearance (with the addition of characteristics indicative of their higher status, even sometimes in the form of a physical handicap), and they disappear once their mission has been accomplished. But what is involved here—as with the ancient Germans as well—is much more the concretization of a functional aspect of a single deity rather than the strict "materialization" of a personified divine being.

Hindu thought introduces another notion, that of the *avatar*. The avatar is not a materialization but rather a veritable embodiment. Given the doctrine of reincarnation, it is normal to think that gods may from time to time incarnate under different identities while retaining their divine quality, concealed beneath the natural human appearance they have donned. This is what is known in religious history as a *hypostasis,* which means the temporarily inferior status of a superior sacred being. In Indian logic the avatar does not pose a problem. Many Hindus are ready to accept the divinity of Jesus as the hypostasis of a higher being, and why not Jehovah?

But the mentality is slightly different in the Middle East concerning the Mithraic religion. Mithra, an ancient god inherited from Iran—and in the final analysis India—truly incarnated as a human being, but his birth is irregular because he was mysteriously engendered by the earth—that is to say, the original Mother Goddess—which matches the ancient Greek theogonies in which Gaia couples with Ouranos to give birth to the race of gods. But taking into account, on the one hand, that Mithra's birth was celebrated on December 25, and, on the other, that the Mithraic religion experienced significant growth during the first centuries of the Christian era, even threatening to supplant Christianity, certain questions arise. Human beings have always held the concept of an incarnated or manifested god, even if only to allow them to communicate and establish a dialogue with a higher being that is the creator and master of all, but which remains inaccessible, unnamable, and incomprehensible because it is infinite and absolute.

On this point Christianity offers something completely different and completely new. Jesus can certainly be considered a hypostasis, but he cannot be considered an avatar. He is the envoy, the anointed one—that is to say the Christ, the only son of a Father God of which he is only an integral emanation embodied in humanity. Jesus is not a deity who abandons the invisible world to incarnate as an avatar on earth. He is still in the invisible world, *but he is also in the visible world* through the process of his full and total incarnation, by his complete humanity. This is no doubt the first time that such a notion appeared in the history of human thought, and it is what makes Christianity profoundly original. But it is obvious that such a notion poses more problems than it seems to resolve if we stick to a historicizing explanation of the facts.

Historicizing has prompted the sharpest controversies concerning the "mystery of the Incarnation" and the concept of the Theotokos. The Christian message, of Hebrew (and even Aramaic) origin, traveled through the Hellenistic world before reaching the heart of the Roman world. The incorporation of the Christian message by the Roman mentality was not without consequence. The Roman mentality had one characteristic that, while not widely known, has been firmly established: It is *historicizing*. The Roman mind—in contrast to the philosophical Greek mind—created history everywhere, even where there was no basis for it. The Roman mind demanded the concrete before all else. This, moreover, was the strength of ancient Rome on the political plane as well as on the military, economic, and juridical planes.

But as Georges Dumezil has shown, while the Indians and Celts thought *mythically,* the Romans were incapable of grasping myths as anything other than history that had been actually experienced and arbitrarily situated at a definite time. The most famous example is that of Horatius Cocles (Horatius the One-Eyed), who, according to Titus Levy, defended the Sublician Bridge against attack by the Etruscans. Horatius was therefore presented as a historical figure, a heroic Roman patriot. In fact, his tale was an existing story from the myth of Odin-Wotan, the one-eyed god of Germanic mythology. The same was true of another "historical" hero, Mucius Scaevola, who was nothing more or less than the Germanic—and Indo-European— god Tyr, the one-armed god who was not afraid to swear a false oath and thereby lose his arm in order to save his community. As for the three Curiatii, who became so famous thanks to Corneille, it is not so hard to see in them the multiple-headed Hydra of Lerne that the no-less-renowned Hercules-Heracles fought against.

There are numerous other examples, in particular concerning the so-called historical king Numa Pompilius, who had secret discussions with the goddess Egeria (from whose name the term *égérie* ["oracle"] derives); she whispered wise counsel into his ear so that he could enact laws to govern his people, enabling him, like Moses, to give the laws a divine value that was beyond challenge by human institutions, a procedure that has been much used to give legitimacy to government.

That said, the historicizing mentality of the Romans influenced the interpretation, even the drafting, of the scriptures, when the Roman Church was imposed as the cornerstone of the entire religious edifice of the West. How can we know whether the Gospels were victims of this same historicizing process? It would be surprising if the Romans had treated pagan mythologies differently from Christian religious texts. Starting from when the Church became a human institution with a hierarchy and rough drafts of dogmas, the Christian message necessarily became a page of world history. The historical existence of Jesus, his divine mission, his nature as both God and man were accepted in a pinch, but it was necessary to explain his incarnation in one way or another. Hence the importance accorded the mother of Jesus, who could not be just anyone, for she was the receptacle of the Divine. Thus, although she was certainly human, she had to be an exceptional human, especially given that it was made explicit that Jesus was the *only son,* and that, consequently, the event would never be repeated, unlike the materialization of avatars in Hindu belief.

It seems that at the very beginning of Christianity the image of the mother of Jesus had only relative importance. The little attention paid her by the Evangelists, aside from Luke, bears witness to this. As for Saint Paul, the true founder of the Christian religion, the question of Mary barely interested him. It was essentially in Gnostic circles that the concept of the Theotokos was developed. Gnostic sects, which flourished throughout the eastern Mediterranean region, sought to establish a connection between the most ancient mystico-philosophical traditions and the message of the Gospels. This connection is sometimes presented as a vague syncretism, but more often as an attempt to create a thorough synthesis. It allowed the rediscovery of an image that was quite difficult to uproot, if not from folk memory, at least from the collective unconscious—the image of a primordial female deity worshipped throughout the entire East but particularly in Ephesus. And it is not by chance that the concept of the Theotokos was first proclaimed at Ephesus, for Ephesus was from the time of greatest antiquity the central and essential sanctuary of all the worship given to the Mother Goddess.

To the various Gnostic theoreticians, the image of the universal Mother Goddess, under whatever name was used to invoke her, was capable of crystallizing all the impulses of the human being to supreme wisdom. The Holy Ghost was then considered a symbol representing the Mother of the Holy Trinity. The word used to designate the Holy Ghost was neutral in Greek but feminine in Hebrew and Aramaic. The Gnostics soon replaced the neutral Greek *pneuma* (literally "breath") with the feminine *sophia* (wisdom), a term that was used for both masculine and feminine in the texts of that time, but which clearly designated the female aspect and nature of the deity. This explains the famous name for the Basilica of Saint Sophia in Constantinople. The *sophia* is the divine creative breath and absolute mold of everything that exists, the essential breath through which all must pass before acquiring form.

Of course, Saint Sophia is a name in the same way as Our Lady of the Good News is a name, and is of little consequence on any plane other than that of popular liturgy. But the Gnostics did not understand it in quite the same way as did Orthodox Christians. For them, not only was Sophia the real mother of Jesus Christ, but she also was the Mother Goddess that every believer had to worship equally with God the Father and Jesus the Son. The Trinity was therefore expressed this way: God-Father, Jesus-Son, and Mary-Mother. The sole problem was to reconcile this brilliant demonstration (perfectly logical insofar as it proclaimed a divine family with two parents and a child) with the Gospel of Luke, where it clearly appeared that the Holy Ghost was the genitor of Jesus and could not in any way be considered a feminine element. But certain theoreticians found their way around this by making Mary–Holy Ghost a kind of androgynous entity who temporarily split in two to fulfill her procreative mission.

Furthermore, it was not this contradiction—however essential—that prompted the indignation of the church fathers; it was much more the fact that it led to the concept of a female deity on equal footing with God the Father, whereas according to the Gospels and their historicizing nature, Mary was only a human chosen by God. To accept the divinity of Mary, it would have been necessary to assume that she herself was a female hypostasis of God. Given the antifeminist nature of Judeo-Christianity, this was properly inadmissible and, given the absence of any references, canonical or otherwise, absolutely unthinkable. This was how Epiphany, one of those distinguished church fathers, who lived between 315 and 403, unequivocally condemned all those who would be tempted to offer Mary her own worship: "The body of Mary is holy, but it is not divine; she is a virgin and deserving of high honors, but she should not be an object of worship for us." It was in this protest that Mary's virginity began to be magnified, although we have no clear idea of what specific meaning Epiphany and his contemporaries attached to the term *virgin*. That was a different problem. It was first essential to demonstrate that Mary was a woman and only a woman, even if she could be acknowledged as a saint.

Another church father, Saint Ambrose, the famous bishop of Milan who had such a strong influence on Saint Augustine, declared, "Mary was the Temple of God and not the God of the Temple. That is why we should worship only Him whose presence gives life to the Temple." This involves, as does every other theological commentary, an assertion that is based on nothing. It can be accepted as an article of faith but not as a demonstration. If we go beyond appearances, however, the assertion is laden with ambiguity. If Mary is the Temple of God, which no one dreamed of contesting, given that Jesus-God took form in Mary, it means that Mary is considered to be a *container*. Because Jesus-God would in this case be the *contents,* is it correct to consider the *container* as inferior to the *contents*? If we follow Saint Ambrose's reasoning, we would logically be led to claim that the perfect (Jesus-God) was born from the imperfect (Mary-woman). We might suspect that such an observation had emerged from very heterodox horizons, and in any case it was hardly compatible with the original assertion. It was therefore an open door to the worst heresies. In any event, it inspired a long process of theological speculation concerning Mary, mother of God, which would not until the nineteenth century lead to the proclamation of the dogma of Immaculate Conception. This was finally a lesser evil, as it prevented Mary from being considered God's equal—in other words a "goddess"—while recognizing her singularity among the human race.

The Gnostics would not have been satisfied with the Immaculate Conception of Mary. Furthermore, the Gnostics expressed themselves not in theological terms, but rather in philosophical ones that amassed together mystical elements, mythological fables, and cosmological speculations. Their idea was to make the so-called pagan traditions coincide with Judeo-Christian teachings. What they found most readily in the pagan traditions was the universal worship of the Great Goddess with many faces, many names, and multiple functions, but in any event the Goddess of the Beginnings, she whom Genesis barely dared evoke with its primordial "waters" over which the mysterious "Elohim" breathed.

This initial linkage led to other meetings. The Judeo-Christian contributions to Gnostic thought were first the image of the heavenly Jerusalem, an image symbolizing future humanity, then the *assembly* itself of participants in the heavenly Jerusalem. This was, in other words, the Ecclesia, the Church ("assembly," etymologically speaking). Jesus himself alluded to this celestial Jerusalem, and he always spoke in terms that stressed the *femininity* of the assembly of the elect. Saint Paul repeated the image and the name and defined it as "our mother"—the origin of the well-known expression "our holy mother the Church." She is the *new Eve* who comes to trample the head of the serpent (and is depicted doing so in medieval statuary); she is the true mother of the living, through whom is communicated to us the spiritual life of Christ, himself the *new Adam.*

It can easily be seen that Mary, mother of Jesus, is entirely absent from this speculation. The Church has come to be considered more as the fiancée (the Shulamite from the Song of Solomon, she who is "black but beautiful") than the bride of Christ, somewhat similarly to how the Israelite nation was considered in Jewish thought as the bride of Jehovah. And if we understand the ritual of the Catholic Mass correctly, the priest (when he officiated with his back to the faithful!), symbol and sublimation of the assembly that is the Church and therefore the female principle, prompts, by the consecration of the host and the Communion that follows, the veritable *nuptials* between this assembly and Jesus Christ, who has descended on the altar.

But this is all very abstract and stems from a thorough knowledge of the question of the relationship between God and God's people. We can then understand why the concept of the *assembly* bride of Christ was slowly amalgamated to the material figure of Mary, mother of Christ, but also *mother of all humanity,* if we believe the Gospels. And if Mary is the mother of all humanity, a perfectly comprehensible *historicized* figure and tangibly attainable, she acquires by virtue of this all the characteristics that once devolved on the universal Great Goddess, mother of all gods and all human beings.

But it was not the Gnostics who prompted the irruption of the figure of Mary into the orthodox theology. Oddly enough, it was an authentic heresy known as Arianism that was in large part responsible. Arius, who was founder of this doctrine and an Alexandrian priest (the city of Alexandria was a crucible in which Western and Eastern influences melted together), refused to recognize the divine nature of Jesus and regarded him as simply an inspired prophet. Based on this negation, he had no choice but to refuse the role of the Holy Ghost in the conception of Jesus and consequently came to deny absolutely Mary's role and distinctiveness, thereby also rejecting every female element in Christian doctrine of the time.

It so happens that Arius collided violently, through long theological discussions, with Saint Athanasus, who was bishop of Alexandria in 328, on this question of the Incarnation. (At this time it was not yet a practice to burn heretics!) In reaction to Arius and his negation of Mary's role (the female principle), Saint Athanasus found himself obliged not only to defend the incarnation of Jesus-God inside of Mary, but to amplify both her role and its uniqueness as well. According to him, if Mary was not the mother of the Word, this Word could not be consubstantial *(homousios)* with the human race, and consequently the Redemption would be meaningless. Therefore, it had to be accepted that Mary was the true mother of Christ, with all the consequences that involved, if the divine nature of Jesus was to be demonstrated in tandem with his human nature. Mary emerged from this chain of reasoning as the crucible in which the fusion of the divine and the human was realized in perfect, albeit mysterious, fashion.

This was the concept that prevailed. In 533 a decree by the Byzantine emperor Justinian declared quite explicitly that Jesus was "consubstantial with the Father as regards his divinity and consubstantial with us as regards his humanity." Accordingly he acts as mediator between God and humanity, for he enables God to speak with human words and humans to address the incommunicable God with human words that at times go beyond their strict sense. But here we fall right back into the same problem: What earthly woman, afflicted with all the stains of humanity, could be worthy of being the Temple of God? This raises another, almost metaphysical issue: What weak and imperfect earthly woman would be capable of withstanding such a hierogamous union with the Perfect One?

Sacred unions between a mortal and a god or goddess are familiar to us from the so-called pagan traditions. Such unions generally engender heroes such as Hercules and Aeneas, but they are often dangerous for the men or women involved in them. Anchises, the father of Aeneas, became lame following his union with Venus. More often than not a curse befalls the individual with the audacity to share, if only for a moment, the power of the gods. It is also notable that it never involves any kind of degeneration for the god or goddess. In extreme cases, the physical defects and decay that may befall the mortal are not signs of degeneration; they are *marks left by the god,* who henceforth singles out this human individual from his peers.

The comparisons that can be drawn between certain Christian concepts and pagan traditions are in no way shocking, and in any event are never by chance. In the case of physical defects that follow human contact with a god, the same belief can be found among Jews and Christians. The example of Moses, who can glimpse Jehovah only through the burning bush, is fraught with meaning in this regard. Another is the hero Galahad looking into the Holy Grail and dying from the transcendental vision it produces. As Moses himself said (Exodus 33:20), "None can look upon the Lord and live." It still involves the same relationship between the perfect and the imperfect, and it is only at the end of a slow initiation (life on earth) that the human being is capable of withstanding the vision of an absolute and infinite God.

These same comparisons have even greater significance with respect to Mary, mother of God, when they have been solidly established by examining pagan beliefs and worship that coexisted with early Christianity throughout the Roman Empire. The worship of Mithra and the symbolic value of the Phrygian god, like his esoteric meaning inherited from the remote Indo-European past, emerge from the same mold of thought that presided over the creation of the

Christian religion, to such an extent that Mithra barely failed to supplant Jesus, at least in the second century C.E., particularly among the Roman legions—who included every ethnic group but the Latin—that occupied vast territories on the borders of the empire, on the *limes*.[1] On this point archaeology has provided us with certitudes: The cult of Mithra was transported in the same baggage as the Christian message. But these two similar religious concepts were not alone. They faced strong competition from another system that had originated in Asia Minor, the worship of Cybele.

This is where everything becomes decisive concerning the creation of the Marian cult—not that the Marian cult directly descended from the Cybele cult, but rather that both systems, despite a basic parallelism, were relentless antagonists. While the condemnation of the Christian sect by Roman authorities was due to the fact that the Christians, by refusing to sacrifice to the gods of Rome, placed themselves outside the law, the worst enemies of the Christians were the devotees of Cybele, who never missed an opportunity to cast oil on the fire during their persecution. A simple example will suffice: In Roman Gaul, persecutions were ferocious in two cities, Vienne and Lyon, the two cities that had the highest concentration of Christians and worshippers of Cybele. Both systems were sharing the same terrain.

The religion of Cybele had invaded Rome and its vast territories at a time when Roman ancestor worship was experiencing a great loss of prestige. No one seriously believed in the official Roman religion any longer; most important, nobody accepted the *agnosticism* of such a religion, which did not preach the survival of the soul after death. It has been too often forgotten that the classical Greek religion and the official Roman religion were only formal rituals intended to conciliate the gods in order to allow humans to lead a transitory life as best they could. The same was true of the Hebrews, moreover,

---

1. [The *limes* were fortified walls along the contested borders of the Roman Empire to prevent incursions by small bands of raiders. —*Trans.*]

before the introduction of Eastern doctrines; even during the time of Jesus, some Jews refused to accept the immortality of the soul.

Greek and Roman authors took offense at the Druidic doctrine asserting immortality. They let it be known on countless occasions that they would have deemed it barbaric and puerile were it not for the fact that it presented certain similarities with the teachings of Pythagoras. It speaks volumes about the depth of this agnosticism that it in no way satisfied the natural tendency found throughout the human race to connect with a transcendent reality. Official Roman religion had therefore become a simple patriotic ritual, a kind of glue that bonded the members of a *civitas,* citizens sharing the same ethnicity. But for those who went beyond the agnostic attitude, it was clearly necessary to look elsewhere for doctrines that could satisfy their yearnings. This was the case with the mystery religions such as Orphism and the Eleusinian type, then the Isiac type, and finally the cults of Mithra and Cybele, which immediately preceded but extended the Christian message that had the advantage of offering a historicized version of the survival of the soul after death.

Like Mithraism, the cult of Cybele was propagated out of Asia Minor, notably Phrygia. This region was a veritable matrix of religions and played its own part in the crafting of the Christian Church. Wasn't it in Phrygia that the first Christians, gathered around John and Paul, found refuge? Wasn't it here that they began the actual "evangelization" of the world of those called the Gentiles? But in this land of violent contrasts, the disciples of Jesus did not find peace. They were exposed to the zealots of numerous other religions, principally the sectarians of the Mother Goddess, in this instance the famous Cybele, often depicted as the Great Prostitute—in other words, she who gives herself to all—crowned by towers (a symbol of might), mother of all the gods, seated in great triumph atop the monster she tames, an image that will become the Virgin crushing the serpent, or even the Lady with the unicorn, soothing the bellicose ardor of this fantasy creature by allowing it to rest its head against her breast. Cybele, heiress of the primitive Mother Goddess, is none other than the reborn face of the ancient Greek Artemis, the Babylonian Ishtar, the Solar Goddess of the ancient Scythians. She is the outcome, in a refined Hellenic milieu, of a slow maturation of the concept of the female deity of origins.

So just who is this mysterious figure who emerged from the dawn of time? Cybele, as she appeared in the first centuries of the Christian era, was still laden with a substratum that goes back to prehistoric times. It is she who is depicted, in surprising fashion, in the realistic form of the steatopygic statuettes from southern France that date from the Paleolithic era, and, in the abstract or at least schematic form, in the great Western megalithic monuments mainly found in Brittany and Ireland that date from the Neolithic period. Cybele is derived from the Neolithic goddess of life and death, of war and fertility, who is the origin of every creature, human or animal. She is the material representation of creative energy, the most popular expression of the generative principle that transmutes and transforms the world—what some philosophers will later call, with a tinge of atheistic materialism, the *Natura naturans,* "Nature in the process of becoming nature," reflective of the permanent creation at work throughout the world that transforms primal matter into the philosopher's stone, the imperfect into the perfect.

Of course, missionaries spread throughout the empire to tell the *history* of the goddess, a tale enriched by the details necessary to the Roman mentality of the essential myth of the *Mater Deum,* the Mother of Gods. The myth shows us not only the parallel between Cybele and Mary but also how this outline, which can be labeled initiatory, responds to a fundamental need on the part of the peoples of the Roman Empire during that specific era.

The outline is as follows: The primordial goddess, who is not the creator of the universe, has been given the mission from the unknown and mysterious divine creator entity to implement the energy of this universe and ensure its harmony. She is therefore a demiurge. But dark and adversarial powers (the Enemy in the Hebraic tradition under whatever name he bears, or the Giants of the Germano-Scandinavian tradition) relentlessly oppose the universe, and the entire work is compromised (theme of the Fall). The terrestrial world would have been annihilated were it not for the intervention of another god, son of the goddess but also of the unknown god, whose mission is to restore balance to the world by annually renewing the initial action of the creator.

The effects of the god-son's role are limited to the length of the yearly cycle, a solar year to be precise, for the origin of this myth is set at the level of a feminine solar deity who holds warmth and radiance but needs another god, in this instance the moon, to reflect them onto the world. In one sense, the Mother holds the potentiality, and the Son, charged with this potentiality, implements it as the one who carries out her orders. This is why the Son, in order to clearly indicate this role, was both *son and lover* of the Mother. At the end of the annual cycle he would have to die, then be reborn with all of nature.

The annual passion and renaissance of the Son constitutes the essential basis of this matriarchal religious system. These events are sumptuously commemorated in the domain of the story, but they are quite real on the material plane: the death of nature on the threshold of winter and its rebirth in spring. The same idea is present in the initiatory outline of Eleusis concerning the goddess Demeter-Ceres, who voyaged to the netherworld in search of her daughter, Kore-Persephone, held prisoner by Hades-Pluto. It is also the original theme of the quest for the Grail; the wounded and impotent Fisher King, who already has a daughter, has become sterile in waiting for the one who will come and rediscover the Grail. Mythological outlines of the same nature are not lacking in Celtic tradition.

There is a wide variety of mythical narratives about Cybele, but all refer to the same basic assumptions. The son, who is called Attis, is associated with a tree: the cedar in the East and the pine in the West. He dies at the end of a tragedy equivalent to the Christian Passion. After several days of mourning, his mother-lover reanimates him and marries him in a bloody hierogamy from which all creation benefits.

But in Phrygia, soon followed by all other countries subject to the worship of Cybele, the tragedy in which Attis died took on a strange, fanatical coloration that has its equivalents in medieval Christian thought. During the festivals commemorating this event, the Phrygian priests, going their predecessors one better and probably under the influence of hallucinogenic substances, surrendered to frenzied dances in which some, in the grip of a mystical delirium, intentionally castrated themselves to fully identify with the bloodied son of their goddess. Some memories of this remain within Christianity. On the one hand, there is the mysterious phenomenon that causes the stigmata of Jesus Christ to appear on the bodies of certain individuals while they are in a state of mystical trance. On the other, there is the celibacy and chastity required for monks and Catholic priests. This chastity is obviously, on a symbolic level, an exact replica of the castration of the priests of Cybele.

In the beginning, the matriarchal religion, with its cruel rites still in compliance with nature, appeared more as a cosmogonical than a theological practice. The performance of the annual rites primarily helped nature function better, with a material profit in mind: the hope for fine herds and good harvests. But little by little this primitive naturalism became charged by a series of metaphysical considerations on the meaning of life and humankind's fate. The influences of Eleusis and the different mystery religions are clear. While the mysteries of Attis illustrate the death and resurrection of a god-son, he had become a model and example for all humanity. Through Attis, through his personal evolution as well as through the help of his divine mother, human beings had hope of being reborn to a higher state after death. Death was no longer an ending but instead a passage. The very notion of the "departed" indicates a passage toward an "elsewhere," going beyond the world of visible realities to attain a suprahuman world. The religion of Cybele therefore became a religion of salvation, capable of transferring the benefit of the resurrection, previously reserved for Attis, to all human beings, even foreigners. This important point explains the stunning success of the new system.

Probably sometime during the second century C.E., the worship of Cybele was enriched with a heterogeneous element, tauroboly, or sacrifice of the bull, that formerly belonged to Mithraism (as well as to ancient Western religious rituals that have left behind only a few traces).[2] Symbolically, the death of the god-son responds to that of the sun-bull. The practice that consists of having the faithful receive the blood of the bull, an act equivalent to baptism by water, displays the part humans take from the god, followed by human resurrection. This is how, when the matriarchal religion was completely freed of its naturalistic attachments and had abandoned its transitory material purposes, the sacrifice of the bull and the baptism by blood took on an initiatory value. Once the initiate emerged from the trench in which he had received the blood, he was, according to the accepted expression, *in aeternum renatus*, "reborn for eternity." There is no need to extend the analogies between these practices and those of Christianity—not that there may not be reciprocal influences, but they are both a response to the anguished pleas of human beings, while the traditional religious systems offered only a happy life that was limited in duration.

The sacrifice of the bull is thus closely connected to matriarchal liturgy. But the sectarians of Cybele added something to it. It was not enough to spread the blood of the bull on the faithful; it became customary to tear off the testicles of the animal. These would be solemnly carried with the horns into the temple of the goddess and placed beneath a commemorative altar. The practice of the adoration of relics, so common in Christianity, also has some connections with this rite.

---

2. For example, according to Pliny the Elder, the harvesting of mistletoe, a famous ritual but one that is generally presented in an incomplete form, was followed by the sacrifice of a bull, which clearly indicates that the Druids practiced *tauro-bolium*. This has been confirmed by numerous Irish stories from the early Middle Ages, notably those from the Ulster Cycle, in which implacable wars are waged for possession of a divine bull, which will finally be killed during the battles. Furthermore, this entire cycle brings to mind a pastoral kind of civilization where the bull sacrifice is essential to ensure the prosperity of the entire herd. The idea of bull sacrifice can also be seen in the practice of bullfighting.

Moreover, to ensure the triumph of their religion, the priests of Cybele had the brilliant idea of associating it with the cult of Rome and the emperor. In the official Roman religion, the dead Roman emperor was deified (ceremony of the apotheosis) and then worshipped in the same way as the other gods. Far from scorning this practice, the priests of Cybele went further and presented their goddess as the protector of the emperor, thereby incorporating the historical figure with the god-son, something that the Latin mentality did not find objectionable. Soon, the goddess adopted the name Cybele Augustus, and the priests obtained an important place in the municipal cult of the emperor.

This speaks volumes about the significance of the bull-sacrifice ceremony. In the year 160 an official bull sacrifice, the first up to that time, was offered for the "emperor's salvation." Emperor Anthony was a devotee of the Mother of Gods, and during this time it was conceivable that the worship of Cybele would become the religion of the entire Roman Empire, making the emperor the son of the goddess. He was promoted as "savior" of the world, the regenerator of nature, and the model of life, like Attis in mythological tradition. This strengthened the concept of a human mediator of divine origin, which was precisely what the Christian message revealed in an entirely different context. Here again we find a response to a profound request from people haunted by the idea of a salvation that could be both collective and individual.

All this largely spills over the narrow framework of metaphysical speculation. This new religious attitude permeated daily life and was denoted by a precise solar-based calendar that gave a privileged position to spring, the season of renewal, and hence the resurrection. The great matriarchal festivals began on the Ides of March. Believers were expected to observe a one-week period of mourning marked by absolute sexual abstinence. Something of this remains in the Christian Lent. Then, before dawn on the day of the spring equinox, March 21 or 22, the Procession of the Pine would take place. A tree was cut down by the priests, the *dendrophores* (leaf bearers), and adorned with strips of cloth like a mummy; a depiction of Attis was carved on one of its branches. The tree symbolized Attis himself, prepared for the funeral ceremony. Once prepared, the tree was led in procession to the temple of Cybele, where it was erected. It remained exposed for three days and two nights, guarded by worshippers who expressed their despair in funereal dirges and plaintive songs.

The Festival of Blood took place on March 24. The most exalted of the faithful slashed their shoulders and arms to water the pine with their blood and thus share in the god's passion. The pine was then taken down into a cellar of the temple, and a long vigil began during which the faithful achieved their purification. (Something of this survives in Masonic rites, in particular the sojourn that neophytes make in the Tomb.) On the following morning in the first light of dawn, when the rays of the sun began penetrating the depths of the sanctuary,[3] the young god resuscitated was seen stretched out on a parade bed arranged at the feet of Cybele's statue. One of the faithful played this highly desired role.

This was the opening of the day of Hilaria, that of universal joy. The images of Cybele and Attis (in Phrygian bonnet) were set up in a cart drawn by four horses; they carried the pastoral staff of the cross, the symbol of command.[4] An amazing procession followed consisting of flute and tambourine players, cymbalists, singers,

---

3. The solstice sunrise of summer or winter played a significant role in connection with certain megalithic monuments (the New Grange tumulus in Ireland, Stonehenge in England, Dissignac-Saint-Nazaire in France). These monuments were built in such a way that the first ray of the rising sun would strike the back of the central chamber. There are equivalents in some Christian churches, where the sun, passing through the stained glass, strikes the altar stone or this or that statue at a given moment of the day. This takes place as if someone had sought to "harness" the solar energy in its purest and youngest state.

4. The pastoral staff can be seen again among the priests and monks of Christianity. As for the cross (already visible as a symbol of power and command in megalithic carvings), it would become the distinctive sign of the Christian bishop and the abbot of a monastery.

torchbearers, and priests and priestesses clad in white and crowned in gold surrounding the high priest, the Archigalle, in his purple pallium. The procession made its way through the streets of the city, stopping at the temples of all the other gods, demonstrating that Cybele and Attis were superior to them—logically enough, as Cybele was the Mater Deum. The day ended with luxurious banquets at which alcoholic beverages flowed in great torrents, which certainly had an effect on the orgiastic behavior of the participants throughout the following night.[5]

These feasts form the apex of the matriarchal liturgy in both their length and their solemnity. But the *secret* part of the worship of Cybele should not be forgotten. The "mysteries," meaning the initiation ceremonies reserved for neophytes, took place on March 28. The neophytes underwent tests about which we have little information but that included sacrifices and a period of strict abstinence. Sacrificial blood may have been spilled over the young neophytes as some sort of baptism. They may have partaken of a communal meal that admitted them to the divine family, as was practiced in Eleusis with the sharing of bread and wine. There may have been a mystical marriage of the new initiate to the Mother of the Gods (and human beings) in the nuptial chamber of Cybele, a cave reached by following a long, winding path.[6] In any event, dur-

---

5. The festivals of Carnivale share this same concern of celebrating the renewal of life through great displays of joy and all the vital impulses of the individual. But once their orgiastic aspects have been stripped away, the matriarchal processions can be recognized quite easily in the Christian processions that travel from "altar of repose" to "altar of repose" and from chapel to chapel at the time of Holy Saturday as well as on Corpus Christi.

6. The mystical marriage of the neophyte to Cybele has many equivalents (even some of a sexual nature) in numerous pagan cults of the universal Mother Goddess. In Babylon there was the union of the believer with an unknown woman embodying Ishtar, the Great Prostitute, in the noble sense of the word. But the mystical marriage is also a feature of Christianity, once it has been emptied—theoretically—of all sexuality, as can be found in the reports of Bernard de Clairvaux and other illustrious saints of their sublime relations with the Virgin Mary.

ing the course of these ceremonies, the neophyte would formally identify with Attis. This was the guarantee that the neophyte would share in Attis's resurrection.

The extraordinary evolution of the Cybele cult and the integration of the Mithraic bull sacrifice took place in a material framework adapted to imperial Roman civilization: the ancient rites in honor of Ishtar and her son-lover Tammuz; those honoring Aphrodite and Adonis, as well as Isis and Osiris; and even those of the mysterious Artemis and Hippolytus, her no less mysterious priest-lover, vowed to chastity. Racine's tragedy about this last pair retains numerous features of its original story. But the cult was obviously an expression of a mythological outline, a metaphysical structure representing the evolution of human thought through the ages.

The primitive Mother Goddess, the Great Goddess of the Beginnings, was first represented alone. Before femininity became tainted with condemnation and suspicion, she was sometimes divided into two feminine figures, viewed as mother and daughter, as in the myth of Demeter and Kore. The dyad of an elder goddess and a younger goddess symbolized the renewal of the former. This dyad is common to Greek, Roman, and Etruscan mythologies, but it can also be found in Japan with the goddess Amaterasu, who is often accompanied by her double. Because Amaterasu is a solar deity, the dyad involves the image of the setting sun (Amaterasu herself) prolonged by the rising sun.

Once the transition from the original matriarchy to patriarchy occurred, the daughter became a son; the myths became those of Isis and Osiris, Venus and Adonis, Ishtar and Tammuz, and finally Cybele and Attis. These myths are identical, involving, according to Przyluski, a "descent into hell that suggests death followed by a resurrection, and a dyad formed by two deities of different age. But whereas Demeter and Kore are two goddesses, Astarte and Adonis are of different sexes. We have therefore moved past the female dyad to the two-sex couple. It is the application of the principle that fertility requires the union of both sexes."[7] Previously, fertility was believed to be the exclusive domain of the female.[8]

Thus, there is a constant in the first centuries of Christianity that must be taken into account when we examine the role of the Virgin Mary: the widespread image of a female deity whose savior son dies tragically and is reborn, making possible the resurrection of the whole of humanity. This image of the Mother Goddess and the God-Son is clearly an archetype, a property of the collective unconscious. The success of the worship of Cybele in the Roman Empire testifies to this.

The Christian message emphasized the figure of Jesus, son of God, who was portrayed during his life as surrounded by male apostles. This androcratic message left little place for women, especially after the almost total elimination of the mysterious Mary Magdalene and what the Gospels call the group of Holy Women. A reading of the canonical Gospels, however, leaves no doubt as to the importance of the female element in the group of those following Jesus. Most crucial of all, the son of God had to be born from a woman's womb. Whoever she may have been, this woman acquired considerable importance in the eyes of the faithful and had little in common with the picture of her furnished by the rare bits of information in these same canonical texts. One way or another, the Church had to find a solution to the problem raised by the mother of Jesus, and it did exactly that at the Council of Ephesus in 431, when Mary was declared Theotokos, Mother of God.

This decree, perhaps one of the most important in the religious life of the West, was immediately extended into popular worship in a very concrete and practical way. It answered an unconscious desire of the faithful haunted by the image of the Mater Deum. As Lederer explains:

---

7. J. Przyluski, *La Grande Déesse* (Paris: Payot, 1950), 163.
8. The reversal of the matriarchal tendency, which I have analyzed at length in *Women of the Celts* (Rochester, Vt.: Inner Traditions, 1986), occurred when the male became aware of his own role in procreation.

Alleged portraits of the Virgin began to make their appearance. One of them, the Hodegetria attributed to Saint Luke, was sent, it is said, by Empress Eudoxia in 438 C.E. to her sister-in-law Pulcheria, who had it placed in the church of Constantinople. The icon was given its own brand of intense adoration for centuries, to the point that the army carried it on a chariot when going on a campaign against the enemy, as once was done with the effigy as Cybele.[9] At the beginning of the fifth century, people began to dedicate churches to her, and during the sixth century, Madonnas with the Infant Jesus became one of the favorite subjects of Christian iconography. The symbolic colors are the same as those used for icons of the goddess; even the accoutrements seem familiar: Mary wears a crown of stars and a star-covered cloak; her feet are placed upon the moon; and she is strangely reminiscent of the effigies of Aphrodite. She sometimes carries an ear of wheat, like the Virgin of Epis *(Spica Virgo)*, or is accompanied by the dove that was dear to Ishtar, treading upon the serpent that had until this time been invariably associated with representations of the goddess; her history teems with legend that had once been those of Ishtar or Juno.[10] This is how the high figure of the Virgin Mary, mother of Jesus and thus mother of God, was injected into Christian devotion.

One thing is certain: You cannot speak to a people in a language members do not understand. The internal structure of the collective unconscious needs concrete images, and it seems necessary to supply them when it wants them, although sometimes the original meanings have been changed. De Smet, a Belgian Catholic priest, observes:

---

9. According to the tenth-century document *Annales Cambriae,* the fabled King Arthur, who is based on a historical figure of c. 500 C.E., won the three-day battle of Mount Badon against the Saxons because he had an effigy of the Virgin Mary carried in front of his troops.

10. W. Lederer, *Gynophobia, ou la peur des femmes* (Paris: Payot, 1970).

Although guided from the very interior of Christianity, this devotion typifies on its own three currents: Jewish (the daughter of Zion), early Christian (Our Mother the Church), and pagan (the goddess). In fact, the nostalgia for the feminine deity and the adoration of maternity is so deeply rooted in the human heart that it is impossible to extirpate it completely. Conforming to the law of the human heart and against dogma, the cult of the Mother of God eventually prevailed. . . . The Artemis of the Ephesians thereby became the "great, glorious, and sublime Mother of God." The most beautiful flower from the religion of nature fills the most glaring gap in the religion of salvation. Isis returns with Horus in her arms. Mary becomes the goddess of fertility, love, and beauty, the most noble of all those history has known.[11]

But this concerns the *folk* image of the goddess, which lurks in the human subconscious and whose functions, on a primary and concrete level, are above all sexuality, reproduction, and fertility. The problem the church fathers faced was accepting this image while going beyond it. Jesus, as God incarnate and especially as the only Son born once and for all, could not, however, be fully identical with Tammuz, Adonis, or Attis. In following up a Greek philosophy, Christianity had taken on the task of spreading the idea of transcendence. Also, the necessary but ambiguous image of the goddess had to be refined, if not rendered sublime, as de Smet explains: "All that Mary could not reuse from the dark and destructive figure of the goddess, principally her sexual worship, the church fathers, the Councils, theologians, and preachers then took by giving it the appearance of a living, spiritual being who opposed the Virgin and God: Satan."[12] Hence the emphasis placed on reutilizing and extending the very common representation of the Virgin crushing the head

---

11. A. de Smet, *La Grande Déesse n'est pas morte* (Paris, 1983).
12. Ibid., 178.

of the snake or the dragon. Hence the emphasis placed on the parable of the wise virgins and the foolish virgins, with all the associations triggered by such a fundamental opposition. Hence, even, the curious relationship in astrology between the sign of Virgo and the sign of Scorpio, the Virgin assuming an ambivalent meaning (pure Virgo and Virgo-Scorpio), which shows the difficulty in considering the Great Goddess of the Beginnings in anything but her totality.

A form of dualism is developing. What appears to be incompatible with the Mother of God is cast into the shadows, taking on the sulfurous appearance of the Enemy. Giving him the disturbing guise of a horned or monstrous deity enables him to act as a kind of foil, a mediating object intended to externalize and concentrate the base impulses of the subconscious. Once those have been extracted from the subconscious and objectified, they become less virulent and less dangerous. But this *dark* side is not thereby annihilated. In fact, it returns in force, although quite marginalized. Przyluski observes:

> The witchcraft trials of the Middle Ages reveal a curious set of beliefs and practices, or pagan remembrances combining with Christian elements. The witches' Sabbath took place in deserted places under the invocation of Diana and Lucifer, who played the role of the god of sun and light. Here the dualism is astral and sexual: there is a tangible connection between Diana, witches, the moon, and night. The Sabbath recalls the ancient mysteries, and the orgy that brings it to a close is related to the ancient ceremonies of the cult of the Great Mother.[13]

In this way the path was cleared to make Mary the great transcendental goddess.

---

13. Ibid., 167.

5

WORSHIP OF THE VIRGIN

One of the essential characteristics of Christianity, at least in its Catholic and Orthodox formulations, is incontestably the worship given by the faithful to figures who are not divine but occupy a privileged place in a presumed hierarchy—generally the saints, but most particularly the Virgin Mary. It is also the chief bone of contention between Catholics and Protestants when they seek, in a laudable display of ecumenism, to restore their original unity.

It is indeed difficult to reconcile the two extreme positions, one seeking to maintain direct contact between the created and the divine creator without the help of any intermediary, not even the pastor (Calvinism and Lutherism), the other defending the role that some intermediaries can play between the human being and God: the priests in earthly life, the saints (those privileged by Divinity) in the world of supernatural realities. On the one hand, human beings are responsible for their acts before God alone and have no time to waste praying or entreating figures who have been declared to be saints in an arbitrary and relative fashion. On the other hand, these same individuals should find on the long road that leads to God obligatory mediators who serve as examples, intercessors, or advocates of a sort and who, if need be, are capable of showing the seekers which way to go.

This debate is more metaphysical than theological; the question is whether it is possible for human beings to grasp God by themselves or only through intermediaries who have already presumably benefited from transcendental experience. The conflict, moreover, is distorted at the outset. Because Protestants are more Augustinian than Catholics (asserting that the human being can be saved only by the intervention of supernatural grace), they refuse this aid, whereas Catholics expect it and intentionally solicit it through *works,* that is to say, exercises of piety—in other words, worship. We find ourselves completely fogged in; or to use a more current expression, everything is in very soft focus.

The problem is far from resolved. Rather than attempting a solution, we must confine our analysis to a better understanding of the scope of the difference between Catholic and Protestant. Throughout Christianity, including all the Protestant denominations, salvation and transcendence are envisioned through the exercise of worship: the most bare-bones possible for Protestants, the most sumptuous for the Orthodox, and the most traditional for Roman Catholics. In whatever form, this worship is, if not an essential condition, at least an important one in the transcendental relationship that the creature maintains—or should maintain—with the creator. Worship is the most practical and common means for establishing a rapport and dialogue between the visible and the invisible worlds. The human mind needs concrete elements to prop up its convictions and to confirm its beliefs as truths. Otherwise the beliefs are just the abstract words of metaphysicians who spend their lives juggling concepts. Mere concepts satisfy no one, except perhaps some brilliant intellectuals cut off from daily life who eventually find themselves spinning in circles within the higher spheres of speculation.

Worship thus presents itself as an action—or a series of actions—intended to establish a durable and permanent relationship between the invisible and the visible, the perfect and the imperfect. It is the embodiment of an abstract thought not only in words—which are very important, although not exclusively so—but also in behavior: in other words, in a series of actions of a religious or magical nature. Despite the prohibitions of horrified priests, magic and religion overlap, especially in the Christian faith. But the border between magic and religion is a delicate topic, so it is better to stick to a prudent reservation: Magic consists of appealing to supernatural powers and compelling them to obey us, whereas religion consists of knowing the designs of supernatural powers and complying with them. Amen. But what to say of this *magical command* of the Catholic priest that compels Jesus Christ to appear on the altar in the form of bread and wine?

Why bother to make something simple when you can make it complicated? The witticism is based on observation of the twisted nature of the human mind. It wants to deny the supernatural, but it supports it whenever it finds the opportunity. Under these conditions, the worship of any religion appears to be a desperate attempt to recover the lost primordial unity (no one knows how it was lost, hence the symbolic value of original sin) scattered through the multiplicity that makes up the world. Just as the purpose of shamanic practices (as Mircea Eliade has shown well) is to restore humankind to the same primitive and absolute state that characterized humans at the dawn of time, the first objective of any religion's worship is to give back to the creature its opening, its *availability,* its "virginity" in some way—to allow it, by substitute methods, to contrive its return to the alleged original purity, in other words paradise, and all the confused notions attached to this concept of paradise.

So worship is primarily a means of substitution. Religion generally guarantees its effectiveness. It obliges human beings to become aware of their nature, their weakness, but also, as Pascal said, their *greatness,* for we cannot know that we are great until we have passed through all the stages of "smallness." Hardly any but the Protestants have seriously doubted this. For them, salvation is earned through faith and not by works, and if they gather to celebrate what they call "worship," it is mainly to achieve "communion" among themselves, not to establish a magical bond with God. This is why Protestants criticize Catholics for what the former perceive to be crazy superstitions and veritable idolatry. Ecumenism in its full realization is not to be expected tomorrow, even if the desire for understanding remains sincere. The spirit of the Reformation, which still predominates among all the various Protestant denominations, was to purify a ritual that had become burdened by too many heteroclite, even clearly ridiculous, elements.

At the end of the Middle Ages, works had prevailed over faith and often appeared void of all meaning. Now—and this is a general rule—any attempt to change is triggered by a radicalization that may not have been anticipated. The abandonment of the ceremonies and worship of the saints by the Protestants formed part of this approach. But it in no way invalidates the justification for the worship of the saints as it was presented in the early Middle Ages.

Early Christianity was concerned primarily with maintaining the memory of the earthly presence of Jesus during fraternal assemblies. *Ecclesia* means "assembly" and nothing else. It does not matter if the assembly convenes in this place or that; God is present everywhere, and the message is spread by human voices testifying to the tradition. One often cited example is the Roman catacombs, where Christians gathered to hide from prying eyes rather than to escape persecution. They felt a need to be apart from the world, to be in a zone of silence and meditation, so as to establish contact with the Divine more easily. But this allowed a revival of the idea of a privileged location, a *sanctuary,* despite the instinctive Christian mistrust of "temples" inhabited by what they called false gods.

It appears that since the earliest prehistoric times, humans have continuously displayed their belief that certain sites have a better capability than others to reunite heaven and earth, offering better conditions for the subtle and delicate exchanges that take place between the visible and the invisible. The Gallic *nemeton,* the sacred clearing in the middle of the forest, is one example. But in the Mediterranean world, the "sacred groves," the caves, the summits of hills and mountains, the islands, and then the buildings erected on these sites, were propitious for all kinds of theophanies (the visible manifestations of a deity), as well as for inspiring the human being's passion for the divine.

And despite the early Christians' desire to break this habit, notably through the contention that God is present everywhere, they did not escape the tendency to favor certain spots. Because they had asserted the historical existence of Jesus Christ and placed it in a specific country, they could not underestimate the exemplary value and "holiness" of towns like Bethlehem, Nazareth, and Jerusalem, for they were naturally and obligatorily charged with imprints from the divine presence. Furthermore, by extension, all those who approached Christ, particularly the apostles, adopted the sacred charge of their teacher and became "saints" themselves. The places where they lived and traveled, the places where they were martyred or buried, obviously benefited from this mystical, not to say magical, aura.

Finally, the first martyrs, meaning those who chose to die rather than deny Christ and who loudly declared their association with the "mystical body" of Jesus, and later the figures who led exemplary lives, in turn became keepers of this aura, which, of course, would be transferred to the places where they had lived or spent time or were buried. The worship of saints stemmed from a desire to preserve not relics in the strict sense of the term, but rather the physical remnants (bodies, clothing, objects) or spiritual remnants (mystical aura) of Jesus Christ and all those who had approached him and all those who had confessed their union with him. What has touched the divine becomes almost divine itself, or at least that seems to be the assumption. This explains the origin of most of Christianity's great sanctuaries, and especially the names they were given, which most often concerned the saints and the Virgin Mary.

But the problem appears more complex than that. While it is normal and natural for Christians to found sanctuaries dedicated to the Virgin and the saints, it seems neither normal nor natural that they were founded—especially by a young Christianity that was dealing with a number of rivals—in the sanctuaries of a paganism that clung tenaciously to many cultures. Nor, in a later period (following Theodosius's edict making Christianity the sole religion of the empire), were these same sanctuaries assiduously frequented by the people before their conversion.

There were two possible solutions. The first consisted of simply destroying the pagan edifices by laying a kind of ban on their installation; the second involved substituting the new worship for the old. But the first solution was most often found to be impractical. The places considered sacred had always been so considered, and it was next to impossible to desanctify their value through the blackening of their reputation, most particularly by placing them under the patronage of diabolic powers. Thus it was eventually the second solution that prevailed, starting with the imperial territory and spreading into the newly Christianized countries.

There are many famous or significant examples. The Christian sanctuary of Mont-Saint-Michel is located on the site of a former Mithraic temple that was itself situated on the site of a Gallic sanctuary consecrated to the "shining god," Belenos.[1] In Carnac (Morbihan), the church dedicated to Saint Kornely replaced a sanctuary of the Gallic horned god Cernunnos.[2] Notre-Dame in Paris was built over an ancient pagan temple dedicated to a mother goddess. In Langon (Ille-et-Vilaine), the existing chapel of Sainte-Agatha (the patron saint of nursing mothers) is the very building constructed during the Roman era in honor of Venus (as demonstrated by the magnificent Gallo-Roman fresco showing the naked Venus emerging from the waves), after having been a sanctuary dedicated to a mysterious "Saint" Véner or Vénérand. With respect to Our Lady of Chartres, the local clerical tradition loudly asserts that this site once housed a sanctuary where the Druids honored a *virgo paritura*. A list of similar cases would be too long to compile.

---

1. For more on this, see Jean Markale, *Le Mont-Saint-Michel et l'énigme du dragon* (Paris: Pygmalion, 1987).

2. For more on this, see Jean Markale, *Carnac et l'énigme d'Atlantide* (Paris: Pygmalion, 1987).

These substitutions, whatever the circumstances that inspired them, whatever dates may be attributed to them, are difficult to contest. Christianity inherited not only places of worship from the religions that preceded it but also cultural practices. Communion, the fraternal sharing of bread and wine, was practiced during the Eleusinian mysteries and during the ceremonies worshipping Cybele. This is but one element among many others, which in no way diminishes the strength and essential symbolic value of the new cult. But it did not all occur smoothly, especially because worship of the Virgin and the saints was required of an illiterate populace, the majority of whom needed images to support their devotion. The imperative of religion is to make itself understood by the greatest number. To do this, Christianity had to find a way to satisfy the human mind, which cannot isolate a problem and transcend it without recourse to concrete intermediaries. This concrete quality appeared immediately in the form of images, mainly statues, that were supposed to represent the hallowed deity or pious individuals.

Such an attitude has often been considered idolatrous. It is an easy charge to make, so it is important to understand what is meant by *idolatry*. Is it the magical belief that the god is present in the statue or the image? If so, would the actual presence of Christ in the Eucharist belong in this category? Is it only a symbolic object, a "medium" intended to facilitate meditation and prayer, that has been charged with an entirely moral significance? Polytheism has often been derided because of the ambiguity of the term *idol,* which means simply "image." Polytheism is accordingly understood to involve belief in numerous gods, each with an individual identity; in reality, the numerous deities are merely concrete representations of the social functions imputed to a deity who is one, indivisible, and unknowable in its absolute existence. Only Calvinist Protestantism has rejected this attitude across the board as superstition and even sacrilege. Islam takes a more subtle position: While banning the human figure, it accepts the symbolic decoration of geometrical motifs. As for Druidism, before it was contaminated by the Mediterranean religions, all testimonies concur that though it rejected the idea of imprisoning deities in animal or human form, it authorized if not encouraged the famous simulacra that Caesar mentions with regard to the Gallic Mercury, which were simple, nonfigurative blocks of stone or wooden pillars.

There is one additional element in this debate. During the first centuries of Christianity, and even long afterward, pagan images became Christian images because of an analogy of form or function. The medieval depiction of the horned devil, for example, borrows its broad lines from Gallo-Roman representations of Cernunnos. The sculpted pairs of Cybele and Attis, Venus and Adonis were easily transformed into Virgin and Child. Depictions of Demeter and Kore were easily confused with groupings of Anne and Mary. As for the countless *matronae* statues, the Gallic Mother Goddess holding a child on her knee, they were easy to pass off as the Virgin with the Infant Jesus.

Furthermore, in ancient times the discovery of a statue was always surrounded by miraculous elements that suggested divine intervention. These marvelous elements are of two kinds.

The first concerns the discovery of a statue thanks to the intervention of an animal, usually a bovine. The scenario is quite specific: A steer continually wanders away to browse at the same place or else stops at the same furrow in the field, refusing to budge but kneeling down when the farmer tries to get it to move forward. It can also be a cow or bull that always moos at the foot of the same tree. These actions excite the curiosity of the people who witness it. They then find beneath the sod or furrow, or in the tree, a generally shapeless or worn statue that someone declares to be the Virgin Mary. As Saillens notes:

Such legends invariably remind us that we once worshipped Isis with cow horns, Cybele, who was associated with the Mithraic bull, and the horned god Cernunnos. It is true that a myth can be spontaneously born several times, but it also true that the bovine, in the mythologies where it figures, is always connected with Earth worship. It held this role even as early as Neolithic times. Now a tradition can be maintained without it being necessarily understood any longer. Bullfights are one proof, as are the processions of fatted cows.[3]

The second kind of miraculous discovery is that of the "return." It is widespread throughout Europe. According to Saillens:

> The image having been discovered in some deserted, even uninhabitable if not outright inaccessible spot, the finder, who is never a priest, brings it back home. During the night it returns to the place where it was found. The peasant then turns to the local priest, who carries it to the parish, but the next morning it is back in its original location. The priest goes in search of it with cross and banner, but it flees again. It proves necessary to build a chapel for it exactly where it was found.[4]

This is the origin of a large number of more or less important and well-known sanctuaries—mainly dedicated to the Virgin. And, of course, whatever reality there may be to the marvelous events surrounding the finding of the magical image, the image itself is necessarily miraculous, and cases can always be cited of miraculous healings or the granting of simple wishes to those who came to see it on pious pilgrimage. But on further reflection, how many of these "miraculous" images were only pagan representations, mainly mother goddesses, abandoned or buried at the whim of circumstance and rediscovered most often out of the desire to maintain the connection between the ancient beliefs and the new? People are not fond of absolute innovations and always need to connect with an ancient tradition; this bears testimony to permanence and thus conveys a certain sense of security.

---

3. E. Saillens, *Nos Vierges noires* (Paris: Universelles, 1945), 57.
4. Ibid., 58.

It goes without saying that these "finds" and the recourse to images, even those that conformed to official Christianity, were not always totally accepted by the sacerdotal leadership. For a long time there was antagonism on this point between town and country, the latter considered inhabited by *pagani* with their nostalgia for pre-Christian cults. In fact, in most of the regions subject to Roman control, save on its northwesternmost borders (Armorican Brittany and the northern and western areas of Great Britain), the Christian religion spread and established itself essentially in the towns and cities. There are many reasons for this, in particular the revelation of the evangelical message through the agency of merchants from the south and the municipal nature of urban life.[5] But the outskirts of the Gallo-Roman towns were still virgin ground, and the aftermath of paganism was still vital because it was integrated into rural life itself (whose conservative tendencies are well known).

Furthermore, as a temporal organization, the Roman Catholic Church had borrowed all the machinery of the imperial Roman administration. This is why, following the disappearance of Roman power, only the Church was able to present a consistent, even monolithic appearance in face of the Germanic "barbarians" then working with it (the alliance of Clovis with the bishops against the other barbarians who had converted to Arianism), and finally integrating them into the Gallo-Roman context. But this was possible because Rome was the capital of Christendom, as it had once been the capital of the temporal empire, and because Christianity had become urbanized. In spite of missions like that of Saint-Martin de Tours,

---

5. The domain that remained purely Celtic was primarily rural, and no large settlements would be found there before the Viking invasions. Celtic society traditionally avoided urbanization; the phenomenon of nonurbanization occurred in the zones farthest away from Rome—or from Lyon, capital of the Roman Gauls. In tandem, oddly enough, another form of Christianity evolved in these same regions, one that may be classified as Celtic. Because it had no urban traits, it was permeated by ancestral traditions, notably vestiges of Druidism. For more, see Jean Markale, *Le Christianisme celtique et ses survivances populaires* (Paris: Imago, 1984).

rural areas were left to their own devices; they were where the most subtle mergers between former rituals and the new practices were accomplished.

Under pressure from the masses, however—most particularly the Eastern populations that were deeply marked by the archaic cults of the Mother Goddess and various deities who were reborn following physical death—the papacy had to resign itself to accepting worship of images as symbolic representations of the divine or sacred. Because it was impossible to root out this ancestral behavior from popular belief, it was thought better to incorporate and channel it rather than see it maintained clandestinely or in some marginal fashion. After all, it was no inconvenience to the Church hierarchy if people who had honored Cybele and Attis in good faith and in hope of their salvation displayed the same zeal in favor of the Virgin Mary and Jesus Christ. The new message overlay the old and altered certain details, but it retained the metaphysical meaning that gave it its strength (a Savior has been born who will allow us, through his example, to claim resurrection in the flesh). The worship of images formerly untainted by any sense of idolatry as evil therefore constituted exemplary support for the new religion's diffusion, working gently to effect what is called the substitution of worships.

But the new converts in the towns, whose religious fervor was more intellectualized, long remained hostile not only to all incorporation of pagan images, but even to the use of purely Christian images, which were reputed to be dangerous because they were too evocative of a past that still clung tenaciously to life in the mind. In the year 835, a council convened in Paris by Charlemagne's son Louis the Pious reprimanded Pope Adrian for recommending the worship of images. Like Charlemagne, Louis the Pious had to deal with the resurgence of paganism; both were responsible for edicts banning the worship of stones, springs, and trees, a clear indication of a return in strength of pre-Christian practices. Charlemagne ordered the destruction of a large number of sacred stones, menhirs, and dolmens scattered across his territory. They had begun to cause offense to the official worship of the Church, of which the emperor was the chief propagator and zealous defender. The Council of Paris did not prevail against the pontifical decisions, and the French clergy had to accept in turn, for good or ill, the extension of worship to images. We can be quite certain that at that time there were a large number of "finds" of statues buried in the ground or hidden in trees, which people hastened to recognize as representations of the Virgin Mary.

This completely natural confusion has been a constant occurrence even into the present day, when it is possible to scientifically date archaeological finds with precision. In his work *Culte de la Sainte Vierge en Afrique,* Father Delattre provided two characteristic examples of this confusion. A Maltese native had brought him a statue representing a woman holding a child on her knees. He did not doubt for an instant that it was a Virgin and Child until one of his archaeologist friends showed him it was an Isis-Horus group from the Alexandrian period. At the home of another native of Malta in a working-class neighborhood, this same Father Delattre had noticed a perpetually illuminated lamp in front of a statuette. This he instantly recognized as a Carthaginian Tanit of the third century B.C.E. and thought it wise to alert the owner to its identity. But the gentleman responded, "It doesn't matter, I had it blessed at church, it is completely Christian now"!

This speaks volumes about the permanence of images and worship, and especially about the serenity with which different populations make the transition from one religion to another. And what should we think of this opinion of Gregory of Tours (in the sixth century), in a letter addressed to Queen Brunehaut, concerning several Christians who "raced to churches and yet continued, abomination, to give worship to demons"? Everything not recognized by the official orthodoxy is reduced to the rank of the demonic, which is not really the best way to get rid of these alternative beliefs, as the pagan survivals in the form of witchcraft show decisively. A Pyrenees native by the name of Vigilance, who died in 410, was indignant at the sight of the faithful worshipping images in the Holy

Land, where he had gone on pilgrimage. He lodged a complaint with Saint Jerome, who tried vainly to make him see reason. Even inside the Church there could be disagreement on the worship of the saints and the Virgin in particular.

Overly realistic representation, however, lessens the sacred power of images. The sacred needs to be surrounded by mystery, as Lucan wrote in the *Pharsalia* concerning the absence of anthropomorphic representations in the sacred clearings of the Druids: "It adds so much more to the terrors of not knowing the gods whom one should dread." This idea was shared by numerous church fathers, and it was only under popular pressure that they resigned themselves to representations of the Virgin and the saints and then encouraged their worship. This is because Christianity, at least Roman Catholicism and Greek Orthodox, claims to be within the grasp of everyone (although it reserves for theologians and intellectuals certain notions that it is difficult not to classify as esoteric, even if the Church has always officially refused to admit it).

It was a matter, then, of using images to spread ideas, because the images were better able than theological analyses or homilies to help the primarily uneducated masses understand the finer points of the Christian religion. In this sense, the cathedral was the Book of the Middle Ages, and its simple language requires no translation. Sometimes, however, images do require commentaries and interpretations; even though they never lose their original power, they risk being no longer understood when mentalities adapt to changing social and cultural contexts.

It is within these complex and problematic circumstances that the history and significance of the Virgin Mary cult should be understood. Three essential dates mark off the historical journey: 431, the Council of Ephesus and the definition of the Theotokos; 1854, the proclamation of the dogma of the Immaculate Conception; 1950, the proclamation of the dogma of the Assumption. But it is quite certain that between these defining events there were many considerations, much trial and error, and many hesitations.

The first church fathers, both Greek and Roman, never directly confronted the problem of Mary and her uniqueness in the human race. The notion of the Immaculate Conception never arises in their writings. To the contrary, while recognizing the holiness of the "woman" Mary, they strove to reduce her by making her *the servant of the Lord,* a very convenient subordinate position that avoids the fundamental ontological question. Mary had merely obeyed God; and, as all creatures should obey God, we should take Mary as an example of obedience, submission, and humility in order to comply, under the best possible conditions, with the mysterious plan that God has drawn for us and the universe. It is for this reason that we should honor Mary, mother of God, and accord her justified worship.

Two ideas were emphasized. The first was that of the Virgin Mary's purity (the issue of virginity will come later), in obvious harmony with the gynophobic tendencies of early Christianity—a perfectly understandable attitude, for it needed to overcome the eroticism of certain Eastern forms of worship given to the Mother Goddess. If Mary could be confused with Ishtar and her successive substitutes in the popular mind, then it was quite obviously necessary to amputate from this new Ishtar all the sexual elements that characterized her. It was unacceptable that God could have incarnated within the womb of a promiscuous woman, and this was emphasized by the base text, the Gospel of Luke, which stressed that Mary was betrothed to Joseph after she found herself pregnant; Joseph's doubts and anger in this regard are quite revealing.

The position of the church fathers was thus perfectly clear: For one to accept that "Mary had been covered by the shadow of God"—in other words, the Holy Ghost—it was absolutely necessary that she be removed from the retinue of the goddesses of antiquity, all more or less erotic and all more or less suspected of numerous copulations (which was logical, given that they were primarily fertility deities). "You and Your mother," said Saint Ephraim in one of his prayers, "You alone are totally beautiful in every respect; for in

You, O Lord, there is no stain, and there is no pollution in Your mother." This is only one prayer and a gratuitous assertion, but it is perfectly consistent with the principle that the incarnation of Jesus-God is a unique event in the history of the world. Jesus-God, even if he was born in strange and exceptional conditions, could not share the birth of the other gods of pagan antiquity, for he had to be completely set apart from the earlier tradition.

Therefore, the image of the Virgin Mary, mother of God, is attached indelibly to the idea of purity, which leads to another notion—that of chastity. And if the Virgin Mary is the model for humanity, her chastity becomes exemplary and must be encouraged. Hence the sexual prohibitions pronounced by official Christianity, hence the chastity demanded of priests insofar as they—in contrast to laypeople, who must perpetuate the human race and share in the creation of other elects for God—have chosen to serve God and the Virgin Mary and thereby identify with their model. This is nothing new; the priests of Cybele castrated themselves—an extreme form of chastity—to identify with the god Attis, and the priests of Diana-Artemis observed celibacy and chastity because they were the theoretical husbands-sons of the goddess, who would never have tolerated any failing on their part.[6]

The purity of the Virgin Mary was necessary to avoid any confusion between her and some Eastern goddess. The outcome, on the one hand, was the assertion of her physical virginity, without any clear idea as to just what that corresponded to[7] in terms of the defi-

---

6. Racine grasped this completely in his play *Phèdre* with the character of Hippolyte. This individual was sworn to the worship of Diana, and this is why he so arrogantly refuses the advances of his stepmother. But (and here Racine innovates on his model, Euripides' tragedy) Hippolyte is in love with Aricie (a Racinian creation) and is even disposed to marry her, thereby breaking the vow of chastity that was imposed on him when he became a priest of Diana-Artemis. This is why he perishes, victim of the vengeance of Neptune—in reality, negative forces unleashed by Diana-Artemis to punish him for his transgression.

7. I have examined at length the possible meanings of the word *virgin* in the different traditions, particularly the Hebrew, in Jean Markale, *Women of the Celts* (Rochester, Vt.:

nition of the Theotokos; and, on the other hand, was an incitement to the chastity of the faithful, priests mainly, through the completely understandable identification of the priest with the deity.[8] On the social and thus moral plane, there was the prohibition cast on sex, the guilt associated with sexual relations outside marriage—considered merely a stopgap measure—and the exile of women, who since Eve have been held responsible for human sin. All this has led to an antifeminism that is sometimes tinged with fanaticism.

The second important idea that prevailed in the creation of the worship of the Virgin was the parallel drawn between the image of Mary and the image of Eve. Mary became the new Eve, an Eve who was purified or preserved (the subtle distinction between these two terms had not yet been reached) and who would restore the harmony of the world disturbed by original sin: "A woman doomed the world, a woman will save the world." This is the solemn assertion of continuity along with transcendence. Mary is the redeemed Eve who permits, through her consensual and exemplary maternity, the redemption of the world by the Son. There is nothing new here; Attis had already been born of Cybele to regenerate a world that was drowning not in perdition (this word is typically Christian) but in sterility, the preface to death and destruction. The same was true in the myth of Demeter and Kore, in which a "young girl" kidnapped by Hades-Pluto was the naturalistic symbol of annual germination. The pagan myth featured the notion of a cyclical regeneration in rhythm with the cosmos. In the Christian myth, history is inscribed in a linear fashion. In this sense, Christianity can claim to be outside time and space because it proposes an abstract

---

Inner Traditions, 1987), 127–33. Most important, beyond any physical qualities, the Virgin is a *strong, free, and available* woman, which fits in with the idea of Mary as a mediator between God and humans—always attentive to *all* her children, to the entire human race—and is incapable of ignoring anyone who turns to her in need.

8. This was accentuated from the eleventh to twelfth century in the theoretical and literary discussions on courtly love, in which the Lady, the secular image of the Virgin Mary, was invested with a certain portion of the miraculous aura. For more on this, see Jean Markale, *Courtly Love* (Rochester, Vt.: Inner Traditions, 2000).

version of the cosmic drama that plays on both a planetary and a constellational scale.

And all of this has been *historicized*—that is to say, placed more or less artificially in a time that is presumed real, allegedly to fix in memory a privileged event from which all future history will flow. It is impossible to say if this mental system belongs to the original Christian teaching or if it is a function of the translation of Aramaic texts into Greek and then into Latin. One academic theory assumes that the original Christian message, which was incomprehensible to the Jews, who rejected it, no longer needs to show proof because it was adapted to the Greco-Latin philosophy, by the Socratic schools in particular. This would explain the historicization of the fundamental myth, whereas this myth, like all myths, would be integrated into another mentality entirely differently, as exemplified by the British-Irish version;[9] it was not for nothing that this so-called Celtic Christianity was attacked and annihilated by the keepers of the Roman ideology. Of course, this is only an academic theory. The question is, as noted, impossible to resolve.

On this linear scale, two fundamental events oppose each other. Listen again to Saint Ephraim: "Two innocents, both simple, Mary and Eve, were equal in all respects. But later, the one became the cause of our death, the other the cause of our life." Tertullian, in his *De carne Christi,* said nearly the same thing. Eve and Mary are two faces of one reality; neither could exist without the other. It seems like the purest dualism. Indeed, these are almost the words of Pascal when he declares that thanks to Christ, humankind's greatness lies in its redemption. Pascal appears to be saying that without the redemption, humans would be insignificant beings with no metaphysical breadth, satisfied with just being and not becoming. But Christ, God made human, allows humanity to cross over the stage of passivity to reach the stage of action: a formidable privilege, and one that gives Mary all her meaning and her fullness. The redemp-

---

9. See Jean Markale, *Le Christianisme celtique* (Paris: Imago, 1984).

tion cannot be spoken of without referring to the one who made it possible—Mary.

This is what the church fathers grasped when they accorded so much importance to the Marian cult and all its visible manifestations, especially its images, and finally the definition of the Theotokos. If Eve is the "mother of human beings," Mary is the "mother of God." But given that this God is also a human, it is easy to assess all the consequences that stem from this with regard to the meaning of life on earth in terms of its usefulness and purpose.

While Eve and Mary are two sides of one reality, Eve appears as the negative aspect and Mary as the positive aspect. This oppositional distinction is marked by the attitude of each of them at the moment of the fundamental choice (which implies from the outset the existence of free will). Eve was under a prohibition: Do not eat the fruit from the Tree of Knowledge. *The demand was therefore already negative.* She responded to the temptations of the serpent—who is not Satan at all but rather the personification of the free will of human beings, with their defects, curiosity, and questions—and acts *positively* toward the serpent but *negatively* toward God and God's prohibition. It remains to be seen if this prohibition was not a snare ("Lead us not into temptation," says explicitly the Lord's Prayer, the primordial prayer of all Christianity). Free will worked, but in the wrong sense, and that led to disharmony in the world.

Was Eve responsible for this disharmony? Yes, because she was free—not because the divine plan foresaw that humanity had to sink into disharmony before being redeemed by another woman, the Virgin of virgins, first creature and perpetual guardian of the "infernal marshes." In one sense, Eve was necessary so that Mary could help save humanity, in the same way that Judas Iscariot justifies himself (in myth, because the reality was something else entirely) because he made it possible for the execution of Jesus to occur. In the world of relativities, there are always two generally contradictory sides, because without these two sides, reality would be impossible to perceive. What gives Mary her greatness is the "pettiness" of Eve, who saw things only in the short term rather than foreseeing them in their timeless extent.

So it was necessary to oppose Mary to Eve, hence the classic representation of the Virgin crushing underfoot the head of the serpent or the dragon of the depths. Without the serpent she crushes, Mary would have no power, no meaning, and no grandeur. The same is true of Saint Michael, who would have no equivalent if he did not figure in a perpetual struggle against the dragon.[10] Antagonisms, even mythological ones, are always revealing of a concrete reality that, by virtue of its materiality, escapes the nonexistence of perfection. This is more than obvious; it is a golden rule. Mary, mother of God, would be nothing without God's action. To the archangel Gabriel's request—the voice of God and manifestation of the Holy Ghost—she answered, "I am the servant of the Lord." Thus she answered the request positively. But this request was not a negative prohibition, as in Eden; it was a positive request addressed to the free will of a woman. After all, Mary could have answered no. And the redemption, humankind's grandeur, would not have occurred.

Starting from this notion of a new Eve, or an *anti*-Eve, it was no longer possible for Mary to be an ordinary woman. First it was necessary to strip her of all the dubious colorations inherited from the pagan worship of the Mother Goddess and turn her into a model of purity. Then, to accentuate her fundamental purity, it was necessary to blacken Eve by giving her the aspects customarily bestowed on the mother goddesses, who were cruel, bloodthirsty, and erotic and yet played a maternal role, as did Eve for the entire human race. The parallel drawn between Eve and Mary was crucial both for countering the rhetoric of paganism's maternal deities and for highlighting the unique nature of the Virgin Mary. Mary was the one mother of a single God and a single humanity, the humanity whom Jesus hoped was fraternal and the one from which the Cathars asserted that the world would be saved only when the last soul found salva-

---

10. See J. Markale, *Le Mont-Saint-Michel et l'énigme du dragon.*

tion. Instead of being an epiphenomenon in the Christian doctrine, the Virgin Mary occupies a primordial place: Without her, nothing would hold together.

But this was all grist for the mill of theological discussion. For these sometimes arduous notions to be understood, they had to be presented in a simplified form placed in the context of the dogma— that is to say, in the context of incomprehensible verities that every member of the faithful obligatorily believes and, in fact, believes blindly. It was therefore essential to graft the wording of the dogma onto customs, practices, and feelings, those relating to maternity being the most widespread and the most accessible to the greatest number of people. And, of course, ritual provided an opportunity to give greater precision to certain phrases of the dogma.

Starting in the seventh century in the Greek churches of the East, a feast was instituted to celebrate the Conception of Saint Anne, or the passive conception of Mary. This feast soon moved into southern Italy and into Great Britain as the Conceptio Beatae Virginis. But this could not have happened were it not for the agency of a figure about whom the Gospels say nothing, the mother of Mary, Saint Anne. The Protoevangelion of James, which was rejected as apocryphal by the Nicean Council, recounts her story with an extraordinary wealth of detail.

The reference to the mysterious Saint Anne is important. She is nothing more or less than *the image of the original Mother Goddess,* she whom all peoples honored under different names, and who was definitively separated from the image of Mary to avoid any confusion. She had returned in strength because it was impossible to get beyond her. But it was less perilous to transform her into the mother of the Virgin Mary than into the Virgin Mary herself.

The East and Far East are very familiar with the Goddess of the Beginnings. In India she is Annapurna, Anna the Provider. She can be found again in Rome under the name Anna Parenna. But in between she had traveled through the Middle East under different names, such as Danae and Tanit, and she gave her name to the Don and Danube Rivers. On the other end of the ancient world, on the far western side, she is the Irish Dana, mother of the Gaelic gods, the Tuatha de Danann. She can also be recognized in Gallic tradition as Dôn, where she is also the mother of the principal gods, and in Armorican Breton tradition in the name Anaon, the "Departed," meaning "the people of Ana." This Ana soon dissolved into the features of Anne of the Protoevangelion, but Celtified to a certain extent, for she was presented in the appearance of a Breton woman who married the Jew Joachim and, after the death of her husband, is supposed to have returned to die in her own land.

The figure of Saint Anne is both simple and complex. The Protoevangelion describes her as a virtuous elderly woman who bemoans her sterility. Her husband, Joachim, is a man of considerable wealth (which invalidates all the scenarios in which Jesus was poor and Joseph a humble carpenter!—these stories are just right for bringing tears to the eyes of the simple folk). But Joachim earned the scorn of the twelve Tribes of Israel for having no child. He therefore requested the Lord to perform a miracle. For her part, Anne did the same:

> About the ninth hour she went down to the garden to walk. And there she saw a laurel, and sat beneath its shade, and prayed to the all-powerful Lord, saying: O God of our fathers, bless me and grant my prayer, as Thou didst bless the womb of Sarah, and didst give her a son, Isaac. And gazing towards the heaven, she saw a sparrow's nest in the laurel, and made a lamentation in herself, saying: Woe is me! Who begot me? And what womb produced me? Because I have become a curse in the presence of the sons of Israel, and I have been reproached, and they have mocked me out of the temple of the Lord. Woe is me! to what can I be compared? I am not like the fowls of the heaven, because even the fowls of the heaven are fruitful before Thee, O Lord. Woe is me! to what can I be compared? I am not like the beasts of the earth, because even the beasts of the earth are fruitful before Thee, O Lord. Woe is

me! to what can I be compared? I am not like these waters, because even these waters are fruitful before Thee, O Lord. Woe is me! to what can I be compared? I am not like this earth, because even the earth bringeth forth its fruits in season, and blesseth Thee, O Lord.[11]

Note the essentially pagan invocation to the elements. At this point an angel of the Lord stands before her and tells her:

Anne, Anne, the Lord hath heard thy prayer, and thou shalt conceive, and shall bring forth; and thy seed shall be spoken of in all the world. And Anne responded: By the life of the Lord my God, if I beget either male or female, I will bring it as a gift to the Lord my God; and it shall be in His holy service all the days of its life.

This was how Anne and Joachim became parents of a little girl they named Mary.

Day by day the child grew stronger; and when she was six months old, her mother set her on the ground to see whether she could stand, and she walked seven steps then returned to the bosom of her mother; and she snatched her up, saying: By the life of the Lord my God, thou shalt not walk on this earth until I bring thee into the temple of the Lord. And she made a sanctuary in her bedroom and suffered nothing common or unclean to pass through it. And she called for the daughters of the Hebrews that were undefiled, and they entertained her.[12]

This was how she who would become the Virgin Mary was born and then grew up undefiled.

---

11. *Protoevangelion of James,* chaps. 2–4, 6, trans. Émile Amann, quoted by Pierre Crépon in *Les Évangiles apocryphes* (Paris: Retz, 1983), 30–32.
12. *Ibid.*

This is the origin of the tradition concerning Saint Anne, whose worship is so important in certain Celtic countries, particularly on the Armorican peninsula of Brittany, where it almost exceeds the devotion to Mary. It is also somewhat amusing to note that this worship and the basic devotion to Saint Anne draw their origins not from canonical texts, but from so-called apocryphal texts that were rejected as such by the official Roman Catholic Church. It is an example of the lack of consistency that characterizes Christian doctrine when we make an effort to look beyond the usual sermon and refer to the fundamental texts. The Protoevangelion allowed worship of Saint Anne to be implemented, consequently permitting the emphasis on the miraculous conception of the Virgin Mary, so it is an important element for explaining the Marian cult. If the conception of Mary in Anne's womb (again, identical to the ancient Mother Goddess) was accepted, it could allow more mystical interpretations.

Accordingly, at the beginning of the twelfth century, the Saxon monks Eadbert, disciple of Saint Anselm of Canterbury, and Osbert de Clare, both influenced by Celtic monachism, declared themselves partisans of a (passive) immaculate conception (in other words, exempted from original sin) of the Virgin Mary. This position, which was well ahead of its time and heavily influenced by Celtic concepts inherited from the Druidism that still lingered in the clerical milieus of Great Britain, was fought by the keepers of Roman orthodoxy on the Continent, particularly by Saint Bernard de Clairvaux. Bernard, who some in mockery of reality stubbornly maintain was the "last Druid in the West," but who was above all the temporal and spiritual master of twelfth-century Europe, addressed a harsh warning to the faithful of Lyon, who had initiated a feast of the Conception of Mary. He fulminated against this "unjustified innovation" (probably because it was from an apocryphal text) and developed the theory that Mary had indeed been sanctified in her mother's womb, but *after her conception.* No one could say that Saint Bernard was a denigrator of Mary, however; he contributed greatly to the development of the worship given to Our Lady!

Nevertheless, he refused to make Mary into a person who was an exception to common humanity. Under the formidable influence of Bernard de Clairvaux, the majority of theologians who followed him, such as Saint Bonaventure, Albert the Great, and Thomas Aquinas, unambiguously pronounced against recognition of any kind of immaculate conception of Mary.

It was another theologian and heir to the Celtic tradition who dared oppose the official doctrine. John Duns Scotus, who died in 1308, taught that animation should precede sanctification not in time, but only in the natural order. He introduced the entirely new notion of *pre-redemption*. It was conceivable that Christ redeemed his mother solely through mercy. The Franciscan Order adopted Scotus's theory, thereby violently opposing the Dominican Order, and displayed its will to make the Immaculate Conception a dogmatic element of the Roman Church.

But the discussion between the different tendencies of the Church was just getting under way. The thirty-sixth session of the Council of Basel in 1439 stood openly in favor of the Immaculate Conception, and Pope Sixtus IV, who ruled from 1471 to 1484, encouraged the celebration of the feast in honor of Mary "conceived without sin." Everything was called into question again, however, by the Reformation. Luther and Zwingle recognized Mary as an exceptional individual, even going so far as to assert her virginity *after* the birth of Jesus. But Calvin categorically rejected any idea of worshipping the Virgin at the same time that he denied her Immaculate Conception. This prompted a reaction from the Council of Trent; without asserting anything, it was satisfied with repeating that no creature could be considered exempt from original sin, adding that "God had no intention to include in this decree the benevolent and immaculate Virgin Mary." This led to the proposal that Mary be given special status among all creatures without going any further than recognizing her absolute purity. In 1567,

Pope Pius V condemned the theologian Baius, who maintained that no one other than Christ was exempt from original sin and that the death and tribulations of Mary were the penalty for either her actual sins or that original sin. Officially, the Church left the door open for the assertion that the Virgin Mary could not have been subject to the same fate as most of humanity.

All this was brought to an end on December 8, 1854, by the solemn proclamation of the dogma of the Immaculate Conception of Mary by Pope Pius IX, following consultations with the entire episcopacy. In fact, this decision, which made the assertion a matter of faith, was only the official recognition of what had long been believed by the great majority of Catholics, which they expressed naively or clumsily in their worship of Mary. Without asking themselves thorny metaphysical or theological questions, the faithful had felt a confused need for the Mother of God to be an absolutely uncommon individual. Unable to make her into a goddess, which would have constituted a return to paganism and the archaic definition of the primordial female deity, they arranged for her to be a human "full of grace" who had earned the right to transcend her human condition by agreeing to be the "receptacle" of God. This was an "apotheosis" to a certain extent in the strict—and pagan—sense of the word.

But the apotheosis could not be complete until the problem of Mary's death was resolved. From the moment Mary took on the guise of a privileged being who was exempted from original sin, a contradiction was created. If the consequence of original sin for Adam and Eve was the punishment of death, how was the Virgin Mary to be relieved of this original sin and still be subject to death?

Here again folk beliefs and cultural practices had evaded to a certain extent, if not at least outstripped, the problem posed by the theologians. Throughout the Middle Ages, numerous legends had swirled about the Virgin, which, without declaring that Mary was immortal, presented her as clad in a glorious body similar to that of the resurrected Jesus, a figure who had the ability to appear in flesh and blood each time her intervention was necessary to render aid to one of the faithful in anguish or want. Themes like that of the Miracle of the Theophile, in which the Virgin retrieves a pact with the devil that the cleric had signed, and that of the Juggler of Notre-Dame, in which Mary plays for a poor poet a role similar to that of the Lady in courtly love, are valuable clues concerning popular convictions about the Mother of God. She was not only always a virgin, not only of immaculate conception, but also *outside time,* endowed with a "permanence" both on earth and in heaven.

This idea can be seen in the performance of her worship. Mary is invoked not only by reference to the suffering she endured as a mother at the foot of the cross, but especially because she represented a *perpetual maternity.* She is the one who regenerates, who allows transcendence. She is, like her son, the Resurrection and the Life. She cannot die because *she is life.* This is a fundamental idea inherited from the dawn of time, and it is clear that it is superimposed over the concept of the Great Goddess of the Beginnings. Accordingly, certain Breton Calvary scenes show Mary holding her dead son on her knees after the descent from the cross, but not in quite in the same posture as in the classic Pietà. Jesus' body does not come down below the Virgin's knees, as if the artists wanted to signify that Mary had reintegrated her son's body within her own to give him new life.

There are sanctuaries in which Mary is worshipped as triumphant, omitting any reference to death, not only her own but also that of all her sons, for Christ on the cross had given her as a son John, who symbolized the human race. This is the case with Chartres. This sanctuary is dedicated not to the *mater dolorosa* but to the triumphant Mother. *And this is why, contrary to the customs of ancient times, there is no tomb in the cathedral of Chartres,* not even the tomb of a bishop or saint that would have shared his luster with the cathedral.

But all this emanates, on the one hand, from folk religion (often quite distinct from the official religion) and, on the other, from marginal—even "esoteric"—speculations (the cathedral builders were no innocents) that stirred and sometimes strongly shook the dogmatic edifice of a religion solidly established in its sociocultural framework.

These kinds of cultural practices and speculations did not fail to provoke theologians. The main goal was to find a consensus that could satisfy everyone while not deviating from the essential outline. Mary is not a deity, she is only the *first creature* of the One Deity, a sort of *materia prima* that the presence of the Holy Ghost transformed. The transformation is similar to the metamorphosis in the *Magister,* or Great Work, of alchemy, the series of operations starting from a primal shapeless matter that has been chosen and is privileged, which eventually leads to the creation of the philosopher's stone, the transcendence not only of matter but of the spirit as well.

The parallels with medieval alchemy are broader still. The philosophers—which is how alchemists were labeled—often described, in veiled terms, the "Holy Matter" of the Virgin's body, in which the Light had been hidden since the dawn of time. The Great Work consisted of rediscovering the light buried within raw matter and exalting it. In the alchemical interpretation, if the philosopher's stone is implicitly contained within the primal matter of the work, then Jesus-God—who is, on a theological plane, the philosopher's stone in all its splendor and potency—is intrinsically held himself inside the body of Mary. This is sufficient justification for the Immaculate Conception: Mary as Theotokos has existed since the creation. She is the *container,* she is the primal matter from which the Light will emanate, she is the Vessel in which the transubstantiation will occur, she is in some way the Grail, the mysterious object whose contents are unknown (the blood of Christ or some divine force, which amounts to the same thing), but which is necessarily something absolute and perfect.

The problem is that the Grail, which is a container (the meaning of *gradal* is "receptacle"), is permeated by the quality of its contents and thereby acquires a sacred nature itself. Even if there is no longer anything in the Grail, the object itself is divine. It is in similar terms that the problem of the Virgin is posed if she is given the same sacred or divine nature as the Grail. Then we are clearly obliged to claim that Mary, as a corporeal being, was not able to undergo the same fate as other human beings. In a word, did Mary, mother of Jesus Christ, die?

A hasty response could be as follows: yes, as her own son, who was nonetheless God, underwent death, and in painful and igno-minious circumstances besides. So why, then, would his mother, despite her unique nature, have escaped the common fate? But it was not the Virgin Mary who achieved the Redemption, it was Jesus himself. Mary only participated in this redemption, she was not its pivot. In the matriarchal myth, in the same way, it is Attis and not Cybele who is both the model and the artisan of the regeneration. But to be precise, Cybele no more dies than does Ishtar, Artemis, or Isis. These images of the permanence and timelessness of the Divine Mother lingered for so long in the collective unconscious that they eventually became indelibly embedded there. It was therefore neces-sary to find a theological solution that would satisfy popular faith while avoiding a return in strength of the archaic pagan representa-tion. It was a delicate operation that was not performed without controversy and was only fully achieved in 1950—quite belatedly, in other words—in the proclamation of the dogma of the Assumption.

The difficulty lies in the fact that not a single canonical text pro-vides the slightest bit of information on the "end" of Mary. More-over, except for Luke, who expounded at length on the Virgin, the Gospel writers did not have much to say about her. She appears only twice in the course of the active life of Jesus, first at the wedding in Cana, then at the Crucifixion. John added the famous detail con-cerning the "universal Mother" in an episode that leaves the impres-sion that the apostle prayed with his teacher's mother. This is pure conjecture. Acts tells us hardly anything more. And yet a tenacious tradition has thrived in the Church since its earliest days concerning the "death" of Mary in Ephesus, where she found herself in the com-pany of Saint John and where, of course, the location of the house where she lived has been found. The city of Ephesus was, throughout antiquity, the veritable capital of the Mother Goddess, particularly Artemis. It was therefore logical for tradition to place Mary's house here, as well as for Ephesus to serve as the location for the council that proclaimed Mary mother of God. This does not invalidate the possibility that Mary was actually in Ephesus, but it does explain the universal scope the worship of the Virgin took on after Ephesus.

The tradition does have some noncanonical scriptural support. It involves an apocryphal text (one officially rejected by the Church) known as Transitus Mariae. It is the sole text to present a story of the death and Assumption of the Virgin Mary. One Greek and two Latin recastings of this text were known, the oldest most likely being the Greek, which went back to the fourth century. Of course, the late date of this text means only that it set down in writing an older story that had been passed down orally. The same observation could be made of the so-called canonical Gospels, or for most of the books of the Hebrew scriptures, or for any mythological story whatsoever from any traditions whatsoever.[13] There is no reason to think that the Transitus Mariae was not the reflection of an authentic reality. In any case, these three early versions gave rise to numerous reworkings, in particular to a very interesting *Book on the Passing of the Very Holy Virgin, Mother of God,* which was attributed—falsely—to a certain Melito, bishop of Sardes in Lydia, at the end of the second century.

The *Book on the Passing* first emphasizes the evangelical episode in which Jesus entrusts his mother to the apostle John: "And from that hour the holy mother of God remained specially entrusted to

---

13. There is no question that the *Iliad* and the *Odyssey* are revisions or transcriptions of earlier oral tales. The same holds true for all the pagan mythological epics of ancient Ireland. These were oral traditions transcribed by Irish Christian monks starting in the seventh century. This in no way reduces their value; at most it might mean some modifications, some very legitimate misunderstandings, and sometimes intentional changes prompted by the desire to bring archaic Druidic thought in line with Christian thought. Should the Finnish *Kalevala,* a nineteenth-century transcription of oral stories going back to the most archaic periods of Finnish civilization, be regarded as apocryphal? What qualifies as apocryphal and what does not remains a very delicate matter.

the care of John, as long as she dwelled in this life. And when the apostles had drawn lots to determine the region where they would preach, she settled in the house of her parents near Mount Olive." There are no other references to this home Mary's family owned in Jerusalem. Other traditions mention Ephesus, where John seems to have gone to spread the Christian teachings.

Then the *Book on the Passing,* mute as to Mary's activities, suddenly leaps to "the twenty-second year after Jesus Christ, having vanquished death, ascended up to heaven." An angel appears to Mary and announces that her death is close at hand, more specifically that she will be "carried up to heaven with her body." Mary requests a favor of the angel: that all her son's disciples be brought back together around her. The angel responds: "All the apostles will be brought here by the power of Jesus Christ."

Mary then prepares herself. "And lo while the blessed John was preaching in Ephesus on the Lord's day, at the third hour, there was a great earthquake, and a cloud raised him up out of the sight of all and brought him before the door of the house where was the Virgin Mary." The Virgin rejoices at the coming of John. She explains to him what the angel had announced and displays her concern about the attitude of the Jews. "I have overheard the Jews holding counsel and who said: Let us await the day on which the mother of this impostor dies and we will burn her body." She then asks John to keep watch over her funeral services and to hold before her coffin the palm given her by the angel.

"Suddenly, by the order of God, all the spotless were carried off by a cloud from those places where they preached the word of God and they were placed before the house where Mary lived." The vigil begins. "On the third day, sleep overcame all those in the house, and none could remain awake, save the apostles, and the three virgins who were the companions of the Holy Virgin." Jesus appears in the midst of a crowd of angels and speaks to his mother: "When I, sent by my Father for the salvation of the world, was hanging on the cross, the prince of darkness approached me; but when he was unable to find any trace of his heart in me, he went away beaten and trampled underfoot. Such I saw him as you will see him in accordance with the common law of the human race, to which you have complied by dying, but he cannot harm you because there is naught in you that is in him, and I will be with you to protect you."

Then the Virgin lies down and dies. Jesus commands his disciples to bear the body of his mother "to the right of the city toward the East" and to lay it in a new tomb. A description then follows of Mary's body, which "shone so brightly that it was only by God's bounty that one could touch it. It was perfectly pure and absent of any filth. . . . The face of the blessed Mary, Mother of God, was like the flower of the lily, and a great odor of marvelous sweetness arose from her body, which had no comparable sweetness anywhere."

The funeral procession is then organized. Along the route, a Jewish priest, full of fury, tries to overturn the coffin. His arms wither into husks. He beseeches the apostle Peter to heal him. Peter addresses the Lord with a heartfelt prayer. The priest is cured and begins to praise the Lord. The apostles reach the Valley of Jehoshaphat and place the coffin in a new sepulcher. Jesus appears anew and asks the apostles what they want him to do for his mother. The apostles answer: "It would appear to your servants right that just as you have vanquished death and reign in glory, you will raise up the body of Mary and take her full of joy into heaven."

Jesus commands the archangel Gabriel to carry the soul of Mary and raise the stone. And Jesus says, "Arise, my beloved who have not suffered corruption from contact with man, you will not suffer the destruction of your body in the tomb." The Virgin stands up and gives thanks to her son. And he speaks words of encouragement to his apostles, and in the middle of a cloud he ascends "back to heaven, and the angels accompanied him bearing the blessed Mary, Mother of God, to the paradise of God."[14]

---

14. *Livre du passage de la très Sainte Vierge,* chapters 3–18, trans. Brunet, vol. 23 of *Encyclopédie théologique of Migne* (Amort: Collet and Vermot, 1856).

This is the lone narrative concerning the Assumption of Mary. The details are specific. The Virgin died like any other human being, just like Jesus himself. But this death was temporary, and it was with her body—which escaped decomposition—that Mary was "carried into heaven," in other words into the timeless and aspatial world promised by the scriptures, the place where mind and body harmonize once and for all and where contradictions cease to be perceived as such. Mary's Assumption, on a philosophical plane, is a *perfection,* a "fulfillment." If such an event really occurred, it would become exemplary and would mean that every human being, under certain circumstances, could attain total transcendence. Certainly the Christian doctrine teaches that Jesus, a man-god, accomplished the same transcendence, but Jesus is both God and man, whereas Mary is merely a woman, even if she has a unique nature. Hence the importance of the image of the Virgin Mary: She is in some way the regenerator, the one who shows the way that *all* her children should take. It is a maternal image, of course, and one that speaks to the vast majority of human beings. But this maternal image attests to a *new birth,* the definitive birth in a world that excludes the transitory, a world that does not know the ephemeral. These philosophical notions, although they are beyond the comprehension of most of the faithful, do explain the importance of the Marian cult.

Over the course of the first three centuries of Christianity, there was nothing unique about the Marian cult; it was intimately connected to the worship of Jesus himself. It was only starting with the fourth century, probably under the influence of the so-called apocryphal tradition, that the first inklings of independent Marian worship began taking shape. As an example, the hymns of Saint Ephraim (d. 373 C.E.) on the birth of Jesus are really songs of praise to his mother. Saint Gregory of Naziane, who died in 390, confirmed the worship given Mary in this time by his story of a young Christian named Justine who, facing a rapist, begs "the Virgin Mary to come help the threatened virgin." Epiphany testified to the existence of the Collyridian sect, whose members tended to worship

Mary idolatrously, and took the opportunity to assert the official position of the Roman Church: "Mary should be honored. But the Father, the Son, and the Holy Ghost should be adored, whereas no one should adore Mary." It was this position defended by Cyril of Alexandria during the Council of Ephesus that became the definition of the Theotokos. Mary is only a woman, but *blessed above all other women* and promised the highest destiny.

Following this recognition of the specific mission of the Theotokos, the Marian cult developed rapidly in both East and West. Numerous sanctuaries, chapels, churches, and cathedrals were erected in her honor, and calendar feasts were instituted. Next to the Purification and the Annunciation, which were originally feasts in honor of Christ, new celebrations appeared, that of the Nativity (with the idea of the Immaculate Conception in the background) and of the Transfer of Mary (which would become the Feast of the Assumption). Finally, officially, the Assumption feast of August 15 became the celebration most in line with the dogma proclaimed by Pope Pius XII on November 1, 1950.

But it was especially during the twelfth, thirteenth, and fourteenth centuries that the worship of the Virgin reached its height, at least with respect to the Christian West, as seen by the number of feast days; the construction of buildings consecrated to Mary; the abundance of sermons, tales, and legends; and even, in a theatrical context, the importance of plays titled *Miracles of Our Lady*.

The Reformation of the sixteenth century modified this swarm somewhat. Certainly Luther did not abandon the Marian cult, quite the contrary. While criticizing certain idolatrous aspects of the worship of the Virgin (and not entirely in the wrong during this time at the end of the Middle Ages), Luther confirmed the traditional belief in the divine maternity, the perpetual virginity of Mary, the specific nature of her conception, and her power to intercede. Zwingle, too, retained the Marian faith, but refused to accept that any could beseech the Mother of God, who was a simple creature of God and not a deity. Calvin, in contrast, refused her across the board and condemned any form of worship of Mary as pure idolatry. This in no way prevented the Marian cult as such from developing over the sixteenth and seventeenth centuries in rural areas, especially on the occasion of the discovery of an ancient lost or buried statue, or even miraculous phenomena such as the appearance of a white Lady to a young peasant girl, generally poor and uneducated. Examples of this nature are countless both in France and throughout the rest of Europe.

In the eighteenth century, the Enlightenment, imbued with the spirit of rationalism and skepticism, dismissed Marian worship as superstitious and obscurantist. But the revolutionary ceremonies in honor of the Goddess Reason were a rebirth of the ancient cults of the Mother Goddess—albeit intellectualized and heavily filtered—and subconsciously extended the processions and numerous feasts of Our Lady. Statues of the Virgin were undoubtedly destroyed, but at the same time new ones were sculpted, decked out with bizarre names inherited from a distorted antiquity and in reality representing the same feminine entity, even if she was reduced to the rank of allegory.

During the course of the nineteenth century, the era of "scientific materialism," the Marian cult took on new life, mainly as a consequence of the impressive abundance of "apparitions" of the Virgin Mary in remote or anonymous backwaters—not, as one might expect, in places consecrated to the Virgin since early antiquity—that were then transformed into meccas of devotion and pilgrimage. The locations include the Chapelle de la Médaille miraculeuse (Chapel of the Miraculous Medallion) on the rue du Bac in Paris, not far from where Chateaubriand breathed his last; Pontmain, in the Maine region on the Brittany frontier; La Salette, in the Alps; and, of course, the most famous of all the Mary sanctuaries, Lourdes.

Whatever the profound reality may be of these "apparitions," it is impossible to deny that *something happened* at these stated locations, and under certain circumstances. The events in question have been gone over with a fine-tooth comb, are supported by numerous testimonies, and have had vast consequences on the behavior of Christians. They can be interpreted according to each individual's conscience and knowledge, but the fact remains that "phenomena" occurred, and they inspired a formidable renewal of worship of the Virgin. They should therefore be considered natural extensions of ancestral worship of the Mother of God in sanctuaries as ancient and famous as Rocamadour, Le Puy, and Chartres. Didn't Luke the Evangelist record that Mary said after the Annunciation (Luke 2:27), "Henceforth, all generations will call me blessed"?

What were the reasons for this worship, and especially for its rebirth? On the surface it seems that in Catholicism, devotion to Our Lady was more important than, or at least of equal importance to, worship of God himself. All the religions of the world have offered hypostases of God for the faithful to worship in place of God, because God by nature is beyond understanding, ineffable, and unknowable. Humans can communicate with the Christian God only through the humanized image of Jesus Christ. Jesus, however, was not only a man but also God, and he often appeared too remote and almost inaccessible. Piety, to be fully expressed, requires an intermediary who can understand humans and transmit their prayers, who can relay and decipher the message from on high. Christian saints served as such intermediaries.

But who was the most saintly, the most "divine," if not the Virgin Mary, who had the honor of carrying God within her body? Without making Mary into a divine hypostasis, without turning even further to archaic reminiscences of the Goddess of the Beginnings, from the Christian viewpoint Mary plays a starring role. Hence the success of the Marian cult, which, against ill winds and ill fortunes, was always reborn from its ashes. In his commentary on the *Magnificat*, Luther notes: "The blessed Virgin Mary speaks after having had a personal experience in which the Holy Ghost illuminated and instructed her." Then, surrendering to a kind of mystico-philosophical delirium, Luther imagines the message Mary received: "She learns that God is a Lord whose sole concern is raising what is low, lowering what is high, in short breaking what is made and remaking what is broken."

The message that Mary learned and revealed to humanity is essential. It is the purest ontological metaphysics; it concerns the entire universe through the permanent divine creation. By the light of this message, we can realize that God is not immobility but instead eternal movement—in a word, that *God is perpetual Becoming*. This is, moreover, what the Druids asserted in so-called pagan Celtic times when, according to tradition, they worshipped on the mound that today supports the admirable cathedral of Our Lady of Chartres, a mysterious statue of a no less mysterious *virgo paritura*, a "Virgin about to give birth," which perhaps was not a foreshadowing of Mary but purely and simply the depiction of the perpetual creation of God in the uterus of the Woman who is most blessed among women.

6

THE BLACK MADONNA

In Chartres there is no lack of images of the Virgin, and all have one thing in common: They are all majestic Madonnas, giving the strong impression that the church wished only the triumphant aspect of Mary, mother of God and keeper of universal knowledge (by virtue of her acceptance of the Holy Ghost), visible in this sanctuary. But it seems that the different images of the Virgin each have a particular role to play in devotion, and consequently a particular meaning to which the different postures and emblems contribute. And while local tradition maintains that the oldest image is Our Lady of Under Ground (at least the statue destroyed during the Revolution), it clearly emphasizes that the one named Our Lady of the Pillar, and only she, is a Black Madonna.

The current statue of Our Lady of the Pillar, standing in the first bay of the north ambulatory, just above the figure of Our Lady of Under Ground, dates back only to the early sixteenth century. The Chartres historian Sébastien Rouillard wrote in his *Parthénie,* published in 1609:

Above the rood loft on the southern side is a tall throne on which, above a round column of very hard stone, is placed the image of Our Lady. The late master Vastin de Fugerets, canon of said church during his life some hundred years or so ago, had said image erected in order that it would be freely displayed to the worshippers without disturbing the divine service of the choir. But the throngs were so constant and their devotion so great, that the stone column became pitted from being kissed by all these devout Catholics. (I, Folio 134, V)

It is probable that this statue illustrated the Virgin's Holy Tunic, which was piously kept in a reliquary and displayed on the high altar. An account written around 1700 by a Rouen native, Lebrun des Marettes, corroborates a testimony of Canon Estienne in 1682 and provides some useful details on this point:

The high altar is quite large; there are no balusters, only some copper columns and angels above the sanctuary. Above the altar there is only one facing to the reredos, and above that a gilded silver image of the Holy Virgin. There is a copper rod behind, on top of which is a golden crucifix that is about a foot and a half in size. At its foot is another copper rod that sticks out about a foot or a foot and a half in front of the altar, and the holy ciborium hangs from its end. (*Voyages liturgiques de France*, 226)

This is obviously not the same statue as Our Lady of the Pillar. Furthermore, Canon Estienne informs us that this Virgin "in gilded vermeil" is three feet high and that it was donated "during the month of May 1220 by Monsieur Pierre de Bordeaux, archdeacon of Vendôme, a priest and honest scholar, who had ordered an image made of the benevolent Mary with two silver angels that are above the high altar" (*Cartulaire de Notre-Dame de Chartres*, III, 162). We can glean a fairly specific idea of what this statue looked like through other documents and drawings. Mary is depicted sitting with her head erect and looking straight ahead, holding the Infant Jesus on her left knee and lifting an object in her right hand. But as the documents show, the devotion inspired by this statue disturbed the peace of the choir, and the clergy of the sixteenth century strove to direct that devotion onto another object. This was the origin of Our Lady of the Pillar, which was placed right in front of the rood screen. The documents tell us that this image was intended to look like the earlier one, which explains its archaic features. So we are definitely dealing with the erection of a new statue at the beginning of the sixteenth century and not simply the relocation of the older one. But why is this depiction of the Virgin black?

In fact the description of the older statue emphasized the "gilded vermeil." And as this statue is an imitation—at least in its basic features—of the older one, this raises some questions. It is still not known if Our Lady of the Pillar is carved from pear or walnut. It is also still unknown whether the "gilded vermeil" was painted on later. Some ecclesiastics currently deny that this statue is a Black Madonna, claiming her dark color is merely *accidental* due to the color of the wood. That is easy enough to say. In any event, Chartres tradition has clearly spoken for centuries about a Black Madonna, and this is obviously not the sole example of a statue on which the Virgin and Child are thus depicted, either carved from dark wood or covered by a coating that emphasizes the black color.

There is simply no reason to doubt that the statue of Our Lady of the Pillar is what is commonly known as a Black Virgin or Black Madonna, even if it is a sixteenth-century work, as it is the more or less faithful replica of an ancient statue about which all that is known is its outside appearance. Just before the Revolution, the Chartres doctor Marie Saint-Ursin had seen this sixteenth-century statue and kept a description of it under the false impression that it had been destroyed. According to him, this Virgin was "a small black wooden figure, clad in rags and tawdry jewels, from the middle of which a child's head emerged."[1] What was this statue he saw? No one knows, but in any case, no doubt is possible concerning the

---

1. Société Archéologique d'Eure-et-Loir, ms. 43 (7), fol. 213, 5 and 214, Municipal Library of Chartres.

existence of a Black Madonna in the Chartres cathedral, no matter which exact statue represented her.

There are many Black Madonnas throughout Western Europe. These objects of worship and even pilgrimage have been a source of much fascination, both for their black color and for the mystery of their origins. If a list were made of all the statues and statuettes in this category, the number would be staggering. Some can be found in humble rural chapels, others in cathedrals. Some are ancient and others are of fairly recent provenance. Some have been destroyed but piously replaced by copies or imitations. Some are regarded as miraculous, others are simply worshipped out of tradition. Some have been discovered through circumstances bordering on the miraculous or the most wondrous happenstance; others have always been there, or at least are claimed to have always been there. And at each site where a Black Madonna can be found, ancient legends surrounding the presence of a sacred fountain, a sacred tree, or a healing spring awaken the shadows of the past, including the worship of the Mother Goddess. It seems that there is a deep and subtle connection between Christianity as it is lived in folk settings and the recollections of religions preceding Christianity. And the dominant image is always the tranquil, reassuring, or triumphant image of the Divine Mother.

In the Ain region, in Bourg-en-Bresse, there is a statue of Our Lady of Bourg around thirty-one inches high that was discovered in a tree. Analysis of the statue showed it was a thirteenth-century work. In the Allier region, in Moulins, there is a Black Madonna of the same size dating from the eleventh century. It was mounted in the fifteenth century and is now housed in the cathedral. But there is another one in the same city, kept in the museum, called Our Lady of Vouroux, and even a third, Our Lady of Coulandon, at the Grand Seminary. The Bouches-du-Rhône has the famous Our Lady of the Guard of Marseille, also known as the Brown. She is a thirteenth-century statue. The one in Aix-en-Provence known as Our Lady of the Seds is equally famous. In Murat, in the Cantal region, Our Lady of the

Olive Trees is a fourteenth-century wooden statue. In the Côtes-du-Nord, in Guingamp, the seventeenth-century Our Lady of Good Aid, which was burned during the Revolution except for its head, replaced an older statue that is sometimes connected with the one in Chartres. Two Black Madonna statues can be found in Périgueux, in the Dordogne. One is at Saint-Front and is called the Black, the other is at Saint-Estienne and carries an inscription reading VIRGO PARITURA.

In Toulouse, which is in Haut-Garonne, there is a nineteenth-century bust of Our Lady of the Gilt-Head, who is also known as the Black One. In the Loire (La Pacaudière), we find Our Lady of Tourzy, a stone statue that was most likely sculpted before the eleventh century. In the Upper Loire region (Craponne-sur-Arzon) there was a statuette, now held in a private collection, that seems to have been a copy of Our Lady of Puy. Another Black Madonna can be seen in Sargues. This heavily painted wooden statue dates from the thirteenth century. In the Loiret we find the famous Our Lady of Cléry, in front of which the kings of France would prostrate themselves. This is a sixteenth-century wooden statue that replaced a more ancient one discovered in the thirteenth century because of a bull that always stopped at the place where it had been buried.

In Orléans itself, Our Lady of the Miracles can still be seen. Known as Saint Mary the Egyptian because of her color, she is a stone statue a little over three feet in height that dates from the sixteenth century. In Villeneuve-sur-Lot (in the Lot-et-Garonne region), Our Lady of Jubilation is housed in a strange chapel that has been constructed so that half of it sits over the Lot River. In the Morbihan town of Josselin, the famous Our Lady of the Roncier, the destroyed original of which has been replaced by a copy, is still the object of fervent worship. This is a typical example of a statue found in a bush, removed to a church or chapel, and then found back in the same bush the next day. In Sainte-Anne d'Auray it seems that the statue, allegedly of Saint Anne and discovered by the pious Nicolazic during the seventeenth century, was a Black Madonna of the purest tradition, before being recarved and repainted by the Capuchins of Auray. The statue was later destroyed during the French Revolution.

In the northern city of Dunkirk, a fifteenth-century Our Lady of the Dunes was discovered in the sands of the shore. The oratory in Valenciennes (dating from 765) houses Our Lady of the Roads, also known as Our Lady of the Wells. In Boulogne-sur-Mer in the Pas-de-Calais region, the famous statue of Our Lady of the Angels (remade in wood in 1823) is an object of major worship. After World War II, this statue was carried in procession through almost the whole of France, leading to the establishment of a cult devoted to Our Lady of Boulogne. In the Puy-de-Dôme region, which is quite rich in statues of this type, the very beautiful Our Lady of Orcival is a wooden statue dating from the twelfth century. Her worship is connected to the presence of water, and there is both a cave and a dolmen in the immediate vicinity. Our Lady of the Port in Clermont-Ferrand is a wooden eighteenth-century replacement of an older statue, discovered in a well according to tradition.

In the Pyrénées-Orientales, we find Our Lady of the Pésébré, also known as Maureneta, which was once in the Saint-Michel of Cuxa Abbey before being moved to Corneilla. And in the curious church of Villefrance-de-Confluent, a seventeenth-century statue of Our Lady of Life can be found. The Fourvière Basilica of Lyon houses the seventeenth-century wooden statue of Our Lady of Fourvière. In Pringy (in Seine-et-Marne) a statue was discovered in a tree next to a fountain. In the Vaucluse town of Barroux is a similar statue carved from cedar that bears the rather obvious name the Brown One.

The two most famous Black Madonnas outside of the one in Chartres are incontestably those of Rocamadour and Puy-en-Velay. In both these places devotion to the Virgin has been indicated since time immemorial. These are Marian sanctuaries of primary importance whose roots go back, beyond all shadow of a doubt, long before the introduction of Christianity into Gaul.

Rocamadour, in the Quercy region (Lot), a well-known tourist destination, is quite exceptional. It was the ancient Vallis Tenebros, the "dark valley," a sheer drop of 650 feet that suddenly opens in the limestone plateau, with a fortified castle at the edge of the abyss, a bouquet of churches and chapels on the side of the rock, and, farther below, a medieval village. At the bottom of the valley, the Alzon River, which may mean "river of the Aulnes," twists and turns through what was once a dense forest. Here we have water, rock, and tree. These are the customary companions of the Marian cult (this is true also of Lourdes). The pilgrimage to Rocamadour was one of the most famous in the Middle Ages. This is where Henry Plantagenet II went to publicly atone, on his knees before his entire army, for the murder of Canterbury archbishop Thomas à Becket. Numerous chapels bearing the name Rocamadour were built throughout Europe as extensions of that devotion originating in the Dark Valley. In Armorican Brittany, for example, there is a chapel for Our Lady of Rocamadour that was built on a kind of natural dike that extends into the sea at Camaret-sur-Mer.

The Black Madonna of Rocamadour is a Majestic Virgin from the end of the twelfth century that has been crudely carved and blackened, then partially covered with silver plate. It sits on a hollowed-out block in a reliquary. Tradition maintains that the publican Zaccheus brought a statuette carved by the Evangelist Saint Luke to the limestone plateau of Quercy. This is obviously pure fiction; the origin of the sanctuary is something else entirely. In 1166 a perfectly preserved body was found at the entrance of a chapel dedicated to the Virgin Mary. For fairly obscure reasons, the people there regarded this body as the remains of a mysterious Saint Amadour, for whom this place is named. The "saint" was buried in front of the altar to the Virgin and another legend spread, according to which Amadour was the husband of Saint Veronica, the one who wiped Christ's face when he was climbing Golgotha. But during the fifteenth century, Amadour was incorporated into the publican Zaccheus, which was a convenient way to get the two traditions to coincide. Amadour does not appear in the official Roman calendar, nor does Veronica or Zaccheus.

Recent research has found evidence that the hermitage of Rocamadour existed long before the discovery of the "saint's" body. A bell can be seen in Rocamadour that dates before the eighth century and is said to be miraculous. It so happens that the chapel was originally dedicated uniquely to the Virgin Mary. And a local profane legend tells how human sacrifices were once made to a black mother-goddess known as Sulevia or Soulivia. This black mother-goddess's sanctuary was located in a cave, the same cavern where Zaccheus hid the statuette allegedly carved by Saint Luke. This is the realm of Gallo-Roman religion. The Sulevias were goddesses of uncultivated land, which accords perfectly with the nature of the Rocamadour terrain.

The village of Alysses, a little farther away on the banks of the Alzon, is said to have been founded by a mysterious Lady who continues to roam the night, mainly in the place known as the Lady's Combe. This Lady is incontestably a funerary goddess, a "black queen," and has more than one connection with the Black Madonna, whether it involves the goddess Sulevia or some other Roman or Celtic deity who is both protector of the dead and guardian of the sacred waters. Once upon a time, peasants during times of drought would come to Rocamadour in search of water. They would mount a procession, led by the clergy, to the Ouysse Springs. Following many prayers, one of the priests would plunge the base of the processional cross into the spring, and everyone would return home with the hope that the rain would soon return.

Similar rituals requesting rain exist in other regions, Brittany especially. The Marian cult cannot be viewed apart from the ancient worship of the waters. The same is true for Lourdes, as in all the chapels dedicated to the Virgin Mary. In the immediate vicinity of these sanctuaries, if not inside the sanctuary itself, there is always a well or a spring, or sometimes a simple pond, or often a washing place that serves as a swimming pool.

Puy-en-Velay is also one of the most frequented tourist sites in France. But mingling with the crowds of tourists are pilgrims following age-old customs. Le Puy was in fact an important center of pilgrimage in the Middle Ages, not only because of the Mary worship that developed there early on but also because the town was an important stop on the route to Saint-James of Compostella, which ran toward Nîmes and Saint-Gilles-du-Gard on the one hand, and on the other was part of the Regordane Route mentioned in the *chansons de geste*, one of the rare roads to cross the Central Massif from north to south and connect the Mediterranean basin with the Loire Valley. Le Puy was never a Roman town, but rather a Gallic settlement. The Romans established themselves on the Plain by Ruessium. This has since become Saint-Paulien, and it is where they brought their deities.

In Puy, whose name was Anicium at that time, the Gallic worship survived a long time without any Roman imprint. The name Anicium itself offers food for thought, as does the name of the butte on which the current cathedral sits, Mont-Anis. Both refer to the name of the Celtic Mother Goddess Ana or Anna, who was known as Dôn in Gaul and as Dana in Ireland. Furthermore, behind this figure the shadow of the Brittany Saint Anne can be discerned, as well as that of the Black Annis, or Black Annie, who haunts the folklore of Yorkshire. The Black Madonna of Puy-en-Velay certainly has some connection with this figure inherited from the purest Celtic tradition.

The site of Puy-en-Velay is quite extraordinary. The old town is built in terraces up the southern slope of an ancient volcano, Mont-Anis. The cathedral and cloister are located about halfway up the slope. Toward the west, a particularly barren volcanic dike is crowned by the Saint-Michel d'Aiguilhe Chapel, one of the oldest sanctuaries in the region. Before the introduction of Christianity, a temple dedicated to a goddess sat at the foot of this Aiguilhe promontory. Whether it was Cybele, Diana, or a Gallic deity, perhaps even that Anis who inspired the name of the site, is not known. At the very top of Mont-Anis is the Corneille Rock, crowned by the very ugly but majestic statue of Our Lady of France.

It seems that the placement of Puy Cathedral (a magnificent Romanesque construction) was determined by the presence not of a spring or well nearby but rather of a volcanic rock known as a phonolite, which is not so extraordinary in this region. This phonolite slab, no doubt a dolmen table, had been previously used in a pagan sanctuary. This is probably the same stone that serves as the high altar, recut and blessed. Until the seventeenth century, a "fever stone" lay in front of the altar to Mary. Pilgrims seeking a cure for their illnesses would try to sleep one night on the stone, particularly Friday night. It is not clear why the clergy would have removed this stone, especially given that the same custom seems to have existed in Chartres before the destruction of the Romanesque cathedral.

Taking the Eastern influences on the architecture of the Puy cathedral into consideration, some have offered the theory that the devotion to the Virgin Mary was inspired by cults from the Middle East. This provides a practical explanation for the color of the Black Madonnas. Mary would simply be the copy of a bronze-skinned Eastern deity such as Artemis, Cybele, or Isis. But this conflicts with the very name of the town, Anicium, which refers to a Celtic deity. Furthermore, archaeologists have found no trace of any Eastern worship taking place on the Puy site. It is more likely that Christianity here directly succeeded a Druidic cult, and no doubt it was a smooth transition. The Romans avoided Anicium and settled in Saint-Paulien. At the time this region converted to Christianity, the first Episcopal seat must have been in Ruessium, thus Saint-Paulien.[2] It was only after the sixth or seventh century that the bishop of Vellaves left Ruessium, which was in danger of declining, to settle in Anicium (which took on the name of Podium, in other words Puy), a community that had remained prosperous.

But Anicium was still associated paganism. In the legal documents

---

2. Paulien is a very hypothetical saint. Ruessium, a Gallic name, made way for a Gallo-Roman name: Pauliniacus (territory of Paulinius), which evolved into Polignac, the name of a famous noble family of the region.

from that era, the words Sancta Maria often accompanied the name
of Anicium or Podium. Very few towns then bore this title, which
suggests a very distinctive fervor in honor of the Virgin that was
probably quite ancient in origin. Furthermore, a legend had spread
that maintained Mary had appeared in Puy during the year 46 or 47.
This was a way to assert the antiquity of the Marian cult in this town,
which was also what the Chartres clergy did when claiming that the
Druids honored in Chartres a *virgo paritura*. Here we find the same
need to base a cult on a much more ancient worship.

In any event, Le Puy was not some remote village in the middle
of the mountains. It was a very important crossroads and relay station on the Route Regordane. The Étain road always passed through
there, and a very close alliance united the Vellaves people[3] to the
Phocéens of Marseille. Puy is the meeting place of two roads; one
from Lyon goes on from there to Rodez and Toulouse (Route
Nationale 88) and a road from Limagne goes on toward Alès and
Nîmes (the via Regordane). Le Puy was an important communica-
tions center extending toward different horizons, and in any event,
the relationship with Marseille was always a beneficial one.[4]

The frequent visits of people from the Mediterranean region
could have inspired the imitation by local artists of statuettes of
Greek manufacture, which would explain the "blackness" of these
kinds of Virgins. But there is no proof that a matriarchal cult ever
existed in Puy. The statue worshipped during these early times was
either an Isis brought there through the intermediary of the
Phocéens or a Gallic mother goddess. It is unthinkable, in a country
this far west and remote as it was in the early Middle Ages, that
there would have been a statue of the Virgin Mary as she was
defined by the Council of Ephesus. Mystery still lurks around this

---

3. *Vellavi*, in Gallic, is a word meaning "the best." The name Velay derives from this
word. The Vellaves were subjects of the Arvernes.

4. For a long time, Velay was part of Languedoc. The Vellave dialect, like the Auvergnat
dialect, is currently Languedocian and not north Occitan.

statue, for the one that was burned during the Revolution in 1794 (a piece of which was fitted into the new statue) was not necessarily the ancient one spoken of in connection with the date 225. There are descriptions of the statue burned in 1794, and even a copy discovered in Capronne-sur-Arzon. But the characteristics of this Black Madonna leave a great deal to the imagination.

It has been said that no statue ever enjoyed greater renown. No statue was more visited, more examined, and more praised. In fact, it was as mysterious as it was famous. Kings and popes made pilgrimages to Le Puy to pray before it. Joan of Arc's mother even earned the nickname "Romée" there.[5] And of course a flood of legends has spread from this "podium" charged with history and enigmas. One of these legends is depicted (what a coincidence!) on a stained-glass window of the chapel connected to the medieval castle in Lourdes. It tells how Charlemagne besieged the pagan king Mirat in his castle of Mirambel. The bishop of Le Puy, present with the army, managed to convince Mirat to dedicate his castle to the Holy Virgin. Given that Mirat had only been trying to save face, he accepted baptism, and Mirambel became Lordum—in other words, Lourdes.

The image from Le Puy-en-Velay had several replicas in France and Spain. Le Puy was also connected to Italian pilgrimage sites. Every year, but especially during Jubilee years—those in which the Annunciation coincides with Good Friday—Le Puy resumed the tradition of Gallo-Roman Lyon by calling the neighboring populace to attend religious feasts, games, poetry competitions, a fair, and tournaments. This was a reminiscence of the Concilia Galliarum, held in Lugdunum, which itself was based on the Celtic tradition, demonstrated in Ireland, of four great feasts of the year. That of Samhain (November 1), during which the entire populace gathered, was the most important.

---

5. The designation "Romée" was given to those who made a pilgrimage to Rome or any equivalent location.

Historically, it is assumed that during the ninth century, the Virgin Mary was the patron saint of Le Puy-en-Velay, and specific worship was given to a statue whose origin lent itself to countless speculations. In 1630, Father Odo de Gissey recounted how shortly after Clovis, one of his successors undertook a journey to the holy sites. Before leaving, he would have passed through Le Puy. Having spent three years in Jerusalem, he had become a friend of the sultan, who allegedly offered him his pick of his treasure. The king consulted the sultan's favorite, who pointed out a black image crafted by the prophet Jeremiah. Once the king obtained this statuette, he would have stored it in Le Puy. Therefore, given its role in the story, the Black Madonna of Le Puy would be a fairly ancient Oriental representation of Phoenician origin. But the testimony of Odo de Gissey, published in 1620 and revised by him in 1644, deserves examination, especially when compared to a description made in 1778 by Faujas de Saint-Fond, inspector of mines and friend of Buffon, who was interested in the extinct volcanoes of Velay and Vivarais. He wanted to understand the method of working hard stone (volcanic rock), which led him to examine the Puy statue. He was very familiar with Odo de Gissey's testimony and cited it frequently in his own analyses. In any case, he is quite explicit on one point: "It is incontestably the most ancient statue of the Virgin that we have in our French churches."

The statue is located in a poorly lit area in which the light strikes it from behind, on a fairly high marble pedestal beneath a kind of small canopy. From neck to feet the statue is swaddled in a cloak of gilded cloth, whose conical form displays "the most barbaric taste." This cloak is overloaded with reliquaries, several of which are augmented with diamonds. "The Infant Jesus," writes Faujas, "who from afar appears pasted to his mother's stomach, displays his little head through an opening of the cloak; slippers of gold cloth can be seen on the statue's feet." Having obtained permission from the canons of the cathedral to give the statue a detailed examination, Faujas had her brought down from the pedestal. He took off her robe and saw a statue about thirty inches in height

> . . . made from cedar, certainly quite old, probably from a single
> block, weighing about twenty-five pounds. She is seated in the style
> of certain Egyptian deities, on a detached armchair that I think to
> be of modern construction. The entire statue is completely wrapped
> from head to feet in bands of very fine cloth that has been very care-
> fully and solidly glued to the wood in the manner of Egyptian
> mummies. The cloths are applied to the faces of the mother and the
> child; the feet are also wrapped; this is the reason no trace of any
> toes can be seen; similar bands cover the hands, but the fingers have
> been emphasized; they are extremely ugly and of the poorest design.

The face of the mother and the child are both black and polished
like ebony: "The face of the mother is an extremely elongated oval
shape that goes against all the rules of drawing. . . . The nose is also
of a disproportionate length and width, and is shockingly twisted.
Its mouth is small, and its chin is shrunken and round."

By all evidence, this was an eighteenth-century work that no one
could label "barbaric." Now it would be described as an "archaic"
work. Odo de Gissey said that the eyes had an intolerable sparkle.
Faujas clarified this; they are "two hemispherical pieces of very common glass; these two pieces are concave on one side and convex on
the other; the convex side is on the outside and imitates the globe of
the eye, whereas the concave part, being applied to an interior surface painted with the colors of the eye, imitates the iris." This gives
the figure "a haggard and at the same time astonished air that
inspires surprise and even terror." There are no ears or hair, but

> . . . a kind of very common black cloth that completely covers the
> top and back of the head and entirely hides the ears. Beneath this
> top wrapping, a second can be seen formed from selvedges of black
> silk, and finally a third in homespun; the entire thing is closely
> bound and tightly wrapped around the head. . . . I should not

forget to mention that when passing my fingers beneath the wrappings I just described, I felt in the area of the neck a kind of semicylindrical relief, about the size of a little finger, that extended from the start of the neck to the nape, where it disappeared.

This is a significant detail. It seems the statue may have had a kind of necklace. Was it a torque of the Celtic kind? In this case, the hypothesis would have to be that this was a Gallic mother goddess. In any event, notes Faujas, "this singularity, seen uncovered and intensively studied, could shed light on the essential quality of this figure, *which may well not always have been an image intended to represent the mother of God.*" The doubt surrounding this statue's provenance could not be any more clearly expressed. The drapery is crudely sculpted in the wood. The cloths are covered in a layer of white gouache on which has been painted "thick and solid colors that imitate those of the Egyptian mummies." Faujas noted several carved symbols that could have been writing and small Greek crosses on the child's robe "which may not be Christian symbols, for the Isaic Table[6] and the obelisk with hieroglyphs in Rome have similar crosses."

It is true that at the end of the eighteenth century, Egyptian style was in vogue and, probably under the influence of Freemasonry and the Rosicrucians, the ancient religion of Isis and Osiris was being rediscovered. Faujas de Saint-Fond concluded that the Black Madonna of Le Puy-en-Velay was nothing more or less than an Isis depicted with Horus "that had been transformed into the Virgin, which did no harm to the religion because good intention was totally responsible." But something else caused him to doubt this interpretation. "The head, which is thin, tapered, and has an enormously long nose, does not share the character of Egyptian faces, which are large and flat." This led him to a second hypothesis: The

---

6. [The Isaic Table, also known as the Bembine Table, is a bronze tablet measuring fifty by thirty inches and decorated with silver and emerald inlay. Once in the possession of Cardinal Bembo, of Italy, it is covered with hieroglyphs and occult symbols. —*Trans.*]

Black Madonna came from Lebanon and would have been imported by Adhémar de Monteil, bishop of Le Puy, one of the leaders of the First Crusade and legate of Pope Urban II in the Holy Land. Unfortunately, Adhémar de Monteil never returned to France; he died in Antioch in 1098.

An earlier hypothesis of this nature was based on a tradition that made Saint Louis, on his return from Egypt, the donor of this strange statue. But on this point Odo de Gissey, though not rejecting the tradition, displayed great skepticism. Father Odo de Gissey, a good, educated Jesuit, could hardly conceive that a statuette could have been carved by the ardent iconoclast and prophet Jeremiah, "the man in the world who most heartily attacked the cult of the image." Thus, Saint Louis may have brought back this statue, but it was not ancient.

The notion that Saint Louis was the donor of the Virgin of Le Puy, however, smacks into one serious problem: In 1095, Raymond IV of Toulouse had offered the cathedral of Le Puy an important sum of money in exchange for which "they would keep a candle brightly burning, day and night, before the image of the Virgin as long as he lived." We have to believe that 150 years before the coming of Saint Louis to Le Puy, there was already in the Vellave city an image of the Virgin of sufficient renown for the powerful count of Toulouse, who did not lack for famous sanctuaries in his own domains, to have sought her protection.

One problem remains insoluble: Was this image a pre-Christian work that came from the East or was it crafted on site during the Gallo-Roman era? The hypothesis of a statue carved in cedar does not hold up. Noting scratches that seemed to have been clumsily repaired over the entire image, Faujas de Saint-Fond voiced the opinion that these were the result of scrapings by rosaries and other objects used to touch the statue, and that the black paint had to be periodically restored in the places where it was missing. This means that *the statue was not originally black, but every effort was made to make it black.*

Furthermore, one peculiarity both Faujas and Odo de Gissey pointed out was that the Virgin's hands were white. Another detail supplied by Faujas concerns a somewhat mysterious cavity whose purpose the inspector of mines did not understand. It was the location of a small reliquary. No other image in this category contains this specific feature. It is explained, says Saillens, "by the exceptional nature of the site of Le Puy. No other French pilgrimage site has processions that are as frequent and as long, nor such mountainous terrain. This statue was a cult statue (because it was a reliquary), but also a processional statue."[7]

But it is probable that this statue was not the sole representation of the Virgin in the cathedral of Le Puy. There must have been another one, the depiction of which appeared on a medal of 1182. It is the same situation we found in Chartres; two statues have been confused, and no one is sure which one this particular description concerns. When the Black Virgin was burned on June 8, 1794, with eight other statues, the heat of the pyre caused it to explode, and to the surprise of those in attendance, out fell a rolled-up parchment, the "relic" in this statue. This work, it seemed, was a reliquary statue in compliance with Church standards, an assertion reinforced by the distinguishing feature of her white hands. But what we do not know is if the statue that was burned was the same one that had been the object of constant worship from the earliest Middle Ages.

It is reasonable to assume that the cathedral of Le Puy-en-Velay held two representations of the Virgin, an ancient Majestic one in wood and a Madonna in stone. The latter was *white,* as she appeared on the 1182 medal and in accordance with Odo de Gissey's description of a seal from 1263, which tells us that she looked entirely different then: She was seated and "held the child in her right arm and a scepter with a *fleur-de-lis* at its tip in her left hand. The child also held a scepter in his left hand. But the figure on the seal today depicts the image that is presently on the altar."

---

7. E. Saillens, *Nos Vierges noires* (Paris: Payot, 1945), 91.

Could this be the object brought back from Egypt by Saint Louis? Surely not, but the fleurs-de-lis imply the king played some role in the affair. Did some kind of substitution of statues take place when the clergy, alarmed at the display of superstitious practices, wanted to eliminate all traces of an object they sensed had emerged from the purest kind of paganism? We do know that the statue described by Odo de Gissey and Faujas de Saint-Fond, and thus the same one that was burned in 1794, had been *intentionally blackened.* From there, it is an easy step to considering this image a compromise between the original archaic, and definitely very pagan, image and the official Majestic version confirmed in 1182 and 1263.

The debate over the Black Madonnas is not close to being resolved. Taking into account the ambiguity of the texts and the diversity of the artistic evidence, we find almost everywhere the removal and substitution of statues, adaptations of their images, and the existence of outright fakes. By this reckoning, we can see in the oldest Black Madonnas Egyptian statues of Isis and Horus, representations of Cybele and Attis, and Gallic mother goddesses, with no theoretical contradictions or any affront to the good faith of those who erected or installed them in medieval Christian sanctuaries. Traditions resist time and religious substitutions, because they represent something profound that cannot be threatened by styles or dogmatic subtleties. The Black Madonnas, although quite Christian in appearance, have their origin in ancient Mother Goddess cults, by whatever name they might individually be known. This is a reality. Another reality is that quite often the Black Madonnas were darkened intentionally, as if someone wished the color to signify something specific. These purposely blackened Madonnas exist in Chartres and in Le Puy-en-Velay and their meaning clearly appears insoluble.

Why would the Virgin Mary be given this black color? And why only in certain cases?

There are multiple theories. One suggestion is that the Virgin Mary had a sunburned complexion, appropriate for a Semite, and that the custom of depicting her as black or simply dark-skinned came from the Hodegetria, the mythical portrait attributed to Saint Luke and said to have been sent by Empress Eudoxia to her sister-in-law Pulcheria, who placed it in the church of Constantinople. Along these same lines, the Jesuit Van den Steen (1556–1637) declared in his *Commentaries on the Bible,* "The Blessed Virgin Mary had a dark and almost black skin like the Egyptians and Palestinians who are burned by the sun. The fact is proven by the portrait painted by Saint Luke worshipped in Rome at the Basilica of Santa Maria Maggiore."

But this is mere fiction. We should remember that Saint Augustine insisted the alleged portraits of the Virgin Mary existing in his time were too different from one another to be authentic (*De Trinitate,* VIII, 6, 7). He goes on to say, "Furthermore, we know not what face the Virgin Mary wore." This did not prevent Saint Epiphany in the fourth century from asserting that Mary had skin the "color of wheat, blonde hair, and pupils the tone of ripe olive." A blonde with black eyes? Why not? Marie-Bernarde (Bernadette) Soubirous described the apparition of the Virgin in the grotto at Lourdes as white and *blonde.* What happened to the suntanned skin of the Virgin Mary in this heap of visions and various interpretations?

A second hypothesis contends that the prototypes of the European Black Madonnas were executed by artists who were themselves dark-skinned and simply reproduced their ethnicity in their artwork. Why not? But Crusaders brought back Black Madonnas, as Saint Louis brought the Puy image from Egypt; and the Black Virgins of France were worshipped long before the time of the Crusades. In this case we must assume that the first depictions of the Black Virgins were Eastern mother goddesses more or less commingled with Madonnas by very zealous Christians who were ignorant of archaeology. This hypothesis does not hold up, however, because all the Black Madonnas that have been listed and described bear obvious Christian characteristics.

A third hypothesis is even more simplistic. It is merely that some statues were carved from black wood or sculpted in dark-colored

Top: *An ancient engraving depicting the cathedral of Chartres*

Bottom: *The cathedral seen from the Eure River*

The north façade

The south façade

Top: *The cathedral's Royal Portal*

Opposite page: *Frontispiece from Rouillard's* Parthénie *depicting the* virgo paritura *worshipped by the Druids*

VIRGINI PARITVRÆ

LE PVITZ DES
SAINCTZ FORTZ

L'AVTEL DES DRVIDES

Our Lady of Under Ground (engraving by Leroux)

Our Lady of the Pillar (the Black Madonna; sixteenth century)

Notre-Dame de la Belle-Verrière (the Blue Virgin Window), a stained-glass window from the twelfth century

stone by chance. This notion led Faujas de Saint-Fond, a specialist in volcanic rocks (basalt), to make his meticulous examination of the Virgin of Le Puy. Basalt is notorious for being almost impossible to work, and ebony was unknown in the West until the thirteenth century. This hypothesis, moreover, can provide no explanation for why "normal" statues of the Virgin Mary were knowingly coated in black paint, and constantly repainted in that same color. Nor can it explain why there are not Red Madonnas or Pink Madonnas, for stone can have these natural colors as well.

A fourth solution has been proposed. The statuettes and paintings representing the Virgin Mary were spontaneously darkened by an outside agent, perhaps fire. Subsequently, great efforts may have been made to faithfully imitate a particular such statue that was viewed with great respect. But this holds up no better than the other theories outlined here. Why, then, would there be White Madonnas? All the statues of Mary would be uniformly black, which is obviously not the case.

A fifth hypothesis is more serious: The so-called Black Madonna statuettes were reproductions of dark-colored paintings. At first glance there might be a grain of truth to this, mainly because the earliest Christian sculptures were most often inspired by Eastern art motifs, and especially because the icons of the Virgin Mary produced in the Byzantine Church are distinctly brown. The Byzantine icons and those of Russia, however, never inspired Western artists before the modern era. Furthermore, these icons, beautiful as they are, never depicted Black Virgins. Their dark color results from the fact that they are covered with an oil-based varnish that darkens fairly quickly and requires periodic cleaning. As Louis Réau says in his book *Les Icônes russes* (Paris: Larousse, 1945), "It is the accumulated layers of oily varnish, in which the smoke from candles had been incorporated, that has given birth to the legend of the 'sadness' of Russian icons."

The portraits of the Virgin attributed to Saint Paul were certainly different, with an absolutely black skin color and wide-open eyes with a somewhat haggard expression, like the image in Le Puy. But these representations of the Hodegetria are far from ancient, despite a so-called apostolic tradition. All that is known for certain is that Cretan studios established in Venice from the thirteenth to sixteenth century executed a series of Black Madonnas, allegedly by Saint Luke, that were dispatched primarily throughout the Balkans and Russia. These images were never intended for the West. This style of depicting Black Madonnas, and even in some cases rendering originally white images black, is connected with something more profound. Whether in the East or the West, says Saillens, "in popular imagination, Mary was blonde. So if the people attached such great value to these black portraits, it cannot be because of their faithful likeness, but because their appearance aged, and furthermore, caused Mary to resemble deities whose memory was still cherished."[8]

The shadow of the great Goddess of the Beginnings still lurks around the Virgin Mary. The quarrel of the iconoclasts was triggered by the desire of certain Christians, and not the lesser ones, to create a gap between the totally mystic and "theological" Christian spirituality and the ancient Mother Goddess cults, which were too stained by mythology to be honest. In 726, Leo of Isaurico issued the first edict against images. In so doing he not only sought to placate the Muslim subjects of the Byzantine Empire but also hoped to break the monks' best means for taking action, and therefore restore a certain order to the Church. Holy images were mostly peddled by monks, and the monks' irruption into the Church (where they enjoyed a special status) and the state made them troublemakers. But the people revolted against the imperial edicts, siding with the monks. For example, in 726, an imperial agent who had broken statues was put to death by a frenzied mob. The worship of images was definitively reestablished in the Eastern empire by Empress Theodora. But in the meantime, and during the worst moments of the iconoclastic repression, numerous monks had left Byzantium and taken refuge in the West, bringing their images with them. We

---

8. Ibid.

could, if need be, see a cause-and-effect relationship between this massive arrival of Byzantine monks and the appearance of the worship of Black Madonnas in the West.

But that does not explain everything. The West clearly played its own role in the appearance of the Black Madonna. It is too easy to claim that the dark color of some Virgins' faces comes from the East on the pretext that the skin color of Easterners is darker than that of Westerners. It is a superficial solution. The oldest painting that seems—there is no decisive proof—to depict the Virgin Mary is located in the Roman Priscilla Cemetery. This painting, which may date from the second or third century, shows a brown-skinned woman holding a child on her knees. It was no doubt a similar fresco, or an equally dark-skinned statuette, that inspired the creators of the "first portraits of Mary" allegedly by Saint Luke. The cemetery of Priscilla is Christian, no question about it. But were all the artists' models Christian? Christianity, outside its broad fundamental options, drew largely from earlier religions for dogma, worship, and symbolic representations. No one has ever been able to prove that the painting in the Priscilla Cemetery is an image of the Virgin. But if she is brown, it is because someone deemed it wise to depict her in a color that was intended to say something.

Let us now abandon the realist's explanations and try to envision a symbolic meaning for the custom of blackening the face of the Virgin, realizing that here too all we can do is theorize.

For some, the darkness of the Virgin symbolizes the profound melancholy of the Middle Ages, especially during its decline, and the approach of the storm that would put an end to the unity of the Church. This explanation is doubly foolish, first because the Black Madonnas date from the early Middle Ages and attained their apogee during the triumphal era of Saint Louis, and next because the supposed obscurantism and melancholy of the Middle Ages were Enlightenment-era arguments to depreciate one of the most fertile times in human history.

Another hypothesis makes Mary both a human sinner and a

Mother of Sorrows. A curious explanation has been appended to this idea: When Joseph saw that Mary was pregnant before he had "known" her, he saw her as black. So what happens, then, to the concept of the Immaculate Conception, which, before being homologous as dogma, was still one of the more positive elements of the worship of Mary? To give Mary a black face symbolizing her membership in the cursed human race is a kind of blasphemy. To transform this darkness into a symbol of Joseph's opinion of her when he saw her pregnant is deficient reasoning. To transpose the suffering of the Virgin Mary beneath this color is a mistranslation; the Black Madonnas are triumphant and majestic Virgins. There is nothing in all the explanations that withstands scrutiny. They are all so puerile and their inanity so flagrant that they do not even merit denunciation.

It is possible, however, to find a symbolic meaning in the Black Madonnas by turning to one of the more bizarre texts from the Hebrew scriptures, the Song of Solomon. Saillens observes, "The comparison between Mary and the [black-skinned] Shulamite is often declared absurd. The main objection is that while the Shulamite is but a fiancée, Black Virgins are generally accompanied by children."[9] But no text of the canonical Gospels claims that Mary was Joseph's wife, and when he arrived in Bethlehem for the census, it was with Mary, his fiancée, who was pregnant.

The Song of Solomon enjoyed a unique role in both Christian thought and rabbinical speculation. The Shulamite inspired eddies and tempests, and there are no fewer than 134 different Hebrew interpretations of this exceptional text, featuring a plethora of symbols, meanings, and expansions. "The sole woman the Middle Ages surrounded with a comparable retinue of symbols is the Virgin Mary," notes Saillens, "and some of these systems were borrowed from the Song of Solomon. To incorporate Mary, 'throne of Solomon,' into the Shulamite, lover of this same king, was child's play for the scholars

---

9. Ibid., 214.

and poets."[10] It was all the more so as they endeavored to depict the Mother of God as "she who is promised to humanity for all time," like the universal Mother whose distinctiveness is emphasized by her black color: "I am black, but I am beautiful . . . pay no attention to my black color; I have been burned by the sun." When we recall that Jehovah had warned Moses that he would be struck by lightning if he saw God in God's infinitude, a comparison is tempting. Mary, visited by the Holy Ghost—in other words, by God—was not struck down by this sublime and infinite contact because she had always been chosen for the Immaculate Conception. But like the Shulamite, she was burned by the sun. The symbol is quite clear, even if this interpretation can remain only hypothetical. In any event, is it even possible to have just a single explanation for such matters?

In fact, there is something else. Simplistic realist theories and all references to symbolism lead to a dead end, to a dissipation of the mind, which can use this or that element in an argument to provide a perfectly logical and acceptable conclusion. In such a situation the mind is running in neutral, because its role is to exist and function with nothing other than itself. The eighteenth-century philosopher Berkeley, an Anglican bishop, maintained that the sole proof of existence was thought and thought alone; hence, the reality of matter was uncertain, for it could be nothing more than the result of internal contradictions of thought. It is true that the mind, to exercise its power, needs to forge myths that it will juggle with all the creative power it can muster.

The Black Madonna forms part of these myths necessary to the action of creative thought. It even seems to be one of the most potent revealers of awareness, for little interest is shown in tracing this question back to its roots, the black attribute of the Virgin Mary, perpetual image of the divine creation, but a creation that is always in motion and can halt this dynamic process only at the price of denying itself. The black color of the Virgin is, of course, a symbol.

---

10. Ibid.

But the symbol is just a precarious clue in the course of a becoming that escapes all who seek to grasp it. Wouldn't it be, by very definition, ungraspable?

The human being needs concrete images, not to comprehend, for this is impossible, but to apprehend reality, which is the Being in its totality, and not the subjective judgment we are liable to focus on this Being by giving it names or attributing qualities to it. In this sense the Black Madonna is an extraordinary transporter of this message, but the message is accessible only when we transcend the form to attain the spirit.

In all traditions, the color black is synonymous with night, darkness, death, chaos, or even, to use an Eastern term, nonexistence, which is not the same thing as death or chaos. The color black is not a color, it is the absence of color, whereas the color white brings together and synthesizes all colors. This allows us to understand the primordial dichotomy between Black and White that has passed into the collective unconscious in the zone of white civilization—in other words, that of the Indo-Europeans and Semites more or less centered on the Mediterranean.

Under these conditions, the Black Virgin Mary necessarily means something: chaos or nonexistence, both terms that are poor translations for something that is unorganized. If we go back to the justification of the entity Mary, mother of God, and if we accept that she represents the first creature emanated from God before the Creation— that is to say, the organizing force of the existential universe—this black color attributed to her becomes quite logical. The Virgin is potentiality, the *materia prima* that has not yet been organized but out of which everything may emerge. It is in this sense that we should understand the dialogue among Jesus on the cross, his mother, and John the Apostle. It is in this sense that we should understand the mission of the archangel Gabriel to the young Mary and her acceptance of becoming the receptacle for the embodied God. The Virgin Mary, thus always virgin (the meanings that can be given the word *virgin* here are irrelevant), is nothing other than the *materia prima* of the alchemical work, a series of metamorphoses that lead to the creation of the philosopher's stone, the crystallization not only of all knowledge, but also of all energies. This raw and common "primal matter" must be "fertilized" by fire and separated into its two opposing elements, what the alchemists called sulfur and mercury.

It would seem as if primal matter, thus the original chaos, was an inharmonious combination of these two elements. Therefore nothing is possible. But the introduction of fire—in other words, the sacred spirit—prompts a return to the original unity, a return that is not without violence and collision. In alchemical operations, it was necessary to "cook" the primal matter under very special conditions that would prompt the introduction of material heat as well as the flame of the spirit. The result of this "cooking" is a black, shapeless material, the first stage of the regeneration of chaos. The alchemists called it the Black Stone and willingly gave it the periphrastic—yet nevertheless metaphorical—name Raven's Head.

The concept of the Virgin Mary, the *virgo paritura* of Chartres and other sites, may be this Black Stone. In any event, this was in the minds of all those who unhesitatingly depicted the mother of Jesus with a black face, therefore recycling the well-known image of the Shulamite "burned by the sun." The Song of Solomon takes pains to counsel the Daughters of Jerusalem, and thereby all humanity, to refrain from treating this black color as a punishment or curse: "Pay no attention to my black color, I have been burned by the sun." Whether it is the Holy Ghost whose shadow covered Mary or the secret fire of the alchemists, the result of the operation remains the same: The primal matter turns black. But this is because, when impregnated by the Spirit, it can give birth to the One who will be the Light, Jesus in the evangelical scriptures, the philosopher's stone in alchemical treatises. These same treatises specify that no one can discover the material philosopher's stone without mentally undergoing the same metamorphosis. There is no longer any dichotomy between mind and matter, for Jesus (or the philosopher's stone) is both body and spirit, human being and God. And if the anonymous sculptors of the Middle Ages wanted to give Mary this black color that has caused so much fascination, it is clearly because they had in mind the spreading of an essential message: From this apparent darkness, the Light will emerge.

Of course, only certain elite knew this meaning of the black goddesses, then the Black Madonnas of Christianity, but the nature of the elites is to transmit to the highest number a core concept in the form of a very simple concrete image. The Black Virgin is not a Christian creation; it is an adaptation to the Christian world of this archaic concept that is present in all religious or mythological traditions. In India, "[I]n the beginning was depthless night. Then manifested the Most High, who was self-existent; he created the water and sowed his seed upon it; this produced the Golden Egg, from which was born Brahma, creator of worlds." This myth of the original darkness is universal. Still in India we have the figure of Kali the Black, who admirably sums up this fundamental assumption:

> You are the image of all, and above all, you are the mother of all. . . . Before the beginning of things, you existed in the form of a Darkness that is beyond Word and Thought, and from you, the creative desire of supreme Brahma, is born the entire universe. . . . At the dissolution of things, it is Kali who will devour all, and for this reason she is called Maha Kala [the Great Blackness], and because you devour Maha Kala itself, you are the supreme, primordial Kalika. . . . Because you devour Kali, you are Kali, the primordial form of all things. (Hymn to Kali)

This is reminiscent of what Isis declared, according to Apuleius: "I am all that was, all that is, and all that will be." And there is little difference from what Saint Paul asserted: "For the earnest expectation of the creature waiteth for the manifestation of the sons of God. . . . Because the creature itself also shall be delivered from the bondage. . . . The whole creation groaneth and travaileth in pain together until now" (Romans 8:19, 21–22).

The "creation" of which Saint Paul speaks is nothing other than Plato's "nature" as presented in his *Timaeus,* which was heavily influenced by Egyptian traditions maintaining that all bodies were composed of a unique substance that was shaped in a wide variety of ways, what Parmenides called the *materia paritura.* It is not too far from here to the *virgo paritura.* And according to the teachings of the Kabbalah, it is the black Shulamite of the Song of Solomon who is this primal material. As Dom Pernéty said in his *Greek and Egyptian Fables* in 1758, "It is thought that the rabbis believed in an original matter, which was less a body than an immense shadow, a dark ghost of the Being, a very dark night, and the lair and center of the darkness. . . . From this latter principle God would have pulled a dark abyss."

But this dark abyss is not necessarily the "night of sin" emphasized by Christian moralists. Given the role granted the Virgin Mary, it is impossible that the color black with which she was sometimes covered could be a consequence of Original Sin. As the Black Madonna, Mary represents all creation before it was created. She is pure potentiality, hence the absence of colors. As sung by the visionary German poet Novalis: "The Virgin is Mother of the World, the Beloved whom nothing can resist, the imperious Night that wins the Universe to its cause. The cosmic Virgin is mirrored in each terrestrial virgin, and we realize that the quest for love is a devotion to the invasion of the Night." The amorous union leads to an annihilation of the individual into a whole, a kind of reintegration into the original mass represented by the universal Mother. Christian doctrine is in perfect agreement with the philosophies of antiquity here, as well as the most diverse mythologies. Black is not a symbol of the "divine death" that some swear by (not without a connotation of suicide). It is a long way from this "divine death," which is finally a kind of negative orgasm, to the "earlier quietude" represented by the Black Madonna. Saillens explains:

Fulbert in Chartres, or any alchemist canon in Le Puy or anywhere else, could see in the Black Madonna a symbol of the universal matter without being inspired to desire that the world fall back into chaos. Fulbert built Chartres; the alchemist toiled on the Great Work. People of that time viewed matter as dangerous but not despicable. Even God wore it, and wore it each and every day. The most humble professions had their patron saints, feasts, and dignity. The stone of the cathedrals proclaimed the possibilities of humanity and matter, the triumph of love over destiny. Life, work, nature, had a meaning, because one day, among other days, "the new Cybele," as the first Christians sometimes called her, gave birth to the Messiah. In those days, when a French crowd wished to express its joy, they shouted: Noel![11]

Traditional alchemy codified these basic assumptions inherited from mythology. Fulcanelli, in his book *The Mystery of the Cathedrals,* writes, "The Black Madonnas, always housed in the crypt, represent the matter on which the Alchemists work." Of course, Black Madonnas are not always placed in crypts, but their other locations may be symbolic crypts. Nonetheless the meaning remains the same—to wit, that these depictions were created to inspire those who meditated before them *to work.* Among the operations of this Great Work, we can note the calcination of the primal material, followed by its putrefaction and dissolution. The second phase of the operation gives the black that is blacker than black. The color white is obtained from this, then the color citrine [lemon yellow], then the color red, that of the Blood that filled the Grail. All the authors stress that nothing can happen to the primal material unless it goes through this black color, this Raven's Head, this "brass that must be made white." As one Hermetic philosopher said: "The top garment of Isis is black; beneath it appears a white robe, a citrine robe, and a red robe."

"The brass that must be made white": This brass is obviously not the combination of metals with which we are familiar. Its name

---

11. Ibid., 244.

[French, *laiton* or *léton*] comes from Leto or Latona, the primordial mother darkness of the white Diana-Artemis and the blond Apollo, one of the ancient faces of the Goddess of the Beginnings. Gladstone, the rigid minister of Queen Victoria, who had a great interest in Greek mythology, penned a curious essay on this subject. "Latona," he wrote, "is a very strange figure. Her name means "the Obscure One," "the Forgotten One," or even "night." She has no attributes. Her sole role is to give birth to two divine children. It so happens that her son was not originally a solar god but a savior god, a Messiah announced by Hesiod, Homer, Virgil, and Horace."[12]

The Puritan Gladstone concluded from this that Latona was a forerunner of the Virgin Mary. So here we are back at the *virgo paritura* of Chartres.

The reading of a cathedral always takes place on several levels, as does the deciphering of artworks that are also objects of devotion. This is perfectly logical; everything converges toward a unique meaning while taking into account the degrees of receptiveness of different audiences, independent of any specific era. "The Philosophers," wrote Dom Pernéty, a Benedictine of Saint-Maur yet still an alchemist, "teach that when white overcomes Matter, life has vanquished death, their king is resurrected, the earth and water have become air, their Child is born, the Earth and Heaven are wed." Couldn't this be the description of the Incarnation of Jesus Christ in the womb of the Virgin Mary, she who has always been "virgin" and

---

12. W. Gladstone, *Homer and the Homeric Age*, vol. 2 (Oxford, England, 1858), 183. Apollo in early Greek mythology (Indo-European, in fact) was a god of healing and resurrection. It seems that the Indo-Europeans had a solar goddess, but at a certain juncture in history, a reversal of polarity occurred. The male deity took on the luminous functions. Apollo, after having defeated the Serpent Python (the Earth Mother), became a celestial god, but retained his role as god of medicine all the same. In Celtic tradition, Apollo was not at all a solar god, as Caesar noted in his *Commentaries,* but rather was restricted to his role as doctor. In Ireland this doctor god, named Diancecht, digs a Fountain of Health in which the wounded will be healed and even the dead can be resurrected.

will be "virgin" forever and who, to be shown in her potentiality, is depicted covered by the color black?

But the common folk will not make any connection to these mysterious alchemical operations, with which the perfect is drawn from the imperfect by applying to matter what religion applies to the spirit. Here again we should recall that Christ is present as resurrected—that is to say, in his material body once it has been purified and transformed, reharmonized with himself in fullness. Without entertaining these subtle considerations, the people see in the image of the Black Madonna the transitory and provisional nature of things, but they know that beyond this there is the whiteness of the triumphant Virgin, she who shines in the stained-glass windows of Chartres with all the splendor of Wisdom.

This is why the images of the Black Madonna are so popular: They correspond to a fundamental notion that is inherent to humanity. If the images of this Black Virgin bear such close resemblance in many ways to the ancient mother goddesses of East and West, is this truly surprising? The Christian doctrine may be revolutionary in placing foremost the precept of love, which may have been largely missing in certain religions of antiquity—notably those of the Mediterranean basin—but it is nonetheless the logical sequel in humanity's metaphysical and religious evolution, by which it integrates into its current form the speculations and even "revelations" of its ancestors.

In Chartres, as in Le Puy-en-Velay and elsewhere, the Black Madonna glows with an inner fire that can be seen only by those who are convinced that "the door is on the inside."

PART 3

THE MYSTERY OF THE DRUIDS

7

THE FOREST OF
THE CARNUTES

The name Chartres is derived from Civitas Carnutum, or rather the locative ablative Carnutibus, "home of the Carnutes." The Carnutes were the Gallic people who occupied the territory that now forms a group of three *départements*, Eure-et-Loir, Loir-et-Cher, and the Loiret (at least partially). These correspond to the ancient feudal domains of Chartres, Dunois, Blésois, and Orléanais. The city of Chartres therefore represented a central position in a Gaul that extended farther north than the current border of France—up to the Rhine—and a little less to the south, where the Garonne was a border of heavy Celtic settlement. This may explain why, based on Caesar's words, it was in the land of the Carnutes that once a year the Druids of all of Gaul would gather, and why "this land was viewed as the center for all of Gaul." Of course we cannot always take literally the expressions "center of the country" and "center of the world," because quite often they concern a purely symbolic *omphalos* in a perfectly ideal "center." The hill of Tara in Ireland, the religious and political center of the island, is far from the actual center of that isle. The old notion of *omphalos,* the navel of the world, is superimposed over many mythological elements inside a sacred geography that no longer has much in common with the actual topography.

Before defining what this central sanctuary of the Gauls in the land of the Carnutes might have been—and after accepting the idea of *omphalos* as inherent to such matters—we should examine the name of the Carnutes. There may be a link between the choice of the place and the role given to the Carnutes, a role that, as in many other cases, may be definable by the name given to the people.

By all evidence, Carnute has something in common with Carnac (Morbihan), which is not Breton, but rather Gallic. To be precise, it is Gallo-Roman, for it is formed with the suffix *–aco,* which has yielded the names ending in *–ac* in Occitan and Breton toponymy and the names ending in *–é, –y,* and *–ey* in Romanesque toponymy. The first syllable, *carn,* is identical and has two acceptable etymologies. The first refers to a root word, *kern,* which means "horn." There is an evident connection with the Gallic horned deity Cernunnos, once worshipped at Carnac, an Indo-European deity of the third function that expresses prosperity and abundance (as in *cornucopia* or "horn" of plenty). By extension we can add the sense of *horn,* the musical instrument, because these were formerly crafted from animals' horns. This is the meaning of the Gallic word *carnyx,* "war horn." But given that horns were a warrior's adornment, and the Indo-European king type was always selected from the warrior class, the crafted horn [*corne* in French] became the "crown" [*couronne* in French], the symbol of royal power. If this etymology is accepted, the Carnutes could therefore be "the people with the horns" (warriors) or "the royal people" (those who have been crowned). After all, their immediate neighbors, the Durocassi, are "the water fighters" and the Eburovices are "the people of the yew." This interpretation appears to comply with what we know of the Gallic peoples.

The second etymology views *carn* as the equivalent of the English word *cairn,* which has become a universal archaeological term designating a prehistoric or protohistoric funeral mound—in other words, a tumulus, a galgal, or any other artificial mound that serves as an individual or group sepulcher. Its original meaning is "pile of stones," and it is likely that it contains a pre–Indo-European root that can be recognized in the Languedoc word *garrigue* [scrubland] and through the intermediary of the derivative *kal,* in the Provençal *calanque* [creek]. By this reckoning, the Carnutes could be "the people of the mounds," which is certainly not incompatible with the fact that their homeland contained the central sanctuary of Gaul.

Mounds play a considerable role in Celtic religion. Not only did the Celts build funerary mounds to house their dead (incinerated or buried; the two practices coexisted), but they also incorporated all the large tumuli from previous ages, the megalithic mounds and covered alleys in particular. This incorporation, furthermore, took place on two levels: that of myth and that of worship. On the one hand, the Celts placed inside the subterranean world of the mounds the dwellings of their gods, their heroes, and their dead: Ireland has a great wealth of mythological traditions concerning the *sidh* (a Gaelic word meaning "peace"), where numerous legends are set. The *sidh* is truly the Other World, but on certain occasions, such as the night of Samhain (November 1, a great Celtic feast day), it was said that the *sidh* was open to any human with the audacity to enter.

This Other World is a wonderful place that resembles the earthly realm, but where suffering, illness, and death are unknown and time is "a day of eternally pleasant weather."[1] On the other hand, because the Celts never built temples (at least before the Roman occupation or Roman influence), their ceremonies took place in sacred places, either in clearings or in locations that had been consecrated as far back as anyone could remember, or, particularly, on the tops of megalithic mounds. Thus, there is nothing to oppose the notion that the Carnutes were "people of the mounds," given that it was their territory where the religious elite of Gaul had decided to meet dur-

---

1. For more on this, see Jean Markale, *Epics of Celtic Ireland* (Rochester, Vt.: Inner Traditions, 2001). The reader will find there meaningful stories on the role played by mounds in the mythology and worship of the island Celts that were not strikingly different from those on the Continent.

ing a predetermined period (which Caesar did not identify, but which was surely November 1, if we take the word of the Irish documents concerning Celtic festivals).

The rare portions of Caesar's *Commentaries* concerning the Carnute people permit only theorizing about them. Caesar never mentions Autricum. He speaks only of Cenabum (probably Orléans) and never indicates the precise spot where the Druids gathered. "At a certain time of the year," he wrote, "they [the Druids] gathered together on consecrated ground in the land of the Carnutes, which is regarded as the center of all Gaul. Converging on this spot are individuals who are involved in disputes that they give over to the Druids for advice and judgment" (VI, 13). That is all. This clue has been seized on as a pretext to claim that this "festival" was a gathering only of the Druids from all of Gaul. It is certain that all the Druids were here at this convocation, and that they came from all over. It is an affirmation of the nature of the Druidic institution. The Druids' kinship with a specific people did not interfere with their ties to a larger international, even supranational community.

But the context remains perfectly clear: Non-Druids also came to this assembly, for it provided them a place where they could debate their issues and request advice and, to a certain extent, judgments. It seems to have been a vast gathering of the Gallic peoples, outside any patriotic connotation or any link with the indigenous people, in a ceremony that combined religious ritual and political counsel. It is therefore likely that one of the four great Celtic festivals of the year was involved.

According to the Gallic *Calendar of Coligny* in the Museum of Lyon, as well as numerous Irish tales, the Celtic year was centered on two dates, November 1 and May 1, with two intermediary dates of February 1 and August 1.[2] February 1, later adopted by Christianity,

---

2. The Celts did not celebrate any festival at the time of the summer or winter solstice. With all due respect to the "neo-Druids" who abound at present and mistake their desires for realities, no document justifies any Celtic solstice celebration. Solstice feasts are pre-Celtic, having taken place in the Bronze Age and the megalithic era.

incorporating the Feast of Saint Brigitte of Kildare (Ireland) and displacing the February 2 holiday of the Purification of the Virgin (Candlemas), was the ancient Feast of Imbolc, which was celebrated at midwinter. August 1, which was moved to August 15, the Feast of the Assumption, was Lughnasa, literally "the marriage of Lugh" and symbol of the sacred union between the god who was master of all the arts (Lugh) and the Earth (the ancient Mother Goddess), with a solemn celebration of the new harvest.[3] May 1, the Festival of Beltane, meaning "the fires of Bel" (Bel or Beli being Belenos, the Shining One, title of the god of light), is the celebration of the herds returning to the fields at the beginning of summer, therefore a feast celebrating work and activity. It was incorporated into profane tradition as the Festival of Work (May Day), then moved to Saint John's Day in the summer for the fire rituals, but was also integrated into the holiday of Easter, mainly with its blessing of the new fire.

The most important festival was that of Samhain, November 1, the name of which means "end of summer" and which was wholly integrated into Christianity as the Feast of Toussaint (All Souls' Day), in which the "community of the living and the dead" is celebrated, just as it was in the time of the Druids. Samhain was the ideal time, when normal time was abolished and became eternity. It was always during Samhain that the mounds were open, allowing the interpenetration of the two worlds, that of the living and that of the dead. It was on Samhain that the dramatic actions recorded in the ancient mythological epics always took place.

Samhain was the decisive hinge of the Celtic year, and there is no lack of documents to illustrate this fact. They show Samhain to

---

3. In modern Gaelic, the month of August is Lughnasa. Lugh is the most universal Celtic god, and his worship can be found both in the British Isles and on the Continent, where he gave his name to cities like Lyon, Loudon, and Laon, which are Lugdunum, "fortresses of Lugh." This Lugh is the Gallic Mercury about whom Caesar spoke, who was quite different from the Latin Mercury and whom the Gallic people worshipped through simulacra, crudely cut pillars of wood or stone, no doubt menhirs or *lec'hs*. Lugh is the god "beyond role" of the Celts because he is the "master of all the arts."

have been a compulsory universal festival in which everyone participated, under pain of punishment if they did not. From the Ulster Cycle: "An assembly was held by the Ulates every year, for three days before Samhain, and three days after, in addition to the day of Samhain itself. This was the time when the Ulates were in the Murthemne Plain, and they held the Samhain gathering every year. There was nothing that they did not do at this time, if it were not games, reunions, pomp and magnificence, good cheer, and banquets."[4] "Conchobar[5] served the people at the Samhain feast because such a large crowd had gathered. It was necessary to feed this huge multitude because any man of the Ulates who did not come to Emain[6] on Samhain night would lose his reason, and his tumulus, his tomb, and his stone would be erected the following morning. There were vast provisions at the home of Conchobar."[7] "Here is the reason the Feast of Samhain was celebrated: because the laws were made by the men of Ireland and none dared transgress them until all were again reunited at the end of a year. And whoever had transgressed them would be exiled from the company of the men of Ireland."[8] "The rules, laws, and duties were set and the opinions of the Irish people were taken at this assembly . . . with the Feast of Tara on Samhain—because this was the Pagan Easter—and all the men of Ireland helped the king hold this assembly."[9]

It is not so difficult to identify the annual assembly in the forest of the Carnutes, mentioned by Caesar in his *Commentaries*, with the Samhain festival so renowned throughout ancient Ireland.

---

4. "The Illness of Cuchulainn," trans. Guyonvarc'h, *Ogam*, vol. 10, 286.

5. [Refers to the great mythical king of the Ulates, the inhabitants of Ulster. —*Trans.*]

6. [This is Emain Macha, the principal fortress of King Conchobar and actual capital of Ulster; today it is Enania near Armagh. —*Trans.*]

7. "The Birth of Conchobar," version A, trans. Guyonvarc'h, *Ogam*, vol. 11, 61.

8. St. O'Grady, *Silva Gadelica*, vol. 1, 319.

9. W. Stokes, *Irische Texte*, vol. 3 (Leipzig: n.p., 1887), 198. Tara was the capital and theoretical center of Ireland in the no less theoretical kingdom of Meath (meaning "middle"). It was a hill that had been held sacred since prehistoric times, an *omphalos* where the people of Ireland gathered when supranational decisions needed to be made.

It displays the same characteristics. And this festival is unthinkable without the Druids. Here is an account by the seventeenth-century Irish theologian Geoffrey Keating:

> The festival of Tara was a royal and general assembly, and all the doctors [Druids] met every three years at Tara during Samhain to organize and renew the rules and the laws, and to approve the annals and archives of Ireland. A seat was also prepared for each Irish nobleman according to his rank and title. Another seat was prepared for each chief who commanded warriors in the service of the king or lords of Ireland. It was still the custom at the festival of Tara to put to death any who committed violence or rape, who struck anyone or attacked anyone with a weapon, the king alone having the power, and no one else, to pardon anyone for such an action. It was still then custom to spend six days drinking together before the session of the royal assembly, that is to say three days before Samhain and three days after, concluding peaces and establishing bonds of friendship between each other."[10]

According to testimonies from the Christian era, the festival of Samhain was deemed to be "a ceremony of idolatry that the pagans had customarily celebrated with numerous incantations, magical invocations, and several other idolatrous superstitions, with the kings, the princes, the chiefs, the lords, the nobles of the nation, and an even larger number of spell casters, seers, and all sorts of magicians and doctors having been summoned."[11]

This throng of magicians, spell casters, doctors, and seers, all belonging to the Druidic class, is a close match with Caesar's description of the assembly among the Carnutes. Furthermore, in the sequel to his *Commentaries,* Caesar gives the specific title of a Druid

---

10. Geoffrey Keating, *History of Ireland,* vol. 2, trans. Patrick S. Dineen (London: Irish Texts Society, 1908), 132.

11. W. Stokes, *The Tripartite Life of Patrick,* vol. 2 (London: Eyre and Spottiswoode, 1887), 278.

named Cotuatos, one of the leaders of the rebellion of 52 B.C.E. that sparked Vercingetorix's campaign. This Druid is presented as a *gutuater*. The term is confirmed elsewhere on four Gallo-Roman monuments, once as a proper name (in Puy-en-Velay) and three times as a common noun. In one of these instances the phrase Gutuater Martis leaves no doubt as to the sacerdotal role it designates: a priest vowed to Mars, who has been superimposed over an indigenous Gallic deity, probably Toutatis or Teutates.

There is nothing intrinsically mysterious about the word itself. It contains the term *gutu–,* which literally means "voice," and the term *–ater* (or *–tater,* related to the Indo-European root of "father"). This priest is therefore the Father of the Voice, or even the Father of the Word; that is to say, he is responsible for preaching, or else his role is to speak incantations, praises, and satires, all of which share an eminently magical nature. In this latter sense, the *gutuater* is the counterpart of the Irish spell caster. But this *gutuater* can be found in circumstances that attest to both the role of the religious center in the Carnutes' territory and the part taken by the Carnutes in the latter phase of the Gallic Wars in 52 B.C.E.

The Romans had occupied Gaul for about six years. Local revolts had occurred continually, as well as the famous war against the Vénètes, which Caesar won only because of a shift in the winds, as the Vénète ships were powered by sails. But in the shadows, a general rebellion was being prepared among most of the Gallic peoples, a revolt whose soul and motor were combined in a single figure, Vercingetorix. This young Arverne chieftain could do nothing, however, without the accord of the Druid clergy. Although Caesar rarely alluded to the role played by the Druids during the campaigns of the war with Gaul, the Druids were behind the scenes, ever ready to step in, for they were the conscience of Celtic society. This was quite easy to see in 52 B.C.E., because the revolt was actually inspired by Druids specifically from the land of the Carnutes.

The time was in their favor. Caesar had returned to Rome. The legions were peacefully hibernating, and their leaders did not have the authority to take any initiatives, save to defend themselves when attacked. Emissaries from all the Celtic and Belgian peoples (Gaul between the Seine and Garonne Rivers and between the Seine and Rhine Rivers) were coming and going constantly. "The occupation," Caesar wrote, "had stirred up these people who were impatient with their subjugation by the Romans. They began to lay plans for war with more freedom and boldness. The Gallic leaders arranged secret meetings among the gods scattered about the middle of the woods" (VII, 1). The secret meetings took place in "remote areas" and "in the middle of the woods," which are characteristic of Druid sanctuaries. It was therefore in religious establishments in the forest centers, near the *nemeton* ("sacred clearing"), and of course under the aegis of the Druids, that the secret conferences of the Gallic chieftains took place. This is a valuable clue because it gives the exact tone of the revolt of 52 B.C.E., especially its religious dimension. Following the meetings scattered across the extent of Gaul, at least among the people supporting the conspiracy, a general meeting took place. Caesar did not say where this meeting occurred, but the context clearly indicates that it was set in the forest of the Carnutes:

> After many discussions of their plans, the Carnutes declared that they were ready to face any danger to save their country and promised to be in the front ranks of the rebellion. . . . At the time, it was not possible to exchange hostages as mutual guarantees, as that would risk betraying their intentions; they would instead swear solemn vows around their military standards stacked together—a ceremony that establishes the most sacred of bonds among these people—to not abandon their promises once hostilities commenced. The Carnutes were warmly congratulated; the oath was sworn by all in attendance, and preparations were begun after a date had been set for the uprising. (VII, 2)

The religious aspect of the Gallic chieftains' commitment could not be any clearer. And it was the Carnutes, keepers to some extent of the symbol of the Druidic religion in Gaul, who committed fully and offered to strike the first blow. For a time, the secret remained well guarded. Not a single one of Caesar's spies was informed of what was being plotted in the sacred clearings of Carnute territory. The plan proposed by the Carnutes was executed down to its smallest details: "When the appointed day arrived, the Carnutes, led by Cotuatos and Conconnetodumnos, men of whom naught could be hoped but desperate acts, swooped down, at a given signal, upon Cenabum and massacred the Roman citizens who had settled there to pursue commerce, and pillaged their property" (VII, 3).

It seems that Cenabum (most likely Orléans) was chosen for its exemplary value. It was not a town, properly speaking—there were no real towns in independent Gaul—but rather a fortress refuge and an important commercial stop on the Loire, at the intersection of the land road running north to south (the famous medieval road of Saint Jacques) and the waterway that connected the Atlantic with the Saône basin and thus the Provincia Romana. The Romans had established commercial trading posts there whose importance grew daily. To destroy these trading posts was symbolically to destroy Roman influence in the region, and at the same time rid Carnute territory, a sacred domain, of the foreign elements profaning it.

The religious aspect of this operation, which at bottom is a kind of expiatory sacrifice, is even more evident in that one of the leaders of the rebellion was Cotuatos, a *gutuater*—in other words, a spell caster—therefore necessarily a priest and member of the predominant Druid class. He would later pay a heavy price for his involvement, a victim of Roman vengeance. Hirtius, Caesar's continuer,[12] described the punishment:

Having arrived among the Carnutes, Caesar demanded that the *gutuater* be delivered up to him as the guilty party chiefly responsible

---

12. ["Continuer" is the term used to describe those authors who completed the numerous compilations begun in medieval and Roman times. For example, continuers finished the Grail saga left unwritten by de Boron. —*Trans.*]

for the war. He was promptly escorted into the camp. Caesar, despite his natural tendency to clemency, was compelled to execute him at the demand of the soldiers crowding round and charging him with all the pains they had suffered in the course of the war. Accordingly he was flogged unconscious before being finished off with an axe." (VIII, 38)

We know what happened next. This was the era of Vercingetorix that started in triumph and ended in disaster with Alésia.[13] But in this war to liberate Gaul, the Carnutes had played a starring role from the first—political, military, and, most significant, religious—which only emphasizes the importance of this *omphalos* or *nemeton* located in the heart of Carnute territory, most likely in a clearing in the middle of the forest.

But what forest? Currently the Beauce is, as it has been for several centuries, a vast plain of farm fields devoted essentially to wheat and cereal grains. The remnants of forest that can still be spotted are no more than a few sparse groves scattered here and there. Only the perimeter of the ancient land of the Carnutes retains enough forested massifs to let us speak of the Forest of the Carnutes. It has been claimed that Beauce, formerly Belsa, means "clearing." But a clearing of such size would merit the label "plain." All this seems quite strange, especially as Caesar never mentions the spot where these famous annual assemblies of the Druids took place. We are again reduced to hypotheses, none of which is truly satisfying.

We no longer live in a time that sees "Druidic altars" in the smallest dolmen buried in the undergrowth of any rural area or bloody sacrificial tables on the famous "basin stones" that are common in some places. But we should not go to the other extreme and see a Gallic temple in every Roman brick construction.

---

13. For more on all these events, see Jean Markale, *Vercingétorix* (Paris: Hachette, 1982), principally starting on page 178.

This is not a supposition, but archaeological and historical reality: Before being occupied by the Romans or assimilated by the Greeks, the Celts never built temples. There are no references to buildings of worship in the Welsh or Irish epics. Greek and Roman authors never mentioned any Gallic temples before the conquest. The famous Temple of Apollo located in the British Isles is the monument of Stonehenge, a Bronze Age construction, an open-air temple. Titus-Livy alludes to a Boïen Temple in Celtic Gaul and Polybius to a temple of the Insubres, but in each of these, the reference is to a place in a forest, with no details about appearance or architecture. Caesar, who knew of what he spoke, designated the Gallic sanctuary by the term *locus consecratus,* "consecrated place" (VI, 13 and 16). If it had been a constructed temple like Roman temples, he would not have failed to mention it. The sole buildings of worship that can be attributed to the independent Celts are limited to the Mediterranean region, like Entremont near Aix-en-Provence, where they had contact with Greeks and Romans and were subject to their influence.

It is only after the Gallic Wars that constructed square-shaped temples appeared, but they were dedicated to Roman deities and no longer had much in common with the Druidic religion. Furthermore, the exile of the Druids, who were legally banned during the reign of Tiberius, suppressed every Druidic reference in social and religious life. If Celtic worship sites still existed, they would have had to be carefully hidden, safe from the indiscreet gaze of the authorities. This is what Lucan reveals in the *Pharsalia,* moreover, when he mentions a sacred enclosure located in the depths of a forest. Round and octagonal temples were now appearing on Gallic soil, whereas not a one was found (outside of the sanctuaries dedicated to Vesta) in purely Roman territory.

This is evidence of something, a remembrance or a habit. It has been suggested that the round temples reflected an ancient circumambulation rite. This rite is also confirmed in the majority of archaic religions. One circled the tomb of a hero as if to surround the tomb with a zone of protection, or as if to symbolically demarcate a piece of ground considered the Other World. Accordingly, the first temples would have been constructed around a hero's tomb; this incidentally explains the ambulatory of later Christian churches, which were most often built around the tomb of a saint or martyr. But that proves nothing. The Irish, according to their epic tales, had the custom of erecting funerary pillars, in wood or stone, at the spot a hero had met his death, but not necessarily at his tomb, and then sang praises of the deceased while circling the pillar. This is a funeral and homage ritual about which there are no specific records.

But in Ireland, where there was no Roman occupation, no temples have been found. Ceremonies took place outdoors on sacred mounds or in the middle of the woods, which certainly did not prevent the site being marked by the erection of a stone or wooden pillar. As for the underground chambers of the megalithic mounds (dolmens and covered alleys) in which the Irish pagans located the home of the gods, they were never places of worship. In principle, they were reserved for the gods; furthermore, most of the time the entrance to these monuments was hidden and thus inaccessible. Finally, the temples were built of wood, so it is said to be understandable that no trace of them has been found. But not a single Irish tale mentions such a thing, which is surprising all the same.

In Britain the problem is slightly different. During the Roman occupation, great tolerance was extended to the British, who were able to practice their religion in complete freedom. The vestiges of a certain number of temples more or less in the Druidic spirit have been discovered, but their architecture shows equal signs of Roman influence. Furthermore, when Saint Ninian went to spread the Gospel to the southern Picts at the end of the fourth century (in the lowlands of what is Scotland today), he built a church that caused a sensation. It was a *candida casa,* a "white house." It is understandable that it was built in stone, and that it was a novelty. This detail proves that the notion of a constructed temple, at least in stone, was foreign to the custom of the primitive Celtic world. And when Dion Cassius observed that the Bretons of Queen Boudicca (Boadicea) offered sacrifices to the gods in the temples, he used the Greek word *hiera,* which means the same as Caesar's Latin *locus consecratus.* On the other hand, Cassius mentions, like so many others, "sacred groves," and he uses the term *alsos,* which is the equivalent of the Latin *lucus* and *nemus.*

To be precise, we find the word *nemus* in its Celtic formulation. One of Ireland's mythical invaders was a certain Nemed, meaning "sacred" in the Gaelic tongue. The word comes from the same Indo-European root word that provided the Latin *nemus.* This root means "heaven" in the spiritual sense of the term, hence the Gallic *niam,* the Welsh *nef,* and the Breton *nenv* (pronounced *nan*). The preeminent Celtic sanctuary appears to have been the *nemeton,* which designated the sacred, celestial clearing at the heart of a forest. According to what we know, the Druids, while taking part in the collective life of their social group, lived apart and never officiated against the backdrop of a village or settlement.

In Great Britain, the Druidic establishment on the Isle of Môn (Angelsey), which was a significant grouping of Druids and their families, was located in a forest. When Lucan speaks of a Gallic sanctuary near Marseille, he places it in a forest. This, he said, is where horrible sacrifices were performed and crude statues depicting the gods *(simulacra maesta deorum)* can be found. A priest officiated in this remote and secret sanctuary, in honor of the *dominus loci.* And then, especially, "the people never come in proximity to the site of the worship and abandon it to the gods. . . . The priest himself dreads to approach it because he fears to come upon the master of the sacred grove" (*Pharsalia,* I, verse 339 ff.). Lucan specified something else: "The Druids lived in deep woods [*nemora alta*] and retreated into uninhabited forests. They practiced barbaric rites and a kind of sinister worship" (I, verse 452 ff.). We know that later an unknown scholiast added some details about this "sinister worship," particularly about the sacrifices to the gods Taranis, Toutatis, and Esus. But Lucan added: "They worshipped the gods in the woods without using temples." This is precise and clear-cut. And he used the term *nemus,* which brings us back to *nemeton.*

What exactly does the *nemeton* represent? "The Celtic sanctuary is more tied to a symbolic or effective notion of 'center,'" Lucan said, "than to a form or a material aspect as it is expressed in its totality by the word that designates the sacred—as a precise geographical location, as a moment in calendar time, as a person, an individual distinguished from the rest of society."[14] The Celts were of the opinion that it was futile or stupid to seek to cage the god or gods. Conversely, they thought there were places, symbolic or real, where the human world could open onto the world of the gods and vice versa; the *nemeton* is this place of sacred exchange. It is the clearing in the forest as well as the entire forest, the summit of a mound, and an isle in the middle of the ocean. How many Christian sanctuaries, churches, and modest chapels must have been built on the sites of former *nemetons!* Springs and their immediate surroundings were also privileged locations, as, in addition to communication with heaven *(nem),* contact could be made there with the vital, fertilizing, and maternal forces that mysteriously emerged from the center of the earth. In this sense, the Fountain of Barenton, in the ancient forest of Broceliande, perfectly illustrates the idea the Celts had of the *nemeton* in its entirety.[15]

Now every *nemeton* is the center of the world. The notion of *omphalos* coincides exactly with that of "sanctuary," and no matter that these sanctuaries are beyond number. They are simultaneously unique and multiple (like the Christian churches) because, to employ a famous expression, the deity is a circle whose center is everywhere and whose circumference is nowhere. The place where contact with the invisible world, the divine world, is established is necessarily an absolute center from which the forces called into play can radiate.

---

14. Guyonvarc'h and Le Roux, *Les Druides* (Rennes, France: Ouest, 1978), 217.

15. The former name of Barenton is Belenton (Bel-enton), in which we find the name Bel (Belenos). This is the name of the Celtic god of light and a variant of *nemeton* (nem-eton). The Barenton Fountain is a "sacred clearing of Bel."

But it is human beings who establish this center, through their intuition. The *nemeton* is never chosen at random. Most of the time, it is located at the site of a prehistoric sanctuary, because sacred tradition demands that certain privileged spots remain so even if the religious ideology changes. We hear of "telluric currents" and "magnetic forces" without any reference to more or less confused esoteric notions. Sacred places are really privileged places, either because "supernatural events" occurred there that defy our understanding (as with the Marian sanctuary of Lourdes) or because the psychic strength of individuals practicing rituals there for centuries eventually permeated the site with what is called an *aura,* or an *égrégore* (this seems to be the case with Chartres). But in any event, there is no scarcity of traditions concerning sacred sites, whether they are "white," meaning holy, or "black," meaning cursed.

But the *nemeton* always sits somewhere apart, even when there are no grounds for fearing a hostile political authority. It was not in response to Roman occupation that the Gallic Druids established themselves in the forests. Everything indicates that the isolation of the Druidic sanctuary was by deliberate intent. This is similar to the idea of the *desert*.[16] Roman Christianity has distorted our understanding of the concept of *desert*. Christianity evolved in the sociocultural and political context of the Roman Empire, which is to say in the framework of an integrally *urban* kind of civilization, including Greek components, thus under the influence of the Greek *polis*.

From the time of the introduction of the evangelical message, a rupture occurred with nature in the Greek and Roman cities. And the first Christian mystics certainly sensed it strongly; starting with Saint Paul, all went on retreat *into the desert*. Etymologically, the wilderness is everything that has been abandoned, everything not subject to human activity. Still today, in the rural French vocabulary, *désert* designates an abandoned spot, lying fallow, where unchecked

---

16. [*Desert* originally referred to untamed or uncultivated regions bearing no sign of human endeavor, and was not limited to describing an arid, waterless region as it is today. —*Trans.*]

plant growth has gained the upper hand. But this in no way implies any idea of aridity and desolation or a lack of water and vegetation. To retreat into the wilderness simply means to go back to nature. This is what the first Christian hermits did. But because the most famous lived in dry, arid lands, it has bred some confusion. For them it was necessary to go into the solitary expanses of Upper Egypt, to the Sahara, or to Libya. But wildernesses also exist outside the gates of great cities. When the medieval monks established their monasteries in remote locations abandoned by most people but still close to human settlements, they were simply following the example set by Breton and Irish hermits, who themselves were following the example of the Druids. Certain Christian monasteries in Ireland even assumed the word *dysert* in their names, which is quite significant.

The concept of the sanctuary that can be everywhere and nowhere but is always the center of the world, and which is always in contact with raw nature, is one of the distinguishing features of Druidism. This is important for understanding the isolation of Chartres in the center of Beauce, a clearing in the heart of a mysterious forest that was sacred because it was natural. It represents the realization that human beings are in constant contact with the cosmos and thus are never truly isolated, even when alone in the middle of the desert. To the contrary, by removing ourselves from the realm of worries that are naught but illusions, we find the great All, whoever that deity may be and by whatever name it may be invoked. This also shows that it is possible to invoke the deity, and it reveals the inanities of some observations on the "primary naturism" of the Druids, incorporated into a set of propitiatory rituals intended to conjure natural but invisible forces. The concept of the Celtic sanctuary proves, to the contrary, a metaphysical and theological consideration of great scope that has never been erased from human memory and which reappeared, oddly alive, in the framework of Christianity.

But this sanctuary, this *nemeton* in the wilderness, is also a teaching center. In Gaul, as in the other Celtic countries, education was entrusted to the first Indo-European function,[17] which in this instance means the Druidic class. So it was the Druids who taught the young. "Young people," said Caesar, "come in throngs to learn from them, and they are held in great honor" (VI, 13), adding, "Many come spontaneously to follow their teachings; many others are sent to them by their families" (VI, 14). The word *druid* has nothing to do with the Greek name for oak, as was claimed by Pliny the Elder. It comes from the ancient *dru-wides,* whose first syllable is a superlative and the second is kin to the Latin *videre* and the Greek *idein,* "to see." Literally, the Druids are "Those who see far" or "Those who know much," which speaks volumes about their social role.

The Gauls "also have highly honored philosophers and theologians that are called Druids. These philosophers have great authority over the affairs of both peace and war" (Diodorus Siculus, V, 31). The Druids were the keepers of an encyclopedic knowledge that touched on all the disciplines known at that time. "They indulge in much speculation," wrote Caesar, "on the stars and their movements, on the dimensions of the world and that of the land, on the nature of things, on the power of the gods, and they pass on these doctrines to the youth" (VI, 14). This teaching was only oral, as the Druids forbade the use of writing: "They seem to have established this custom for two reasons, because they did not want their doctrine divulged nor, on the other hand, that their students, priding themselves on writing, would neglect to train their memory. For this is a common thing, when one is aided by written texts, less effort is made to remember them by heart and one lets the memory rust" (VI, 14). This explains the length of time required for these studies: "It is said among them that the young learn a considerable number of verses by heart, so many that some remain twenty years at their study" (VI, 14).

There is also this, which explains the art of speaking among the

---

17. [This language refers to the three basic classes or castes as defined by their social function—the Indo-Eurpoean tripartite division of society. —*Trans.*]

Celts: "We Gauls connect eloquence," a Druid told the Greek philosopher Lucian of Samosata, "not with Hermes, as you do, but with the mightier Hercules. . . . We believe that Hercules himself grown wise was able to achieve, through the power of his eloquence, all his exploits, and through the power of his persuasion, get past all obstacles. His rapid shafts, in my view, are no other than his words: keen-pointed and true-aimed to wreak damage on the soul; as you yourselves say: winged words" (Lucian, *Hercules*). Whereas, Strabo notes, "if coaxed, they [the Gauls] so easily yield to considerations of utility that they lay hold, not only of training in general, but of language-studies as well" (Strabo, IV, 2).

Another curious observation is that although the word *druid* has nothing in common with the name for oak (with all due respect to those who continue to spread this insanity!), there is in every Celtic language an undeniable connection between the word that means "science" and the word that means "tree." The Indo-European root °*wid* is close to the Gallic word *vidu,* which means "tree," the word that gave us the Welsh and Vannetais *koed* and the *koad* of other Breton dialects. Nor is it hard to recognize this term in the Chartres region itself, in the name Perche-Gouët, which designates the western part of Carnute territory. Is this simply a homophonic chance encounter? Is it a case of the phonetic Kabbalah? It is easy to conclude that this is a simple case of homonymy, but then how to explain this same ambiguity in other Indo-European languages, concerning the Germanic Odin in particular?

Odin-Wotan (Woden in Saxon) goes back to an ancient Wothanz attested to by Tacitus, in whose name German specialists saw the root °*wut,* which means "sacred fury," and thence complete science. This is quite apt for the character imputed to the Odin of the Norse sagas, the one who intentionally blinded himself in one eye in order to become a "rune master"—which is to say, to see magically. Runes are magical inscriptions carved in wood as if by chance, just like the spells made with tree branches (mainly hazel and yew) by Irish satirists. And the root °*wut* has a strange kinship with the Germanic name that is also recognizable in the English word *wood*. Furthermore, one of the poems from the Scandinavian *Edda* describes Odin as hanging from a tree (a shamanic ritual that can also be found in pagan Ireland), from which he frees himself by the strength of the runes he casts.

Odin-Wotan is the god of knowledge, the preeminent magician god, who cannot help but bring to mind Gwyddyon, son of Dôn (the Mother Goddess), hero of the fourth branch of the Welsh *Mabinogion*.[18] This is because Gwyddyon, while it does suggest the root word °*gwid*, meaning "science" (the Armorican Breton *gwiziek,* "scholar"), can also easily stem from the root of the Gallic *vidu,* meaning "tree" (this becomes *coit* in Middle Welsh before taking the form *coed*). The association may be even stronger; Gwyddyon is the hero of the strange Welsh poem attributed to the bard Taliesin, the *Cad Goddeu,* or "Combat of the Bushes,"[19] in which British warriors are transformed into trees thanks to his magic, or, rather, magic science.

If Odin-Wotan and Gwyddyon, both of whom are genuine Druidic gods, are connected to the ideas of science as well as wood, it is not unlikely that the Druids' name as well as their function share the same ambiguity. There should be nothing surprising about the relationship between science, especially religious and magic science, and the plant element. The fundamental myth of the Tree of Knowledge permeates the traditions of all peoples. And while the Druids are "those who know much," they are also the "People of the Tree," those who officiate and teach in the sacred clearings in the middle of the forests. This may well explain the presence and especially the magnificence of the cathedral of Chartres. Without falling into the romanticism of Chateaubriand, who saw an exaltation of the forest in the Gothic vaulting, one may wonder about the continuity that sought to erect a "forest of stone" entirely dedicated to the

---

18. See Jean Markale, *L'Épopée celtique en Bretagne,* 3rd ed. (Paris: Payot, 1983), 59–76.

19. See Markale, *Les Grandes Bardes gallois,* new ed. (Paris: Picollece, 1981), 74–81.

Virgin of Wisdom right in the heart of an ancient forest that was sacred at the time of the Druids.

These fairly general considerations make the sanctuary of the Carnutes stand out. It was a place of worship, a gathering place, a place of knowledge, and the *omphalos* of Gaul. The problem is its exact location. Caesar's testimony, as we have seen, in incontestable as to the existence of the sanctuary, but unfortunately the proconsul did not specify the site.

So it has been said that Beauce means "clearing." But the study of Beauce place-names reveals an almost complete absence of names of Gallic origin, except in the Eure Valley. The toponymy of the Beauce is eminently French, not even Gallo-Roman, and scarcely Gallo-French. One explanation suggests itself: The villages and towns there were founded relatively recently, which suggests that the place was formerly sparsely inhabited. It is tempting to propose that a vast forest, cleared at a later date, extended throughout the region. There is a strong probability that the Beauce does represent the territory of the ancient Carnutes.

Two possible sites for the sanctuary mentioned by Caesar have been suggested. The first is Saint-Benoît-sur-Loire, the former Fleury-sur-Loire in the southeastern confines of the Carnute land. Caesar said the sanctuary was located on the border of Carnute territory. Some arguments in favor of this identification are reasonable. Fleury was close to the frontier separating the Carnutes from the Senones of Sens. As noted by the great Celtic specialist Joseph Loth, Fleury-sur-Loire is an equal distance from Lake Constance, the Raz de Seine, the mouths of the Rhine, and the Garonne Valley. It is the exact center of ancient Gaul, close not only to the frontier with the Senones but also to the frontiers of the Biturigii and the Éduens. That is not positive proof, for an *omphalos* does not have to be the geographical center of a country; the example of the Irish Tara makes this sufficiently clear. But Fleury-sur-Loire is at the center of a triangle in which significant archaeological discoveries of Gallic objects have been made, with the finds at Neuvy-en-Sulias being particularly revealing of a sacred area.[20] Finally, the erection of the famous monastery that became Saint-Benoît-sur-Loire on this site cannot be due to chance. The Benedictines, the first monastic order organized in the West, merged quite quickly with the Colombanians of Irish origin during the Merovingian era under the aegis of Saint Colomban and his disciples, the most active element in Christianity.

But a number of Celtic customs and concepts made their way through this channel into continental monachism. An examination of the Romanesque capitals of Saint-Benoît-sur-Loire provides undeniable evidence of an Irish Celtic influence, if only in the sphere of symbolic decoration. Moreover, the Abbey of Fleury was one of the beacons of Western Christianity, one of the religious and even political poles of Gaul, and then France, during the first half of the Middle Ages, before being surpassed and marginalized by the founding of Cluny and then Citeaux. There is nothing incongruous about making the Romanesque Abbey of Fleury-sur-Loire the continuation of the sacred sanctuary of the Carnutes—quite the contrary.

There is one major objection to Fleury-sur-Loire as the site of the sanctuary, which takes nothing away from the site, nor from the importance of the Benedictine Abbey, nor from the Celtic survivals that can be seen there. Caesar, who passed through it several times with his troops, knew the site. It is not a remote location in the middle of the forest. It was in the neighborhood of a heavily traveled route. If it had been the location of this large central sanctuary, Caesar would not have failed to mention it.

A second hypothesis places the Carnutes' sanctuary in Suèvres, in Loir-et-Cher, on the banks of the Loire east of Blois. Suèvres is the ancient Sodobria, otherwise called Sodo-Brivum, at the intersection of a number of Roman roads (Gallic roads renovated by the Romans), from Paris to Blois, from Chartres to Bourges and

---

20. These small bronze ritual objects are currently on display at the Orléanais Museum in Orléans. But while their spirit is clearly Celtic, their manufacture is Gallo-Roman, therefore after the conquest.

Poitiers, and from Orléans to Tours. Suèvres is at the eastern borders of Carnute territory, but still fairly far from the frontier shared with the Biturigii on the south and the western border with the Turones. The territory around Suèvres is also quite rich in archaeological finds, and numerous remnants of prehistoric, Gallic, and Roman constructions can be seen there. Furthermore, a strange stone carved with symbolic motifs has been discovered there that unfailingly brings to mind an *omphalos,* like the famous Fal Stone at Tara in Ireland or the now less renowned Meigle Stone in Scotland, or again the *omphalos* of Kermaria in Brittany, or, finally, back in Ireland, in County Galway, the Stone of Turoe.[21]

But the identification of Suèvres as the central sanctuary of the Carnutes also runs into a very serious objection. If the sanctuary had been in this location, given its importance and renown, its use would have been extended, as in Saint-Benoît-sur-Loire, by a Christian building. Now all that is left at Suèvres is a small village much like any other. The permanent nature of the cults and the concern to ensure the permanence of the concept of the "navel" of the world would have contributed to making Suèvres an important religious site. This is simply not the case, and it weighs heavily against the argument for this site.

So just where is that ghostly and yet real sanctuary of all of Gaul, which could gather a crowd of Druids and their faithful at this Samhain festival that all descriptions concur in describing as grandiose? A third hypothesis emerges: Chartres.

One of the foremost arguments in favor of Chartres as this site is the Beauce, once an ancient forest that was cleared only in rela-

---

21. The Fal Stone on the hill of Tara was the magic stone that "shouted when a future king sat upon it." It was a sacred stone in the ideal center of the world where the visible and invisible merged. The Meigle Stone, which is of Pictish origin, offers the division of the world in four directions with four figures forming an authentic swastika. The Stone of Kermaria, currently in the Quimper Museum, is of Gallo-Roman manufacture, but with archaic elements. As for the Stone of Turoe, which sits currently in a field that is not its place of origin, it is covered by undecipherable symbolic motifs.

tively recent times. Chartres's position is ideal for a sanctuary, and moreover, Chartres is still a sanctuary. A second element is that Chartres is the sole place to have preserved the name of the Carnutes. People can continue to vainly claim that Cenabum was the most important settlement of the Carnutes, but it is not Cenabum that perpetuates the name of those who once lived there. So why then Chartres, which does not appear to have been a settlement of much importance during the time of Caesar? Caesar did not even mention it. It is probably because Autricum's role was more religious than economic or military, and the city has never ceased to play this religious role. A third argument is that Chartres is located not in the middle of the former Carnutes' land, but far to the north, and quite close to its frontiers with the Aulerci Cenomani and the Aulerci Eburovices. From the geographical perspective, there is no reason to think that the Autricum mound could not have been the religious center mentioned by Caesar, far removed from the major routes and in the heart of a forest that until that time had been more or less impenetrable.

But there is a fourth argument, which, in a roundabout way, is no less interesting. It concerns the presence of a hillock to the east that is almost a twin to the mound on which the cathedral sits and a mysterious saint by the name of Chéron, who would have been an apostle of the Chartrian area. The legend of Saint Chéron is distinctly edifying. He was a native of Rome, of a rich family, who succeeded in his studies and had been ordained a deacon. After giving away all his worldly possessions to the poor (a classic theme in this kind of story), he was sent to Gaul by Saint Clement, accompanied by Saint Denis and Saint Pothin. (The inclusion of "Saint" Denis, who is merely the Christianized version of the dismembered god from the pre-Hellenic Dionysios tradition, is enough to give food for thought as to the historical value of this legend.)

During his journey, Chéron performed several miracles, and on his arrival in Chartres, where he found a small Christian community, he healed a paralysis victim, which prompted numerous conversions straightaway. Having made up his mind to go to Paris, he stopped on a butte to the east of the city and asked his companions, in the event that he died, to bury him at that very spot. It so happens that several leagues farther along in his journey, in a place that has since acquired his name (Saint-Chéron-du-Chemin), the unfortunate saint was attacked by brigands and decapitated. The next day, his friends, alerted in a dream to what had transpired, made their way to the place Chéron had chosen to house his tomb. There they found the saint's body, miraculously transported to the spot by angels. They buried him there. The site became Saint-Chéron, a monastery was built on the mound, and numerous miracles were obtained through the saint's intercession.

This pretty and pious story was especially widespread after the ninth century, and it served the Chartres clergy well. Sadly, it arose from a confusion of the facts, which would be fairly amusing on its own and merely food for jest if it did not contain an important element concerning the original site of the Carnutes' sanctuary. According to R. Joly, on this mound named Saint-Chéron, "there existed, in near proximity to the beginning of the road to Paris, an ancient cemetery in which Christians had been buried and which would soon after become a venerated site that in Gallo-Latin was called a *sanctus caraunus*. After the Gallic language had fallen into oblivion, no one remembered what the term meant, and it was imagined that Caraunus was a man's name, specifically the name of one of those buried there, for whom piety invented the edifying life of an apostle and martyr."[22]

In other words, the name Chéron is derived from *caraunus*, but this word is not a proper name; it is a common noun whose root is exactly the same as that for the Carnutes. The phrase *sanctus caraunus* simply means "holy mound" or "sacred mound." This is significant, for Carnutes may mean "People of the Mound." It

---

22. Roger Joly, *L'Histoire de Chartres* (Roanne, France: Horvath, 1982), 218.

becomes quite arresting given that the sacred sanctuaries of the Gauls were located in clearings, most often atop mounds that were already sacred sites either by tradition or because of the presence of extremely ancient tombs. The mound of the religious and political center Tara in Ireland was also a burial ground dating from prehistoric times. It so happens that on the Saint-Chéron mound there was once a *charnier* [mass grave or charnel house], a term that comes from the same root word *carn,* which means this was a prehistoric or even Gallic cemetery. And it is likely that the name *sanctus caraunus* goes back to the earliest antiquity.[23]

During the time of the Carnutes, there was a funerary mound on the hillock that now bears Saint Chéron's name, thus in Chartres. Not far from there, one of the city's neighborhoods is called Quarter of the Covered Stones, which is proof that a certain number of megalithic monuments had been on this spot, dolmens or covered alleys in particular, providing another justification for the name of the Carnutes. And under these conditions, why couldn't there have been similar monuments on the mound on which the cathedral currently sits? This hypothesis at least has the merit of showing that a cathedral like this was not built on this site purely by chance, and that an ancient worship never utterly vanishes: It transforms and adapts to the new ideology.

It is impossible to believe that the famous sanctuary in which the Druids gathered at the time of Caesar and Vercingetorix has vanished without leaving a trace. It is the very presence of the mysterious Cathedral of Chartres.

---

23. All this has been demonstrated by Abbé Guy Villette in a large study made in 1975, one that remains unpublished because it is unsettling, but which has been deposited in the Toponymy Department of the National Archives, the Departmental Archives, and the Municipal Library of Chartres. Any excavation is currently impossible at Saint-Chéron, as the site has been entirely torn up by numerous construction projects.

8

GARGANTUA'S ITINERARY

here is an odd detail on the flagstone paving of the Chartres cathedral in the center of the labyrinth that church authorities once attempted to conceal from visitors. It is a copper nail that is struck at noon every June 24 by a ray of sunlight filtered through stained glass. This has inspired numerous analyses; many of them, unfortunately, sacrifice all common sense on behalf of utterly unverifiable esoteric theories. In fact, the nail is the survivor of three copper buttons placed in the labyrinth by a certain canon Estienne. This strange ecclesiastic was an ardent fan of mechanical engineering and astronomy, and he had obtained authorization to install a "meridian" inside the cathedral. He was also given permission to pierce a hole at the edge of a window to let through a ray of light. Where it falls on the floor is easy to mark at different times of the year, notably on solstices and equinoxes. Meridians of this kind, and sometimes more complex ones, also exist in other religious monuments like the church of Saint-Sulpice in Paris, just as there are labyrinths in other cathedrals, if only those in Reims and Amiens.

The explanation of this nail and the ray of light that strikes it on Saint John's Day in summer is therefore perfectly ordinary; there is no need to seek answers in the hazy and mysterious notions of currently popular esoteric traditions. But no insult is intended to the memory of Canon Estienne in claiming that he may well have had some idea he wanted to transmit. After all, even if it is only a simple meridian, it is the concept of the central point, the *omphalos,* that emerges, and everything seems to point to the possibility that Estienne had sought to reinforce, by a scientific device, the conviction that the cathedral is an ideal and sacred point in the storms of the cosmos.

The device does indeed involve a cosmic reference. The symbolism of the labyrinth is quite expressive. It depicts the universe in all its twists and turns, all its complexity, but also in its primal unity, because it holds the totality within. Furthermore, this simple and complex universe is projected on the ground, expressing the well-known principle "As above, so below." The human being enters the labyrinth, explores the universe, and finds his or her own path. This is the point where the Light comes in. It was not by chance that Canon Estienne sought to take advantage of the meanders of the Chartres labyrinth on which to spill a ray of light, even if the sworn purpose was one of purely scientific astronomy. Wouldn't this ray of light be Theseus confronted by the Minotaur, or even Apollo in the Delphic cavern battling against the serpent Python?

All this has a very tight correspondence with Gallic mythology and the folk tradition that is its incontestable heir. And this is the appropriate point at which to introduce Gargantua, even if, at first glance, it hardly seems possible that a giant skillfully recuperated by Rabelais could have any resonance with a sanctuary dedicated to the Virgin Mary—although the Virgin Mary is very often depicted stepping on a snake, and even crushing its head underfoot.

In Gallo-Roman statuary of Celtic inspiration—and specifically Celtic, despite the Roman technique—there is a statue type known as the Rider of the Anguiped. This is a mounted god shown striking down a giant serpent-tailed monster. According to the dedications, this god is Jupiter Optimus Maximus, meaning "the very good and very great Jupiter." He obviously has no features reminiscent of the

Roman Jupiter and must have been superimposed over a Gallic deity.

"The symbolism of these monuments," writes Duvall,

> is visibly of a cosmic, metaphysical order. As for the group itself that crowns the ensemble, it expresses the triumph of light that sees all over the hidden subterranean forces (as with the giant who appears to be emerging from the ground and his serpent-form nature that emphasizes his chthonian character—day getting the best of night, pure forces prevailing over the impure, perhaps eternal life over death, and occasionally, the imperial peace over the barbarian world). At present it is only in Gaul that this expression of the complex power of Jupiter has been found.[1]

It so happens that this divine figure incorporated into Jupiter is well known in Irish mythological tales: He is Dagda, the "good god," one of whose titles is Ollathir, meaning "Father of all." He is a kind of giant, a voracious glutton with sexual prowess that is magnified tenfold, father of the famous Brigit (also named Etain and Boann), goddess of poetry, music, eloquence, and crafts (a kind of Minerva), with whom, in a very revealing symbolic fashion, he has incestuous relations. This leads to the birth of the god Oengus, the Mac Oc, or Young Son. The extremely complex myth of Dagda holds the key to the problem raised by the "Virgin of the Druids." But on the Continent, this divine entity Dagda is represented by the character of Gargantua.

Rabelais did not invent Gargantua. He is a giant from folk tradition who left his memory not only in the collective unconscious but also in French toponymy long before Rabelais published his famous work in 1534. Embroidering on preexisting themes, Rabelais used this character from folklore to express his own ideas on humanism, tradition, philosophy, and religion. Two years before

---

1. Paul-Marie Duval, *Les Dieux de la Gaule* (Paris: Payot, 1978), 74.

Rabelais published his "Gargantua" in Lyon, a short anonymous story (probably by a certain Billon d'Issoudon) appeared in the same city entitled "Les Grandes et Inestimables Chroniques du grand et énorme géant Gargantua" [The Great and Inestimable Chronicles of the Great and Enormous Giant Gargantua]. Gargantua was a well-known figure, and the time was favorable for exploiting folk themes, as is shown by the success not only of Rabelais but of authors like Bonaventure des Périers and Marguerite de Navarre as well, who drew abundantly from what is called folklore.

The name Gargantua is Celtic. It can be seen in the simple form of Gargan in many place-names, not just in France but also throughout the rest of Europe (for example, Monte Gargano in Italy). Contrary to what is often claimed, the name is not derived from the Latin *gurgem,* meaning "throat" (a folk etymology suggested by the gluttonous nature of the character), but instead comes from two Celtic words that are quite recognizable in Armorican Breton, *gar* and *cam,* literally meaning "with curved thigh" or "lame."[2] Gargantua is one of the faces of the lame Indo-European god who is keeper of the "secret fire," meaning the light of intelligence, and whose physical defect paradoxically confers exceptional power.[3] In the Greek texts concerning the Gauls, those of Diodorus Siculus in

---

2. Likewise, Gargantua's mother, Gargamelle, derives from the same sources. Gargamelle is the "lame giantess." I first supported this etymology in my *Tradition celtique au Bretagne armoricaine* (Paris: Payot, 1975), 22–26, based on a folktale from Camors in Morbihan. This story presents an odd character, the gergant, who gets rid of his enemies by throwing salt on them. This is a known characteristic of the medieval devil Pantagruel (whom Rabelais likewise did not invent and whom he transformed into Gargantua's son). I again presented this etymology in my book *The Druids* (Rochester, Vt.: Inner Traditions, 1999). Up to the present, few authors have repeated this etymology even to contest it, except for Claude Gaignebet, in his magisterial and prominent work on Rabelais entitled *A plus haute Science* (Paris: Maisoneuve, 1986). This book is an exceptional tribute that highlights the importance of Rabelais in the transmission of popular culture, as well as the role he played in the attempt to regenerate a moribund Christianity by returning to the vital springs of mythology.

3. The most characteristic example is that of Odin-Wotan, who acquires his gift of clairvoyance by accepting the loss of one eye.

particular, the name Hercules has been superimposed. Hercules was a great traveler and destroyer of monsters but also a civilizing hero and founder of the sacred city of Alesia.[4]

In "Gargantua," Rabelais made the giant, or rather his mare, responsible for felling all the trees in what was to become the Beauce. Rabelais did not invent this; his source was "Les Grandes et Inestimables Chroniques." But the circumstances are not exactly the same, and it seems that the anonymous story that appeared in 1532 was closer to a mythological outline that remained strongly present in the collective memory.

The tale is actually connected to Arthurian tradition and involves the intervention of Merlin. On seeing King Arthur at odds with some dreadful enemies—in this instance, giants (a detail that corroborates the British tradition concerning an invasion of the British Isles by giants)—he decides to help the king and literally *manufactures* a giant. The story is quite strange and is worth a detour. "Merlin had himself transported to the highest mountain in the east, bringing with him a vial of Lancelot's blood that he had collected from his wounds. . . . Furthermore, he brought the nail clippings of the beautiful Guinivere, around ten pounds' worth." It sounds like a complete farce, but it is nothing of the sort. Lancelot is *the best knight in all the world* and Guinivere is the *absolute model of all women*—on the profane level, of course, as the Virgin Mary occupies this position on a higher level. Keep in

---

4. Alesia is a generic name given to several fortress sanctuaries in Gaul. There were nine of them in the territory of ancient Gaul, including Alise-Sainte-Reine of Burgundy. But no one, outside of the pseudo-archaeologists of Napoleon III, has claimed that Alise-Sainte-Reine was the Alesia of Vercingetorix and Caesar. All the texts concur in refuting this identification and placing Alesia in the Jura region, probably at Alaise or in Salins-les-Bains, especially in the painstaking research of Mr. Guichot of Besançon, an ardent proponent of the site of Fort-Saint-André on a hill above Salins-les-Bains, a site that currently seems to be the most propitious. The authentic Gergovis placed on the Merdogne Plateau by a decree of Napoleon III is actually located on the fortification that rises near Clermont-Ferrand. What is most important in the legend of Gargantua is that this figure is connected to the founding of a sanctuary, a revealing facet of his divine role.

mind the clue concerning *the highest mountain in the east.*

"Merlin created an anvil of steel as large as a tower and three hammers to match, which he beat so impetuously it sounded like thunder coming down from the skies." Next, "he had the bones of a bull whale brought in and poured the blood from the aforementioned vial upon them; and set them atop the anvil; and rapidly these bones were reduced to powder; and then by the heat of the sun, the anvil, and the hammers the father of Gargantua was engendered. Afterward, Merlin brought in the bones of a cow whale and mixed them with the queen's nail clippings, which he then placed upon the anvil as before, and from this powder was created the mother of Gargantua." Nor did Merlin neglect to shape a "huge mare" from a carcass he found on the mountain.

The details of the bull whale and the cow whale invite a smile. But the entire literature of the beginning of the sixteenth century rests on an accumulation of wordplay, of which Rabelais remains the best-known exponent. Rather than viewing this story as a joke, note the sun's intervention and the role it plays in the properly artisanal manufacture of Grandgousier and Gargamelle, as these are the figures being described. In "whale" (*baleine* in French) is the name, or rather title, of the Gallic god of light, Belenos, meaning "the Shining One," whose consort is Belisama, "the Very Shining One." If we understand this "fable" correctly, the manufacture of Grandgousier and Gargamelle and then the conception of Gargantua *on the highest mountain in the east,* we will have more than one link with the sun's course across the sky, especially as that course ends at Mont-Saint-Michel, meaning the western edge of the world. Couldn't Gargantua's itinerary be the journey of Light inside a definite cycle?

The anonymous tale from Lyon takes a salacious turn here, but it leads to the birth of Gargantua. When he reached the age of seven, on the advice of Merlin, Grandgousier, Gargamelle, and the giant child mounted the large mare and left the mountain of the east, heading west. The itinerary begins to become interesting here. Following a huge leap by the mare that carries them to Rome (why not?), we find the travelers in Switzerland, Germany, then Lorraine. The geography is fanciful, although it is, in the author's opinion, for the use of "all good knights and gentlemen," an elegant way of saying that one should read between the lines. From here the journey's direction becomes quite precise. It is necessary to go toward Champagne and the Beauce so as to end the journey at Mont-Saint-Michel.

The journey of Gargantua can be reconstructed with the help of valuable clues provided by place-names and the study of folk traditions. The places said to bear Gargantua's imprint are countless, but it is necessary to be selective. Incontestably, the large mare takes Gargantua and his parents through Grand in the Haute-Saône, which is a *locus consecratus,* a sanctuary dedicated to Grannus, one of the cognomens of the Gallic Apollo. The word *grannus* has the same origin as the Gaelic word *grian,* which means "sun." A derivative of this word can be found in the name of the heroine of Irish epics, Grainne, who is a prototype for Yseult the Fair. Furthermore, a very interesting Rider of the Anguiped statue has been discovered in Grand, which obviously brings us back to the labyrinth of Chartres.

The journey continues. The travelers find themselves in Troyes in Champagne, the mysterious city where a converted Jew, Chrétien de Troyes, was the first to that date to dare write about the Grail, and also the first systematically to depict Lancelot of the Lake as the lover of Queen Guinivere, which was not the case in the original versions of the Arthurian legend. The city of Troyes was an important center for propagating the medieval Jewish Kabbalah. Troyes also witnessed the early development of the Cathar groups and the gatherings of the first Templars. Gargantua's stop in Troyes has an undeniably symbolic value that connects the legend of the giant to a great many other traditions.

But from there, still in the direction of the setting sun, they must next proceed to Sens, the fortress city of the Sénons (meaning "the Ancient Ones"), the capital of the Fourth Division of the Lyonnaise Province and a religious metropolis for a good portion of Gaul, including the city of the Parisii and that of the Carnutes. There is a Roman road going from Sens to Orléans, and this road passes Château-Landon, where "Les Grandes Chroniques" maintains Gargantua fought in battle, then goes by Sceaux du Gâtinais, which is a former thermal spa (Aquae Segestae). The following leg of the journey is Toury, where there is a dolmen called "gravois de Gargantua." It is also told how the giant drew the water out of the Moret Pond, then returned on the next day and filled in the hole he had left by exhaling all the water. This brings us to the borders of Champagne and the Beauce, the frontiers of the territories belonging to the Sénons and the Carnutes:

> When the large mare was inside the forests of Champagne, the flies began stinging her rear, she who had a tail some thousand feet long and equally wide. She began swishing it, and the large oaks began falling as if they were thin as reeds; and the beast continued in such a fashion that not a single tree was left standing and all lay broken on the ground.
>
> And thus was the Beauce made, for at present there is no wood, and the people of this region are compelled to heat with straw or thatch.

In this same Beauce there can be found at least a dozen megaliths whose origins are attributed to Gargantua. And there are also traditions:

> One day, Gargantua was traveling in the Beauce bearing a load of wood on his back. Taken by hunger, he entreated an old woman he met leading a herd of cattle to give him something to eat. The old woman offered to let him restore himself from her herd, and he ate all of them. As compensation, he left the herdswomen his load of wood, which kept her warm that entire winter."[5]

---

5. *Bulletin de la Société des excursions scientifiques* 5 (1904): 78.

We might think we were hearing a very distorted version of Hercules stealing the cattle of Geryon and hiding them in a cave.

So here we have Grandgousier, Gargamelle, and Gargantua in the Beauce. That the mare knocks down the trees of the ancient forest of the Carnutes should be considered symbolic of a civilizing activity. But this action can be twofold. On the one hand, it involves clearing the land to allow the planting of wheat; on the other hand, it also concerns the establishment in this wilderness of a *spiritual wealth* that, in his very persona, Gargantua represents. Just as Hercules, transposed by the Greek Diodorus Siculus into the oral Gallic stories he recorded, is revealed as a civilizing hero who weds the king's daughter and restores peace and harmony in a still-savage land in which he founds a sanctuary—in this instance Alesia—Gargantua's passage through the land of the Carnutes leaves behind an essential transformation of the countryside, including the famous clearing belonging to the Druids.

It seems that the anonymous tale of "Les Grandes Chroniques" strongly emphasized this passage through the Beauce. From here, Gargantua continues his journey to the west. He arrives in the Perche region. It is snowing—as related in a folktale collected by the great folklorist of the Beauce and Perche regions Filleul-Pétigny—and the snow prevents the giant from walking quickly. So he takes off his shoes, and his two boots remain on this site near Mortagne-au-Perche. They are now two buttes whose names are Champaillaume and Chartrage. The latter name is quite significative with respect to Gargantua's itinerary.

The remaining part of the journey is uneventful, if one may say so. Gargantua and his parents follow the "uphill path," which is the itinerary of the pilgrimage toward Mont-Saint-Michel, through Sées, the former capital of the Sagii, the residential seat of a bishopric. From there they cross through the large Norman forests, over the crossroads of Goult and Carrouges, which is a *quadrivium,* near which there is a very hard rock that bears a kind of groove-shaped depression said to be an imprint left by Gargantua's chariot. This is followed by the Andaines Forest and Domfront, with its Breech of Gargantua, which according to local tradition holds on one of its sides an opening that leads to a Cave of the Dragon. Next is Mortain, where lurks the memory of a mysterious saint Gorgon, who could well be a Christianized form of the giant; and Saint-Hilaire-du-Harcouet, not far from the Sée River, whose waves are said to have been "swollen" by Gargantua's urine. The route now opens onto Mont-Saint-Michel, Mont-Dol, and Tombelaine, which, as everyone knows, are three boulders thrown by Gargantua as an expression of his great anger against the inhabitants of this region. But it should not be overlooked that Tombelaine formerly shared with Mont-Saint-Michel the name Mont-Bélénos. As Dontenville notes:

> Certain topographical facts strike the observer with surprise. Barring omission, France possesses only two places called Tomb(e)laine. They are separated by a great distance. One is the rock . . . in the bay of Mont-Saint-Michel; the other is Tomblaine in Lorraine, on a ford of the Meurthe, a little upstream from Nancy, a ford that was still important during the fifteenth century and from which a polished and perforated ax has been pulled. The butte may have been razed, but what is striking in any case is that to within a decigrade, the Lorraine Tomblaine and the Norman Tombelaine are on the same parallel, the 65 G7 or 8.[6]

This means that Gargantua's journey as described in "Les Grandes Chroniques" is not due to chance. He leaves from somewhere in the neighborhood of Mont-Donon, the Celtic equivalent of Mecca, to end up at Mont-Tombe—in other words, at a Mont-Bélénos, which also served as a mecca for Celtic spirituality before it became one of the most remarkable Christian sanctuaries in the whole West. And this itinerary necessarily passed through the

---

6. Henri Dontenville, *La Mythologie française* (Paris: Payot, 1973), 112.

Beauce, meaning the land of the Carnutes, which housed the great central sanctuary for all of Gaul. There is food for thought here. This journey is necessarily *sacred,* symbolic. It goes from east to west following the path of the sun. Its starting point is a sanctuary consecrated to Belenos, and it ends at another sanctuary consecrated to Belenos.

Again, this itinerary went through the Beauce. The name of Chartres is not explicitly mentioned, but it is significant that there are a large number of megaliths attributed to Gargantua all around Chartres. And what to think of the Chartrage Butte in Mortagne-au-Perche, which lies outside the land of the Carnutes but is in the direction of the setting sun?

The first observation is the evidence that Belenos must have something in common with Gargantua. Belenos is only a title meaning "brilliant" or "shining," and this title can be conferred on any deity, provided the god sufficiently evokes the idea of *light.* Certainly, Gargantua's itinerary looks just like a diurnal course of the sun, but that does not mean that Gargantua-Belenos (the attribution of the title suggests itself) is a solar god. In fact, the Celts *never had had a solar god,* with all due deference to those who literally accept the nomenclature of Latin authors; given that they were writing for a Roman audience, they could only superimpose Roman names over Gallic names.

The transition of Gargantua to Grand should shed some light on this delicate subject. It was the Romans who identified Grannus with Apollo. They also clearly identified Borvo, the name of the god of springs, with this same Apollo. And it is quite likely that Mont-Bélénos, before becoming Mont-Tombe and Mont-Saint-Michel, may have been a Mont-Mercure. Does this mean that the Romans also identified Belenos with Mercury? That seems entirely possible, given that the Gallic Mercury is none other than the pan-Celtic god Lugh, Master of All the Arts, a radiant but not a solar figure. All the more likely, for Mercury was often dethroned by Saint Michael, the shining archangel who also could never be mistaken for any kind of solar symbol. Grannus, the name bestowed on the city of Grand, is a masculine form explained by the tendency of the Romans to consider their most important gods male. No one has ever said that the Gauls, before the arrival of the Romans, worshipped a solar *god* by the name of Grannus. The masculine form may conceal a feminine form. After all, Roman mythology is not exempt from such reversals, and the famous Janus could well be a masculinization of an ancient Goddess of the Beginnings by the name of Di-Anus, literally meaning "old woman deity." Why not use as a reference the Irish word *grian*, meaning "sun"? It is feminine, as are all the names for the sun in all Celtic and Germanic languages.

It is therefore linguistically unthinkable that the Celts, or the Germans for that matter, had a *solar god.* An episode recorded in the *Book of Conquests,* a vast compilation of the most archaic traditions put together in Ireland in the twelfth century, is quite meaningful in this regard. It concerns the arrival in Ireland of the Sons of Milo, meaning the Gaels. They find themselves in the presence of the Tuatha de Danaan, the earlier occupants who are in fact the race of Celtic gods. Now the Tuatha de Danaan (meaning the "peoples of the Goddess Dana"—again the concept of a mother goddess) had three kings, named Mac Cuill, Mac Cecht, and Mac Greine, grandson of Dagda (therefore the equivalent of Gargantua), who were married to the three queens, Banba, Eriu, and Fotla (all three eponymous with Ireland).

The text states: "Mac Cuill, meaning Sethor, the hazel was his god; Mac Cecht, meaning Tethor, the plow was his god; Mac Greine, meaning Cethor, the sun was his god."[7] As Son of the Hazel, Mac Cuill is representative of the Druidic function, hazel *(coll)* being a tree used in magic and divinatory practices. As Son of the Plow, Mac Cecht is representative of the producing class, with the specific characteristic that his function concerns agriculture. He would

---

7. *Textes mythologiques irlandais,* vol. 1, trans. Christian-Jacques Guyonvarc'h (Rennes, France: Ogam-Celticum, 1980), 14.

therefore be a laborer god, an exception among the Irish, who were essentially a people of herders, not farmers. This is, in fact, the sole mention of such a deity in Irish mythology. Finally, as Son of the Sun (think of *sun* as a feminine noun), Mac Greine can only represent the second class, that of warriors. This is the functional tripartition common to all Indo-European peoples. The main issue is why the warrior class is under the patronage of the sun.

The explanation resides entirely in the role of Woman, not only in Celtic society, but also in that society's foundational myths. Woman appears as the true keeper of sovereignty, and she divides this sovereignty among the warriors, who are the driving forces of this potentiality. This is shown quite clearly in some Irish epics, mainly those concerning Queen Medbh of Connaught, who "bestowed the friendship of her thighs" to any warrior she needed to ensure the success of a mission or to guarantee the integrity of her people's joint property. It is also a latent presence in the medieval Arthurian epics in which Queen Guinivere is the absolute center of Arthurian chivalry, inspiring each knight to work toward the good of the collective she symbolically embodies.

Finally, it is what emerges from an intensive analysis of the famous courtly love of the twelfth and thirteenth centuries, in which the Lady is seen to be the center and pivotal point of every action, every deed, and all transcendence. Courtly love—a literary style, of course, but also a philosophy of male and female relations[8]— reveals itself at the very moment when the cult of the Virgin Mary, absolute model of all women, imposed itself as it did in Christian Europe. The symbolism is clear: The sun is the dispenser of heat and light, and it is toward the sun that the stars, who owe it their lives and their movement, gravitate. The example of Yseult the Fair, a historicized image of an ancient solar goddess, is positive proof.

In some versions of the legend, Tristan cannot live for more than

---

8. See Jean Markale, *Courtly Love* (Rochester, Vt.: Inner Traditions, 2000).

a month without physical contact with Yseult, otherwise he will lose his strength and die. Is this not a clue that Tristan is a *moon-man*, whereas Yseult is a *sun-woman*? The same is true in Germano-Scandinavian mythology. When the hero Sigurd-Siegfried, after killing the dragon Fafnir and his initiator Regin—and therefore in possession of supernatural powers—frees the sleeping Valkyrie, the myth becomes quite explicit, even if the three or four versions of the episode vary as to the details. This Valkyrie, clad in a warrior's breast-plate, is in the middle of a castle surrounded by a wall of flames. The hero crosses through the flames and frees—or conquers—the Valkyrie. Subsequently, Sigurd-Siegfried's fate is undeniably and inexorably linked to that of the Valkyrie, as that of Tristan is linked to Yseult following the test of the potion.[9]

The castle surrounded by flames is the sun and the Valkyrie at its center is the sun goddess. As everyone knows, the Valkyries, the "seekers of heroes," are essentially women warriors. There may be a connection with one of the functions of the Virgin Mary, specifically at Chartres: "We do not see that the Virgin of Chartres ever had any association with the fertility of the earth," observes Saillens. "And, conversely, we have observed that she was a warrior; she contributed to the victory of Bouvines; she convinced Edward III to sign the peace of Brétigny; her replica at the Drouaise Gate routed the Huguenots."[10] It should never be forgotten that Our Lady of Chartres is a triumphant Virgin.

This illustrates the complexity that surrounds the divine solar figure of the Celts. More generally, it raises a matter concerning all the Indo-European peoples. It is not so certain that originally the Greeks, and even less so the Romans, had a true solar god. Among the Germans it is even more vague, and it is not enough to classify this or that figure as a "solar hero" to resolve the enigma. The situation is just as confused among the Indo-Persians, despite the

9. See Jean Markale, *Siegfried ou l'Or du Rhin* (Paris: Retz, 1984).
10. E. Saillens, *Nos Vierges noires* (Paris: Universelles, 1945), 199.

recently introduced Indian Surya and Ahura-Mazda, who was essentially the ontological Light, opposed to Ahriman, the darkness, in the framework of the Zoroastrian philosophical system. The Mithra of the Roman era, the *Sol invictus,* no longer had anything in common with the Vedic Mithra and was content to borrow the sun's symbolism. Then there were the Scythians, who remained much more archaic and had a solar goddess, the famous and cruel "Scythian Diana" who animates the legend of Orestes and Iphigenia and whom the Greeks made into their Artemis by softening her character to a considerable extent—and, more important—with a kind of astrological transposition gave her the features of a lunar goddess. There was no myth comparable to Osiris among the Indo-Europeans. Does this mean that solar worship is not of Indo-European origin?

This is a difficult question to answer categorically. It seems that the solar cult, of Nordic origin, was primarily the work of the peoples antedating the Celts, particularly the megalith builders and the peoples of the Bronze Age. In any case, it has been proved, thanks to archaeological finds, that solar worship flourished, particularly on the shores of the Baltic, during the entire Bronze Age. So it is possible to suggest some hypotheses. For example, it has been said that Belenos "could well be the Celticized representative of the Bronze Age solar worship."[11] And the famous temple of Stonehenge in England, which dates from the latter part of the Neolithic era and was laid out during the Bronze Age, is definitely a good example of this archaic devotion to the daystar.[12] But beyond the physical proofs for the existence of this worship, we know strictly nothing about the metaphysical implications that justify it.

The Gallic Belenos, who seems so important, has a kind of female equivalent, Belisama (very shining one), who has left traces in the toponymy of the Perche region, if nowhere else, with Bellême

---

11. Guy Rachet, *La Gaule celtique, des origines à 50 avant J.C.* (Paris: J'ai Lu 1975), 148.

12. See Jean Markale, *Carnac et l'énigme de l'Atlantide* (Paris: Pygmalion, 1987).

(Orne), not far from a sacred spring in the forest, a spring dedicated to "infernal gods." In Vaison-la-Romaine, in the land of the Gallic Voconces, an inscription in Greek letters to Belisami has been discovered. In Saint-Lizier (Ariège), an important religious center of the Middle Ages, another inscription, in Latin this time, makes Belisama the agnomen of Minerva. But in Bath, England, a renowned site for water worship, a goddess by the name of Sul was venerated during the time of the Brito-Romans. Caius Julius Solinus also combined her with Minerva while specifying that a flame burn perpetually in her temple, which brings to mind the fire maintained at Kildare (Ireland) in honor of the goddess Brigit, and later in the Christian Abbey in memory of Saint Brigitte. By all evidence, Sul is a name for the sun and designates a sun goddess.

So why then Minerva, who is one of the five deities cited by Caesar in his *Commentaries*? A connection has been suggested between the sparkling of fire and Minerva, daughter of the god of the sky, as the personification of lightning. This is not a very convincing argument. It would perhaps be better to envision the problem from the angle of the Celtic Minerva, who is incontestably the Irish Brigit, who is a *triple goddess,* meaning she has three faces or three names. This was quite common among the Celts, the Gauls in particular, who always represented their mother goddesses (the *matronae*) in groups of three. Now, this triple Brigit, daughter of Dagda, is simultaneously Boann (the deification of the Boyne River), Bodbh (the crow), and Morrigan (the "great queen," goddess of love and war). But as Brigit (meaning "the powerful one"), she is also Etain (meaning "the reborn") and Macha (the mounted goddess). Interestingly, this deity is simultaneously a poetess (therefore a Druid), a warrior, and mistress of the crafts and sciences. She therefore on her own covers *all* the Indo-European functions. If there is an image that prompted the crafting of the Theotokos, it is clearly that of Brigit, the powerful goddess with the luminous, solar nature, the bestower of knowledge, strength, and wisdom. On the metaphysical plane, wouldn't she correspond precisely to that radiant, triumphant Virgin Mary who is also the Throne of Wisdom, which the Church sought to represent at Chartres?

This is what makes Gargantua's itinerary, as it has made its way down to us from an anonymous fifteenth-century story, so important. That story incorporated a long series of traditions going very far back, in what some call a French mythology but which is truly Celtic in essence. Gargantua, presented as a civilizing hero, loses none of his ambiguous nature: He builds but also destroys. Now these exactly match the characteristics of the Irish Dagda, who is his equivalent. Dagda owns a club of a very special kind. When the god strikes an adversary with one end of the club, he kills him. But when he strikes a dead man with the other end, he resuscitates him. A splendid image of godly ambivalence!

And Dagda-Gargantua, during the course of his journey—which could be a veritable pilgrimage to the source—institutes sanctuaries: Tomblaine; Saint-Benoît-sur Loire; Cléry, near Orléans (where there is a famous Black Madonna); Chartres; Mortagne-au-Perche, not far from Bellême with its Chartrage Butte; Sées (where a renowned statue of Our Lady was worshipped); Carrouges, where, as should be the case at every crossroads, Hecate protects nightly travelers; Domfront (where there is a very beautiful Romanesque church, Notre-Dame-sur-l'Eau); Mortain, with the memory of the mysterious "Saint" Gorgon; and finally Mont-Saint-Michel, the ancient Tombelaine. This pilgrimage itinerary follows the course of the sun. Gargantua gives his journey a luminous coloration. And when passing through Chartres, he establishes the *clearing,* meaning the Beauce, with all its resonances with the great central sanctuary of Gaul in the land of the Carnutes, those People of the Mound who have preserved for all time both the memory of the dead buried in the mounds and the complex rituals to evoke the Divine.

Gargantua is a luminous hero and folkloricized image of an ancient god who brings to humanity not only sunlight but also the light of Intelligence, the divine fire, that secret fire of the alchemists. Gargantua is the lame god of the old Indo-European mythologies.

But the physical defect that characterizes him magnifies his power and his ability to be the quickest and the most skilled, in the same way that the one-eyed Odin was the preeminent Seer, he who could see elsewhere. In the statuary of the chapels of Armorican Brittany, the blind bard Saint Hervé is often depicted led by a dog who physically guides him, but he holds a book in his hand. He is able to read this book because it is immaterial, a symbol of wisdom and inner knowledge. It is necessary to understand the Black Madonna in the same way, as afflicted with an apparent flaw that masks and magnifies her power. If she is covered in black, does this not make it easier to grasp that she holds the Light within?

The cathedral of Chartres answers this question in the affirmative: Everything here is conceived, built, and organized to allow divine wisdom, the wisdom hidden beneath the dark features of the Virgin, to shine. It is in vain that one opens the doors to enter the sanctuary. One must resolve to accept once and for all that these doors are not the most important, because there is always a door on the inside. The invitation of the builders of Chartres is therefore very clear-cut: Seek the *real* door, that of the Light.

9

OUR LADY OF
UNDER GROUND

In Chartres, although the statue known as Our Lady of the Pillar is the most ancient, and although she is a Black Madonna, it is Our Lady of Under Ground that most excites the imagination and, more significant, the piety of the faithful. The relatively young age of the statue in the crypt of the cathedral cannot drive from people's minds that it was Our Lady of Under Ground who, in tandem with the so-called Tunic of the Virgin, inspired popular piety and ensured Chartres's success as a place of pilgrimage from the early Middle Ages on.

It goes without saying that the name Our Lady of Under Ground is not exempt from this notoriety. There is something mysterious and secret about it, not so much because it can lend itself to so many analyses of the possible discovery in a cave of a statue going back to great antiquity, but because the notion of the *subterranean* speaks to the collective unconscious. The Virgin is the model and most perfect example of the Mother. What, then, could be more normal than highlighting the "subterranean"—the cave, which is the most common feminine and maternal symbol, and, in the final analysis, the most concrete—to demonstrate that humanity is the daughter of the Earth Mother?

All that concerns Our Lady of Under Ground, however, gets lost in an artistic vagary of the most beautiful effect. Historians as well as theologians have great difficulty finding their bearings in a labyrinth that, without trying to make a play on words, threatens to remain as mysterious as the one that can be seen on the floor of the current cathedral. If Gargantua has been transformed into a kind of Beauce pilgrim—he who is the likeness of an ancient Celtic deity who existed long before Christianity—it must surely be accepted that his journey to Chartres could not have been due to chance. And while the Chartres clergy, during the Middle Ages and even after, did all they could to lend credence to the notion that Our Lady of Chartres was unlike all the other Virgins, that she was unique and, most important, "pre-Christian," it is most probably because they had in their possession elements that may have been secret and mysterious but which were nonetheless indicative of a thoroughly historical reality.

That these elements were problematic and at the very least suspected of being pagan is incontestable. That these pagan elements were recuperated and transposed because they could not be uprooted from ancestral folk memory is absolutely beyond the shadow of a doubt. The statue of Our Lady of Under Ground, whatever may be said about it, whatever its exact origin, whatever the motivations behind the clergy's magnification of it, raises certain questions that touch the history of religions and religious doctrine itself as well as archaeology and history proper.

To examine these questions, we must search among the various texts for those that are, if not the most reliable (there cannot be any scientific reliability in matters of religion), at least the most ancient. They can shed some useful light on the supporters of a Marian worship that has a historical reality, even if this reality can only be proved to have existed in relatively recent periods.

Only a document from 1389 known under the title of *Vieille Chronique* makes any formal confirmation of the worship given to Our Lady of Under Ground. This text is a collection of traditions concerning the origins of Chartres written by an anonymous cleric on the orders of then Bishop Jean Lefèvre;[1] it was inserted in the manuscript of the *Cartulaire de Chartres* between a list of miracles that occurred in the cathedral and an obituary. The bishop of Chartres's motive was to cut short the legends that were circulating at that time and to clarify matters to some extent, at least officially, and in compliance with the most orthodox position. The author claims to have interviewed elderly people who told him that the church of Chartres was founded long before the birth of Christ, in honor of a Virgin ready to give birth to a savior. These same individuals added that a prince of that land, in approval of this foundation, had made the image of a Virgin holding a child on her lap, which was placed in a secret place next to the idols and immediately worshipped by the people of the region; the *pontiffs of the idols* presided over the ceremonies that took place at this site.

It should be noted, as it is quite important, that the word *druids* does not appear in the manuscript. It exists only on a page inserted during the sixteenth century. What is certain is that this 1389 manuscript mentions a kind of Marian devotion that *preceded Christianity* and specifically states that this devotion was analogous to the worship of idols.

Several decades before the writing of the *Vieille Chronique,* the chapters of almost all the churches in France had supported, before Pope John XXII in 1322, the claims of the church of Chartres to be the oldest in all France. They had even declared: "Accepted that the Benevolent Virgin, mother of God, had chosen for her venerable temple, when she lived among men, the church of Chartres . . ." Such concurrence is amazing, considering how many churches and monasteries of the time quarreled incessantly over which was oldest. So what does this consensus on Chartres mean? Had they forgotten that the first church of the Gauls was in Lyon? To present such

---

1. The exact title is *Tractatum de aliquibus nobilitatem Carnotensis ecclesiae tangentibus,* meaning "Treatise of things touching on the nobility of the church of the Carnutes." See M. Jusselin, "Les Traditions de l'église de Chartres," in *Memoires de la Société archéologique d'Eure-et-Loir* 15: 1 ff., 100 ff.

claims, they must have had, if not historical proofs, at least some confounding arguments.

This is all rather mysterious. Furthermore, what is the actual location of this "secret place" that housed the image of the Virgin ready to give birth? It could only be the crypt. Saillens writes:

> The two wonders of Chartres were the Tunic of the Virgin (her *chainze*), donated by Charles the Bald, and the crypt. The first, the marvel of all Christendom, was a simple relic; the second was a remnant of paganism. There is certainly no lack of crypts in France, but this one was beyond compare, for it contained a miraculous well some hundred feet deep and a cave called Prison of Saint Savinien and Saint Potentien, separated from the well by a thick wall pierced by a narrow corridor. In this cavern, where the faithful never entered, reigned, illuminated by the candles, a small black immemorial image.[2]

It is taking a big leap to venture that the image was black, but nevertheless it can be hypothesized that a primitive statue—which has nothing in common with the one that was subsequently described—could have been placed in a crypt, or rather a cave that was hollowed out either by humans or by nature. At the beginning of the twentieth century, the archaeologist René Merlet thought there had been a back crypt that may have served as a *martyrium*[3] in an earlier basilica. He went on to say: "There are serious reasons to believe that during the first centuries of our era, there existed close to the sacred well a temple dedicated to a local divinity." To support his argument, Merlet cited a sixteenth-century Chartrian historian named Duparc, who reported that in his own time, "remnants of ancient altars to idols were discovered" beneath the high altar of the church. But during the sixteenth century, scientific

---

2. E. Saillens, *Nos Vierges noires*, 197.

3. [A *martyrium* is a structure built over the resting place of a martyr. —*Trans.*]

archaeology was still in its infancy. The question is whether they were pagan remnants or Paleo-Christian substructures.

The closeness of the well is intriguing. According to Saillens:

> Of the two mysterious elements in the crypt, the well and the statue, the well is certainly the oldest. For a long time it was the most potent. During the eleventh century it was still called the Strong Place, *Locus Fortis*. At the time the legend developed that Christians would have been thrown down this well. . . . The name became the "Well of Saints-Forts," marking a retreat of the pagan memories. During the seventeenth century both well and "prison" were encompassed by the name "the Saints-Lieux-Forts."[4]

But during the seventeenth century, necessarily before the date of 1655, the well was filled in, probably to forestall the performance of rituals deemed too pagan, and the "prison" was sealed off by a wall so thick that it hid the opening of the well.

It was not until 1902, during the systematic excavation of the cathedral cellars by archaeologist Merlet, that the well was rediscovered. It was definitely the same one described in the ancient texts. It is located in the north gallery of the eleventh-century crypt attributed to Fulbert, in the second rectilinear bay off the curved corridor that corresponds to the ambulatory of the cathedral. What can be currently seen of the well dates from the early years of the twentieth century, including both the coping and the niche that partially shelters it. This is because the entire upper portion of the well had been intentionally destroyed during the seventeenth century. The well section was originally square and measured some four feet on a side. It terminated on a kind of ovoid basin hollowed out of a bed of flint. It was dug without any masonry as a cover in the very resistant volcanic rock formed by the upper layer of Beauce limestone. Recent topographical readings show that the bottom of the

---

4. Saillens, *Nos Vierges noires*, 197–98.

well is located a little bit below the level of the Eure River, almost eight feet. According to Merlet, it is significant that this well is strangely reminiscent of those that have been found on the sites of ancient Gallic elevated fortifications.

The name Lieu-Fort (literally, "strong place") would have come, again according to Merlet, from then neighboring Gallo-Roman fortifications. The site on which the cathedral was built could certainly be the location of one of these ancient Gallic fortresses, the sanctuary's chevet having been constructed on the culminating point of the mound, some five hundred feet high. We know, through the testimony of several authors native to Chartres, that the inhabitants of the town placed great trust in the water from this well. From the eleventh to the thirteenth century, and even later, people came to perform novenas in the southern gallery of the crypt, where, in the proximity of the Virgin's altar and the well, a kind of hospital had been established for the sick and invalid. The name given this hospital was Hospital of the Saints-Lieux-Forts. We also know that Fulbert was cured of "Saint Anthony's fire" (ergotism) after having drunk the water from this miraculous well, which would explain why he wanted to enclose the well within the crypt of the new cathedral, which until that time had been outside its walls.

Toward the end of the twelfth century, the name Puits des Saints-Forts won out. It was obviously under the influence of the legend concerning Saint Savinien and Saint Potentien, as well as the assumed founders of the Chartrian church. The first people to convert to Christianity were allegedly tossed down this well. Another version pushes the time of these events to that of the Viking invasion. Everything is in flux with this Saints-Forts tradition, but we need to give strong consideration to the fact that long before this well had been placed under the patronage of the "strong saints," it already enjoyed a reputation for causing miracles and was the object of pilgrimages, according to the words of a chronicler from the end of the ninth century. This monk, Paul, recounts how people came from the four corners of the Chartres region, which provides strong enough evidence to presume the pilgrimage was of ancient standing, and certainly extended into pagan times.

Furthermore, the Chartrian region is not poor in fountains and sacred springs. In his work *La Religion des Gaulois,* Alexandre Bertrand counts forty-four in the *département* of Eure-et-Loir. And he adds this commentary:

> It is quite remarkable that the majority of the springs in the Chartrian region, ancient center of Druidism, are located in villages that were dependent on the abbeys. The clergy of these abbeys would certainly not have tolerated these superstitions if they had not viewed them as sacred traditions. . . . Several of these springs became baptistries; chapels and churches were erected next to others. In one the spring is located beneath the porch, in another beneath the rostrum, and elsewhere beneath the high altar itself.

This is likely what happened at Chartres. And this is also how the Chartres Madonna became, in the words of René Merlet, "to the northern French, the preeminent Virgin, distinct from all the others."

There is, however, something bizarre here. Villette writes,

> The well was considered, rightly or wrongly, as respectable and sufficiently tied to the religious history of Chartres so that, after several reconstructions during the Middle Ages, it was decided to preserve it despite the technical difficulties this presented. On the other hand, if its miraculous virtues were recognized, it is hard to understand why it was destroyed in the seventeenth century, precisely at a time when people strove to see the mark of Antiquity everywhere.[5]

That is correct: We do *not* understand.

---

5. J. Villette, "What We Know About the Well in the Grotto of the Cathedral," *Notre-Dame de Chartres* 22 (1975): 18.

Thus, we need to go back to the statue of Our Lady of Under Ground. A disconcerting historical anecdote relates that around the year 1013, a Chartrian scholar by the name of Bernard, who had been a student of Fulbert and who taught at Angers, visited the Occitan Midi accompanied by another northern cleric. He was, we are told, shocked to see, in the churches of Aurillac and Conques, images other than that of the Crucifixion offered for worship to the faithful. Waxing indignant, he and his companion adopted the same attitude as the Gaul Brennus, who entered a Greek temple and mocked the depiction of the gods. And they even uttered the word *idolatry.*

The reaction of the two clerics seems quite significant; if they were offended by the depictions of the Virgin in Aurillac and Conques, it is because there were no such images in the sanctuaries they normally frequented—in other words, Chartres in particular. This implies that at the beginning of the eleventh century, there was no statue of Our Lady of Under Ground, nor any other images of the Virgin Mary, for that matter. There is a strong possibility that the clergy of that era, at least in northern France, were still in the state of mind that animated the Gallican church at the time of Louis the Pious. The sole devotion officially accepted at Chartres was to a relic, the Tunic of the Virgin. Bernard would therefore have considered nonexistent any possible devotion to a well and a statuette *located outside the walls of the sanctuary*. But we know that Bernard, having visited Conques several times, witnessed some very moving miracles and returned from his travels much more well disposed to sculpture in churches. Furthermore, following the fire that destroyed the old Carolingian cathedral, the well and the statue were encompassed within the cathedral crypt at the will of Fulbert, who had been miraculously cured by the water from the well. And the artists who had worked at Moissac were asked to provide the decoration of the new building, which suggests that henceforth in Chartres, statuary was accepted inside the sanctuaries.

Contemporary archaeology leans toward the existence of a

statue of Our Lady of Under Ground before the eleventh century—
in other words, Fulbert's era. Merlet comments:

> This worship, given both to a statue and a well of quite archaic
> appearance, existed since the eleventh century; information is lack-
> ing for times earlier than that. . . . The cathedral would have been,
> like so many other churches, erected on the site of a pagan sanc-
> tuary. As for the statue of the deity honored in this sanctuary, if it
> resembled the image of the Virgin about to give birth, it is because
> it most likely belonged to the group of mother goddesses, certain
> specimens of which bring to mind a simulacrum of the Mother of
> God sitting down and breast feeding the Holy Infant.[6]

Why not? But what Merlet did not know, or rather what he did
not notice, is that the famous group of mother goddesses, numerous
examples of which can be seen in all the museums of Europe, is not
Gallic; it is Gallo-Roman. If the original statue in Chartres dates
from Druidic times, as indicated by local tradition, it could not be a
statue of the Gallo-Roman Mother Goddess dating from a time
when the Druids, persecuted and practically forbidden to teach had
almost all disappeared. This is not a hypothesis; it is a reality. From
the time of independence, the Celts never represented their gods in
human form; the testimonies of Caesar, Diodorus Siculus, and
Lucan are convincing enough on this point to put the matter beyond
discussion.

The only other possibility is that it was a Gallo-Roman artistic
depiction, which does not mean that the spirit of the sculpture was
not Gallic. It is a simple mater of dating, but important insofar as
the Druids are claimed to have been involved in the erection of this
virgo paritura. This casts no doubt on the existence in Chartres, on
the site of the current cathedral or the crypt, of a pagan sanctuary
dedicated to a maternal female deity. After all, one of the church

---

6. R. Merlet, *La Cathédrale de Chartres* (Paris: Henri Laurens, 1909), 9–11.

fathers, Justin, declares in his *First Apologia* (LXIV, 1) that even in his time "one erected near springs the statue of the virgin Kore and called her the daughter of Zeus; this was the invention of demons." The diabolical reference is classic in these circumstances, but it certainly provides a valuable clue: The pagans (Greek in this instance) erected statues of female deities near springs. The entire worship of sacred fountains is outlined here. This also reveals the continuity of cults no matter what the dominant ideology may be.

Moreover, to a church father, although aware he was recounting "deviltries," Kore was a virgin. Could the underlying notion be that the Virgin, linked as she should be with Mary, is not a Christian notion, but rather one that has long existed in all the religions that preceded Christianity? The answer is definitely yes, and we know this to be true, even if our judgment is contaminated by our immoderate usage of the word *virgin* in its narrowest sense, that of a woman who has never been penetrated by a man. By stressing Mary's virginity, and by restricting its meaning to an exclusively physical condition, Christianity completely adulterated the sense of the word, whose derivation is from a root (the Latin *vir* or *vires*) that simply means "strong" or "powerful." And yet at Chartres itself, everything is placed in the cathedral to emphasize this incomparable power of the Virgin Mary.

So why not acknowledge that devotion to Mary, mother of Jesus, may well have succeeded earlier devotion to a powerful Virgin, mother of a savior god or regenerator of the world? Without any need to go out in search of Kore, daughter of Demeter (Ceres), and the mysteries of Eleusis, it can be assumed that the same belief in a female deity dispensing abundance and prosperity, both material and spiritual, existed among the Celts before the Roman occupation. The main question is whether this female deity was represented by a figurative statue or by one of the simulacra mentioned by Caesar and Lucan. This simulacrum could be either a wooden pillar or a rock that had been left unworked but was charged with an intense mystical *aura*.

Again according to René Merlet, the statue mentioned in 1389 appears, going by its descriptions, to have been "a very barbaric work," perhaps even "the replica of an even older work." He notes, "One cannot help but be struck by the similarities it reveals with certain Gallo-Roman figurines. I am speaking of those statuettes in terracotta or even wood that have been discovered at various occasions in our land."[7] Yes, but the terra-cotta figurines are very reduced in size and would not be suitable for public worship. Most of the time these statuettes were artworks reserved for private citizens, or else they adorned the altars of certain hearths.[8]

According to Saillens,

> This replica no doubt originally reproduced the color of its antique model, and was expected to do so as it was in pear wood, the sole wood of our land that can darken perfectly. Around her Black Majesty, whose pagan origin was not utterly forgotten, a legend formed that put everything in order; moreover, this legend implied nothing that would run counter to dogma: The Church always believed in an earlier Revelation. It could only be expedient to protect the pre-Christian symbols."[9]

But this cannot be stated definitively, for while Our Lady of the Pillar is indubitably a Black Madonna, it has never been proved that Our Lady of Under Ground was of the same nature.

At this point, it is worth taking a look at some of the more ancient descriptive testimonies. While there is no mention of Druids in the *Vieille Chronique* of 1389, we see them coming out in

---

7. Ibid., 7.

8. There are numerous examples of domestic worship, in particular in the foundations of houses excavated in Alise-Sainte-Reine. But these terra-cotta figurines show the imprint of Romanization, even while they may be expressions of an entirely different Celtic concept.

9. Saillens, *Nos Vierges noires*, 61. It is entirely plausible that the original statue was of pear wood, but this has not been proved.

strength at the end of the sixteenth century. It is probable that the predilection for classical antiquity made stylish in the Renaissance did not prevent the people of that time from taking an interest in "Gallic" remnants. De Bellay had praised the merits of the old national epics of the Middle Ages in the name of the "defense and illustration of the French language." Bonaventure des Périers, Marguerite de Navarre, Noel du Fail, Rabelais, and many authors who remain anonymous drew largely from the traditional stories that had been spread through the French countryside.

More important, the megalithic monuments began to seriously intrigue intellectuals, who of course viewed them as pre-Roman and thus Gallic constructions, imagining the dolmens as large tables for bloody sacrifices, whereas the people continued to believe them to be "tables of the giants" or "Gargantua's turds." And so, at the time of Henri IV, in 1609 to be precise, a certain Rouillard published a curious work on the Chartrian antiquities that he entitled *Parthénie,* which included a frontispiece depicting the *virgo paritura* in the cave of the Druids, right next to the Well of the Strong Saints, with odd kneeling figures that allegedly represented the Druids. Rouillard appeared very knowledgeable about the Druids and their customs, rituals, and systems of thought. For the first time, he clearly identified Chartres as the central sanctuary of the Carnutes of which Caesar spoke, but he established a difference between the sanctuary itself and the Druidic "college": "As for their schools, they were in the town of Dreux and neighboring hamlets located at the entrance to the forest, still presently called the houses of the Druids; for they had chosen such solitary locales as far removed from noise and easy access, consequently more appropriate for attending to the study of Philosophy."[10]

Although this all results from a false etymology of the name Dreux, which Rouillard said was derived from the Druids (in reality it is the name of the Durocasses people, subjects of the Carnutes),

10. Rouillard, *Parthénie,* 26, V.

there is nothing opposing the idea that the Dreux Forest once housed Druid schools. It is even quite probable, and the Celtic-era remnants discovered in the Dreux Forest and its immediate surroundings, notably in Fort-Harrouard, only lends support to that hypothesis. Furthermore, it is interesting to note that in the sixteenth century, there was a desire to differentiate the sanctuary, reserved for worship and assembling, and the schools, havens of peace and tranquillity favorable to the long studies awaiting the apprentice Druids.

But Rouillard is truly the first, also, to signal that the adored statue in Chartres Cathedral was of Druid origin. He even claims that it was erected "one hundred years before the birth of Our Lord." If this was the case, the statue could not be Gallo-Roman at all but uniquely Celtic, as the Romans had not yet set foot in "hairy Gaul" (untamed Gaul, as opposed to the Gallia Togata that was the Provincia Romana, otherwise known as the Narbonnaise). Under these circumstances, it could not have been a figurative depiction. Another seventeenth-century historian, Charles Challine, goes much further: "Some maintain that this image was dedicated to the Virgin more than twenty centuries before she came into the world." The exaggeration is interesting insofar as it shows that certain traditions claimed the statue dated back to an era long before the Celts. In this case we would have to envision a female representation from the late Neolithic—in other words megalithic—period, which is indeed absurd, as we shall see.

For a third historian, Savard, author of an unpublished *Parthénie*, it was only two centuries before Mary's birth that the statue was erected. This clearly brings us back to the Druids. But there is one curious detail in Savard's text. He informs us that when the prophecies regarding the birth of Jesus were fulfilled, three Chartrians—"a Levite druid, a jurisconsult, and an edile"—were sent to Mary. It is odd to recognize in these three ambassadors the representatives of the three Indo-European class functions. And this brings up some questions about the famous Three Magi. Were they only Persians, or might they have been priests and philosophers belonging to various peoples and religions? Given that in a majority of texts from classical antiquity the Druids are often called "philosophers" or "mages," there is legitimate reason to think there were Celts among the Magi Kings.

That said, the three Chartrian ambassadors, according to Savard, would have addressed the Virgin Mary in this fashion: "Thereby know, illustrious Lady, that our fathers erected an altar in an ancient forest, carved the image of a girl holding an infant in her arms, and dedicated it to a Virgin ready to give birth; in order that posterity may preserve that happy memory, they added this script: *Virgo Pariturae.*"[11] This famous dedication, however, is not on the statue itself but rather on its base.

The canon Estienne provides another testimony. It was he who sought to establish a meridian within the cathedral and placed three copper nails in the labyrinth. His scientific concerns did not prevent him from musing about the Druids. He was also much less an "innocent" than he appears at first sight, for in a text he wrote in 1682, he took great pains to describe "the places where the Druids made their sacrifices." His sources are the Greek and Roman authors, and Lucan particularly inspired him. One passage from the *Pharsalia* seems to have truly caught his attention:

There stood a grove
Which from the earliest time no hand of man
Had dared to violate; hidden from the sun
Its chill recesses; matted boughs entwined
Prisoned the air within. No sylvan nymphs
Here found a home, nor Pan, but savage rites
And barbarous worship, altars horrible
On massive stones upreared; sacred with blood
Of men was every tree. If faith be given

---

11. A. Lecoq, "Recherches sur une ambassade chartraine à Nazareth," in *Mémoires de la Société archéologique d'Eure-et-Loir,* 6:64. [Savard is the author of an unpublished edition of this same *Parthénie* quoted by Lecoq. —*Trans.*]

To ancient myth, no fowl has ever dared
To rest upon those branches, and no beast
Has made his lair beneath: no tempest falls,
Nor lightnings flash upon it from the cloud.
Stagnant the air, unmoving, yet the leaves
Filled with mysterious trembling; dripped the streams
From coal-black fountains; effigies of gods [simulacra]
Rude, scarcely fashioned from some fallen trunk
Held the mid space: and, pallid with decay,
Their rotting shapes struck terror. Thus do men
Dread most the god unknown. 'Twas said that caves
Rumbled with earthquakes, that the prostrate yew
Rose up again; that fiery tongues of flame
Gleamed in the forest depths, yet were the trees
Unkindled; and that snakes in frequent folds
Were coiled around the trunks. Men flee the spot
Nor dare to worship near: and e'en the priest
Or when bright Phoebus holds the height, or when
Dark night controls the heavens, in anxious dread
Draws near the grove and fears to find its lord.
    (III, vv. 450–480, ENGLISH TRANSLATION BY SIR EDWARD RIDLEY, 1896)

Here we are in a phantasmagoria. The *nemeton* is a place outside both time and space, and especially beyond the ordinary world. This is where the sacred manifests, but only to those with access there—in other words, the priests. And Lucan stresses that the statues of the gods were crudely fashioned. He even provides an explanation: A deity whose features cannot be visualized is much more mysterious, hence much more feared and adored. This is confirmation of the Celtic refusal to fix in concrete terms that which is incommunicable, ineffable, and incomprehensible, the infinitude of God. Such a sentiment could only attract the Christian clergy to the Druidic religion. But as we know, the people need the concrete; they want images that serve as a material support for their meditations and prayers.

It was therefore in these sinister "sacred groves," near gushing fountains, that the seventeenth-century "antiquarians" chose to effect this subtle synthesis of ancient Druidism and triumphant Christianity. The canon Estienne declared that "it was in these places the mages of Antiquity erected this beautiful figure in honor of a Virgin ready to give birth more than three or four hundred years before her birth."[12] If we understand this correctly, devotion to this *virgo paritura* does not replace the worship of other deities represented by the simulacra, the wooden or stone pillars. All this is quite odd. Another canon of the same century, named Souchet, claimed that the belief in this statue of the Virgin erected by Druids was a "popular error."[13] But then why did so many other "antiquarians," who were clergy members to boot, endeavor to assert the reality of this statue and its patronage by the Druids? There is an obvious contradiction here. In fact, whatever this statue of the Druids may have looked like, there can be no doubt that something existed long before the introduction of Christianity, and in the context of the Druidic religion.

The two oldest descriptions of the statue of Our Lady of Under Ground date from the end of the seventeenth century. These descriptions are of the statue as it was at that time and not necessarily the original, of course. But they can give an idea of what it was intended to depict. The historian Pintard provides the most precisely detailed descriptions:

> The venerable image that can be seen standing in a niche above the altar (in the crypt) appears to be carved from pear wood that smoke of the lamps and tapers that are lit each day have turned into a rich dark color. The Virgin is depicted sitting in a chair holding her son on her knees. He is giving the benediction with his right hand while his left is holding the globe of the world. His head is

---

12. L. Merlet, *Catalogue des reliques et joyaux de Notre-Dame de Chartres*, 171, based on a manuscript (G 403) in the Departmental Archives of Eure-et-Loir.
13. Souchet, *Histoire du diocèse de la ville de Chartres*, vol. 1, 172.

bare and his hair short; the robe he wears over his body is very tight and folded back by the belt; his face, his hands, and his uncovered feet have taken on an olive-brown color. The Virgin is wearing over her robe an old-fashioned cloak in the shape of a dalmatic [a priest's garment] that is rolled up over her arms and seems rounded in front of her knees, which is as far as it descends. The veil that covers her head falls to her shoulders, from where it is thrown over her back; her face is very well made and well proportioned in an oval the same color as that of her son. Her crown is very simple, adorned on the top by fleurons in the shape of ash leaves. The chair has four pillars of which the back two are twenty-three inches high and those in front are seventeen, over a foot in width, including the chair; the entire figure is hollow in back as if it were a tree bark three inches thick that has been crudely carved, save for the faces, which are quite finished.[14]

The canon Estienne provides an almost identical description of this statue. He does, though, add a few details: The leaves of the crown are oak leaves; the Virgin is wearing shoes while her infant is barefoot; the eyes of the Virgin are closed, whereas those of Jesus are open. And the canon astronomer suggests this curious interpretation: "These ancient philosophers [the Druids] only depicted this virgin mother with her eyes closed to show that she who they were honoring in this form was not yet born, and her child's eyes were open to let it be known that they believed he existed before all the centuries and for all eternity."

This observation is both theological and metaphysical. It speaks volumes about the deep motivations of the canon Estienne, who set such store in proving pre-Christian devotion to the Virgin by Druid "philosophers." It is an acknowledgment that the Virgin is actually God's first creature, one who has existed ever since the world began. But her existence is purely potential as long as she has not agreed to

---

14. Pintard, *Histoire chronologique de la ville de Chartres*, N.A., ms. 29, 37.

receive the Holy Ghost and conceive the Child-God. To use the language of philosophy, the Virgin Mary was always *immanence,* as shown by her closed eyes, and could only become *permanence* at the moment she accepted the role of mother of God, when she could finally open her eyes. As for Jesus, being God, he is eternal, therefore he assumes both *immanence* and *permanence.*

The idea is quite attractive. The drawing that accompanies canon Estienne's manuscript does show a Virgin with closed eyes. This drawing is dated 1682. The crown does not have oak leaves, however, but acorns. A drawing earlier than this one by a year that was inserted in Pintard's manuscript is almost the same. The work of a certain Claude Chauveau, the drawing depicts the Virgin not from the front, but slightly profiled toward the left. The entire work is reversed, meaning that its creator intended to use it for an engraving. We also have several copies of an engraving from this same era, signed Leroux. Here again, the Virgin's eyes are closed, but the crown is adorned with oak leaves. As for the copy of this statue currently located in the Carmelite House of Chartres, it corroborates the descriptions of Pintard and Estienne: The Virgin's eyes are closed and her crown is decorated with oak leaves.

But then why did Rouillard, in the frontispiece of his *Parthénie,* depict an entirely different mother-and-child grouping? Nothing is recognizable. The Virgin wears a veil and her head is surrounded by a halo, whereas the head of her child is radiating flames. Furthermore, Jesus is standing on his mother's left knee. And of course the pair is on a kind of base on which there is an inscription reading ALTAR OF THE DRUIDS, the entire work embedded in a cave opening, with the Well of the Saints-Forts depicted on the side.

The characteristics of the Our Lady of Under Ground described by Pintard and Estienne and drawn by several seventeenth-century artists, show that it belongs to the same type of Majestic Virgins that were beginning to spread through France and the rest of Europe at the beginning of the twelfth century. There can be no doubt about this, so it serves as proof that this statue was not ancient and had replaced another statue worshipped before that time. But why was the statue replaced? Probably because the archaic statue had too many details smacking of paganism to be present in a Christian sanctuary. Rouillard was fully aware of this in 1609, for he used his frontispiece to depict some kind of idealization (and not reconstruction) of the original figure. Rouillard's frontispiece serves as a kind of confession: The statue worshipped in his time had replaced an earlier one.

This brings up a question: Just what did this archaic statue that had been allegedly erected by the Druids long before the birth of Mary look like? The two answers that immediately come to mind are both logical but mutually exclusive, and in any case purely hypothetical.

First, the ancient version of Our Lady of Under Ground was one of a Gallo-Roman group depicting a Gallic goddess mother holding a child on her knees. But in this case the Druids could not have any involvement with it, for in Roman Gaul, Druids could no longer openly officiate.

Second, the ancient version of Our Lady of Under Ground was a kind of simulacrum, an "idol" made of wood or stone that had been erected by Druids in independent Gaul. But in this case the idol could not be anthropomorphic and no one could have had any real idea of what it was intended to represent unless a tenacious oral tradition had preserved it in memory.

These two responses—hypothetical, remember—are logical but contradict each other, and are hardly satisfying. The first eliminates the Druids, but this does not conform to Chartrian tradition. The second eliminates the *concrete* image, but this does not conform to the so-called folk tradition, which always formed attachments with concrete and representative objects. And yet it seems to have been established that the city of Chartres since its origins has been regarded as a sanctuary dedicated to the Virgin. Efforts were made throughout the Middle Ages, and not only in Chartres, to confirm the early existence of Marian worship in the land of the Carnutes. This cannot be a simple whim or merely the desire of the residents of Chartres to elevate their own importance. There must be some truth to this story; *there must be something to it.*

It is therefore necessary to get to the heart of the matter. Until the end of the nineteenth century—and even today in certain milieus where "esoteric" syncretism has wreaked havoc—Druidism has been or still is linked to megalithic monuments. The clichéd image of the bearded Druid sacrificing his victims on a dolmen, mistakenly believed to be a sacrificial altar, is derived from this notion. Archaeology has corrected the erroneous interpretation. But if folk tradition connects Druidism to the megaliths, it may be because there is a certain bond, even though vague and fairly minor. After all, the Irish mythological texts view the megalithic mounds as the dwellings of ancient gods. This localization is certainly not due to chance, and it clearly raises a question that cannot be skirted by hiding behind some archaeological certitudes. After all, some Roman sanctuaries became Christian churches, and most Christian chapels are placed on older sites of worship, either Greco-Roman, Celtic, or prehistoric. Certain monuments were also redeployed or recycled; there are countless examples.

Furthermore, a religion never dies completely. Elements of beliefs or rituals always survive from the older one and carry with them habits that the triumphant young religion installs within itself. It is not at all surprising, then, that Druidism would have inherited something from the peoples the Celts found in the Western European territories they took over in 700 B.C.E. These autochthonous populations were not exterminated by the Celts; rather, the Celts incorporated them, which means the Celts must also have incorporated some of their lifestyles and mentalities as well. This conjunction was the foundation of the new community called the Celtic civilization, one of the components of which was Druidism.

What remains to be determined, of course, is the exact proportion of this legacy. But we have already seen that the solar cult, as it appears in the Celtic civilization, seems to be a Bronze Age legacy. Belenos is more a pre–Indo-European god than a Celtic god. And the famous Cernunnos, the god with a stag's antlers, symbolizing and embodying the third Indo-European function, that of the producers, does not seem at all Celtic. He overlays the protector deity of the autochthonous peoples who were incorporated and *put to work* by the conquering Celts.

Under these conditions, the worship of the Virgin in Chartres, while it is indubitably Christian in its medieval and contemporary form, could well have been no less indubitably Gallo-Roman, after it had been Gallic, and *after having been prehistoric*. It perhaps involves a legacy that goes back millennia and not merely several centuries. The stumbling block for this whole matter is the original image of the *virgo paritura,* which can only be concrete, realistic, and figurative. It cannot be Gallic. Why couldn't it go back much farther in time?

There was no ban on anthropomorphism in megalithic times; the petroglyphs discovered in the dolmens, although they can be simplistic, are most often figurative. In numerous megaliths of Morbihan and in Ireland, the image of a female deity can even be recognized, the one that archaeologists have dubbed the "bud-shaped idol." She seems to have been a classic goddess of life and death, as both purveyor of earthly goods and protector of the dead in an Other World, symbolized by the dolmen chamber or the grotto. Not far from Chartres in the Eure Valley in the commune of Changé-Saint-Piat, this image of the Neolithic goddess is clearly visible in a covered alley in the middle of a field. The same general form can be recognized on the supports of the Flat Stones in Locmariaquer (Morbihan), which are the most typical of their kind, or on the famous pillar of Maneer-Hroëk, still in Locmariaquer, where the idol is more complex, with the addition of mysterious symbols clearly indicating her sacred and divine nature.

It is reasonable to assume that the Druids, officiating at prehistoric sacred mounds, would have incorporated this ancient image of the female deity. It is no less reasonable to presume that they may have integrated the worship of the Goddess of the Beginnings into their ceremonies. This has led me to formulate another explanation for the statue of Chartres, which is just as hypothetical but also perfectly logical, and has the merit of establishing the permanence of beliefs and devotions in certain privileged spots.

A third answer suggests that Our Lady of Under Ground in her primitive form was not a statue (which the Druids would never have erected), but instead a carved stone, a *petroglyph* found on the support of a dolmen, or the wall of a cave, at the very site of the current cathedral and not far from a sacred well whose water was believed to have miraculous powers.

The Chartrian tradition, both popular and clerical, emphasizes the cave in which the Druids would have placed the image of the *virgo paritura*. This has inspired much musing on the underground passages of Chartres. It has been claimed that the caves, numerous in the ground below Chartres, are the remnants of ancient galleries that connected to the cathedral and even led to exits outside the wall of the ancient city. People have imagined "secret temples" and a "holy of holies" reserved for initiates (we are never told initiates into what), who alone knew the secret entrances. From here to imagining even more bizarre ceremonies, performed even today by the authentic keepers of Western spirituality, is not a long step—and it is a step that has been taken.

The reality seems much less fanciful, although it remains mysterious. But proofs are required. Is anyone capable of bringing such proofs to light? Systematic excavations are certainly undertaken in the cathedral's cellar, but these are merely soundings. It is impossible to work here as one would in the open air, on a prehistoric site that is not topped by any construction. Excavating the cellar of a cathedral could compromise the stability of the entire edifice, which is hardly desirable. But this does not mean that certain searchers have not discovered something beneath the crypt, and especially beneath the original Carolingian cathedral. It is difficult to confirm and equally difficult to topple certitudes believed established for all time. It is difficult to interpret what emerges from the most remote past.

It can be asserted *hypothetically*, however, that beneath the cathedral of Notre-Dame de Chartres, more exactly beneath the location of Our Lady of Under Ground in the crypt, next to the Well of Saints-Forts, there is a dolmen (probably crushed) or a cave carved out of the limestone (probably filled in) that displayed a petroglyph depicting the Mother Goddess, most likely one of those well-known bud-shaped Neolithic idols, that was the object of fervent worship in the remote past. Our Lady the Virgin is the universal Mother, the First-Born, she whom human beings have always considered to be the *materia prima* of all beings and all things. How would the presence of such a representation of Our Lady of Under Ground somewhere beneath the current cathedral be contrary to the exaltation of the powerful and triumphant Virgin, this Throne of Wisdom who shines so brightly in the admirable sanctuary of Chartres?

THE VIRGIN OF
THE DRUIDS

$\mathcal{I}$f the medieval clergy of Chartres, especially that of the later six-teenth century, took so much trouble to assert that the Virgin of Chartres had been worshipped long before the birth of Mary by Druids of the Carnute region, it is because they had good reason to. On the one hand, there was a folk tradition that did not cast doubt as to the existence of a Marian cult before the introduction of Christianity. On the other hand, it was an intelligent way of demonstrating that, despite differences in interpretation and justification, there is but one spiritual message delivered to humankind, and all versions of it have the same theological and metaphysical implications.

This showed a laudable concern for ecumenism even then; it took into account not only the families scattered inside Christianity itself but also the great philosophical options shared throughout the world. It was also recognition that in entering the West, the evan-gelical message had found very favorable intellectual and spiritual soil, the figure of Christ arriving to fulfill a need: the speculative projections of pagan priests whose mission was to prepare their peo-ple to hear and understand the "Good News." The Druids, as can easily be imagined, quite naturally found themselves designated the privileged intermediaries between a Christianity declaring its role as the keeper of a single, definitive Truth, and a spiritual endeavor consisting of a relentless quest for this Truth by somewhat makeshift means. The theory they were promulgating amounts to this: The Druids had labored to prepare the people for the supreme revelation.

This view is open to debate, but it did exist. The example of Celtic Christianity, as lived by the peoples of Celtic origin, would tend to verify this claim, because it is historically proved that the transition from Druidism to Christianity occurred smoothly, with no constraints, and in an absolutely natural manner.[1] The two doctrines must therefore have had certain points in common. And the Druids, although subsequently depreciated and reduced to the rank of simple magicians, were always regarded in antiquity as philosophers of great value.[2] The necessary patronage of the Druids for the worship—and even the doctrine—of the Virgin Mary is therefore confirmation that in certain ecclesiastical milieus, great value was attached to this seemingly incongruous line of descent.

Of course, the sixteenth-century clerics who defended the line of descent knew little about the Druidic doctrine. They saw it through the few testimonies left by the Romans and the Greeks, and especially through folk tradition, which is a faithful keeper of mythic outlines but a wretched guardian of interpretive details. It seems that it was the overall outline that led them down this path, but it is quite certain that they would have been incapable of explaining how and why the worship and consideration of the Virgin Mary went so far

---

1. This is quite significant in the case of Ireland, which, never having been occupied by the Romans, converted very easily to the Christian doctrine although nothing obliged the Irish to do so; furthermore, they proved themselves to be the most ardent propagandists for Christianity across the entire continent during the Merovingian era. See Jean Markale, *Le Christianisme celtique et ses survivances populaires* (Paris: Imago, 1984).

2. Although they did not understand the Druidic doctrine, the Greek and Roman authors of antiquity always praised it highly. They related it to the Pythagorean doctrine, and some even claimed that Pythagoras was a student of the Druids, while others said the Druids had been inspired by Pythagoras. See Jean Markale, *The Druids* (Rochester, Vt.: Inner Traditions, 1999).

back into the mist-shrouded times of the Druids and other incorporated philosophers.

Today we are much better informed on this matter, especially because it has been shown how the old mythic Irish stories—which corroborate precisely the fragmentary Greek and Roman data—have been stripped down, translated, and analyzed. There is a mass of information there, each item more valuable than the next, that can allow, if not a definitive explanation, at least a considerable clarification of the continuity of the Marian cult from the earliest prehistoric times to the present.

There is one basic element that should be considered first. In the mythic process of the inhabiting of Ireland, considered by itself the image of the world, five postdiluvian invasions took place corresponding to five stages of civilization and the evolution of the human mind. But there was an earlier invasion before the deluge, an invasion personified by a Primordial Woman named Cessair (meaning "hail"). In this first invasion, which lasted but fifty days (reminiscent of the Pentecost), "fifty women and three men was the number of those who were in this ship," according to the *Book of Conquests*. The female element is therefore dominant, and Cessair represents fairly well, metaphysically speaking, the concept debated so often inside Christianity of the Virgin, the first being created by God before the creation of the world. Cessair is none other than the universal Virgin, the Mother of All, the primordial demiurge.

In this conception, the word *virgin* does not have the meaning it has taken on in Christianity and only in Christianity. All other traditions endlessly poke fun at physical virginity, unless they make it into a value-added feature of a woman to be delivered as a "virgin" to her husband, who will therefore be the one to make her a real woman. Furthermore, the word *virgin* comes from an Indo-European root that means "strength" and "potency." This root is found in the Latin *vir*, "male," *virtus*, "courage," and *vires*, "forces"; in the Greek *ergon*, "work" and "energy" (from the ancient *werg*); in the Gaelic *fir* meaning "man" and *ferg*, "activity." The Virgin is literally "the

Powerful One," and that is all. But this gives sufficient indication of the *potentiality* she represents. It is in this sense of the term that we should understand the speculations of the church fathers when they declared Mary virgin before the conception of Christ and still virgin after the birth of the Child-God. All the rest, including the distorted moralizing of professional preachers, is just so much dust in the eyes, not to mention brainwashing for rather obscure motives.

With this in mind, it can be said that Cessair is an image of the primordial Virgin, one of the aspects of the Goddess of the Beginnings. But her story is quite brief, practically nonexistent. She will reappear with other traits in the mythological history of the Gaels. Many can lay claim to this title, starting with Dana, mother of the great Irish gods, the Tuatha de Danaan. The name Dana—Dôn in Wales—is archetypal. It can be found almost everywhere. It is the Danaë of the Greeks, who are also the Danaoi, meaning "sons of Dana" *(Timeo Danaos et dona ferentes . . .).*[3] It is the Tanit of the Phoenicians. It is the Annapurna of the Indians and the Anna Parenna of the Romans; the Anis of the ancient city of Anicium (the modern Puy-en-Velay); the Black Annis of Yorkshire folklore; and the "holy" Anne of Christian traditions, revised and corrected by the Armorican Bretons—grandmother of Jesus, certainly, but a woman who in some cases has a tendency to supplant her daughter, Mary, in the affections of the people.

In the seventeenth century, at the same time that the peasant Nicolazic discovered near Auray a statue of "Saint" Anne after she had appeared to him several times, the Jesuit Christopher de Vega constructed a mythico-theological outline about Mary's mother:

In the beginning, God created heaven and earth (Hoachim and Anne, the parents of Mary). Now the earth was shapeless and empty (Anne was sterile), and darkness (suffering and confusion) lay over

---

3. [This is a quote from Virgil's *Aeneid:* "I fear the Greeks, even when they come bearing gifts."—*Trans.*]

the face of the abyss (over Anne's face), and the Spirit of the Lord moved over the waters (over the water of Anne's tears, to console her). And God said: "Let there be Light!" (let there be Mary, the blessed Virgin). And the gathering of the waters (the gathering of the graces), God wished to call *maria*, the "seas" (or Mary).[4]

This sounds a bit far-fetched, to say the least. But the play on words, which works only in Latin, between the neutral plural noun *maria* (seas) and the feminine singular noun Maria (Mary) deserves extensive analysis. That this all comes from an apocryphal gospel known as the Protoevangelion of James does not lessen its interest.

There is a little-known episode in Irish myth that sheds some light on the theme of the Virgin. It appears right at the beginning of a tale recounting one of the most beautiful love stories in Ireland, that of the beautiful Etain and the king of the Other World, Mider. This prologue recounts the conception of one of the oddest figures in Gaelic tradition, Oengus, the Mac Oc, but it is steeped in a troubled atmosphere of adultery and incest that does not lend itself to being compared with the Holy Scriptures, at least when read literally. A great distance can divide the spirit and the letter, and there are many points in common that appear totally at odds at first glance.

There was a famous king of Ireland, of the race of the Tuatha de Danaan, by the name of Eochaid Ollathir. He also had the name of Dagda, as it was he who produced miracles and determined the storms and harvests. . . . There was a woman at the home of Elcmar of Brug. Eithne was her name. Another name she bore was Boann. The Dagda desired her physical friendship. The woman would have given in to Dagda if she had not been in fear of Elcmar because of his great power. The Dagda then sent Elcmar on a journey. . . . The Dagda cast great spells on Elcmar to prevent him from

---

4. Quoted in E. Saillens, *Nos Vierges noires* (Paris: Universelles, 1945), 201.

returning in time, meaning too soon. He sent him during the darkness of night and kept him from feeling thirst and hunger. He sent him on a long journey in which nine months seemed as but a day. For he had said he would return in between night and day. During this time the Dagda went to Elcmar's wife and conceived a son with her, whose name was Oengus. The woman was healed of her sufferings when Elcmar returned. He noted not her transgression—that is to say, that she had slept with the Dagda. However the Dagda took his son away so that he could be brought up in the house of Mider in Bri Leith. . . . He also bore the name of Mac Oc for his mother had said: "Young is the son engendered at morn and born between that time and the evening."[5]

This story calls for several explanations. First, Mac Oc means "young son." But his other name, Oengus, means "single choice." Elcmar is the brother of the Dagda. His name means "dark." But he is also known as Nechtan, which is the Gaelic form of Neptunus. Under this name he is a god of freshwaters, but as Elcmar he is the owner of the Brugh, the most famous megalithic mound of all; it refers to New Grange, above the valley of the Boyne, whose river bears the name of Boann (or Boinn). Dagda means "good god," and his cognomen Ollathir, "Father of all," is reminiscent of the title of the Germanic god Odin-Wotan, Alfadir, meaning the same thing. Dagda, one of the most powerful members of the Tuatha de Danaan, had a Gallic equivalent in Gargantua.

The person of Eithne-Boann is a bit more complex. Boann or Boinn is in fact the name of the Boyne River, and this name can be divided into Bo-Vinda, which means "white cow." In all likelihood, this ancient Bo-Vinda is the origin of the Arthurian Vivian, the fairy who "ensnares" Merlin the Enchanter, and is also the famous Lady of the Lake, the adoptive mother of Lancelot of the Lake and the

---

5. *Textes mythologiques irlandais,* vol. 1, trans. Christian-Jacques Guyonvarc'h (Rennes, France: Ogam-Celticum, 1978), 242.

one who bestows the sword of sovereignty, Excalibur (Kaledfoulch, "hard thunder"). In Ireland, in addition to Eithne, Boann has many other names. She is also Etain, then Macha, and even Bodbh, "the crow." And she is even better known under the name Brigit, the Potent One, mistress of poetry, arts, and crafts, and virgin warrior. In reality, *Brigit is the daughter of Dagda.*

The complexity of the mythical scenario is now quite visible. The father engenders a son with his own daughter, under the cover in some way of Elcmar, who serves as a putative father. This is obviously reminiscent of something else. Doesn't Christianity teach that God the Father created Mary and that through the intervention of the Holy Ghost, he engendered in Mary his only son, Jesus? In other words, God-Father created Mary (his daughter) and coupled with her in the form of the Holy Ghost to engender the Son. By virtue of the dogmatic principle of the Trinity (one sole God in three personas), one can only arrive at the following conclusion: God is Father, Husband, and Son of Mary all at the same time. This may appear shocking to those who read sacred texts literally, but these kinds of narrative symbols always borrow rather bold formulations that reveal a message that cannot be expressed directly.

Furthermore, in this Irish mythological episode, the Mac Oc clearly appears as the figure of a young god. He is in fact Dagda regenerated, as he has gone through a new birth and was engendered in the space of a day that is symbolically equivalent to eternity. The following part of the story enlightens us even more. Oengus demands a legacy from his father, Dagda, who arranges that he be given the kingdom of the Brugh by Elcmar himself by means of a subtle game in which Elcmar allows himself to be snared. Oengus demands the Brugh kingdom for the space of one day. But as this day is the festival of Samhain, time is abolished, and the symbolic day becomes the equivalent of eternity. Mac Oc will therefore be the sole owner of the Brugh for eternity, which means that he will rule in turn over the world of the mounds, the world of the gods.

The figure of Boann merits the most attention. Her physical

virginity is obviously not at issue, and the story has a tendency to exaggerate her transgression, adultery at Elcmar's expense. Several texts exist concerning Boann's "purification." They are heavily altered because they come from ancient versions that their transcribers would not have easily grasped. These transcribers were medieval Irish monks, who would have been confused by the archaic assumptions belonging to a very different system of thought.

Nechtan, the other name of Elcmar, husband of Boann, possesses (he is a deity of fresh water) a marvelous fountain, the Segais spring. One can immediately see the relationship between the Virgin and the Fountain or the Well. Following the birth of Oengus, Boann wishes to purify herself. Now, Boann is none other than the goddess Brigit, and this Brigit was more or less commingled with the mysterious Saint Brigitte of Kildare, whose feast day is February 1, the date of the pagan Celtic Festival of Imbolc (which was held in Brigit's honor). This raises crucial questions, especially as February 2 in the Christian calendar is Candlemas, feast day of the Purification of the Virgin Mary after she gave birth. There are far too many coincidences for this not to be hiding a continuity of worship and belief. Boann declares: "I will go to the beautiful spring of Segais, so that there is no doubt as to my chastity. I will circle the living spring three times in the direction opposite the sun's course, without lie."[6]

Two observations leap to mind. First, Boann seeks to assert, before humans and gods, her *chastity* (not her virginity), as if she had never given birth to Mac Oc, and in complete good faith. This sounds like the speculations of the church fathers on Mary, who was finally declared forever virgin, even following the birth of Jesus. Second, her rite of circumambulation is in reverse of the sun's course. Such a rite still exists in Armorican Brittany in customs associated with healing fountains. The counter-sunwise circumambulation clearly indicates an intention to regenerate, to go backward, to

---

6. Translation, Guyonvarc'h, *Textes mythologiques irlandais*, I, 269.

achieve pure reintegration, which allows us to consider the Segais spring as a fountain of youth. But as another Irish text says, it was "a secret spring located in the prairie of the *sidh* of Nechtan. Whoever went there did not return without their eyes bursting, none that is save Nechtan and his three cupbearers." The magical operation of rejuvenation and purification is therefore not within the ability of everyone, nor is it without danger.

The transcription continues:

> Once Boann went there out of pride, to experience the powers of the spring, and she said that there was no secret power that could touch the power of her beauty. She made a complete circle of the spring facing toward her left, three times. Three waves emerging from the spring broke over her. They took with them a thigh, a hand, and an eye. She turned toward the sea to flee her shame, and the water followed her to the mouth of the Boyne.[7]

It has been since this time that the Boyne River, to which Boann gave her name, has existed. Obviously the legend claims to explain mythologically the origin of the river, and this kind of procedure is quite common. But it seems that the transcriber or transcribers of the legend sought to emphasize Boann's guilt by presenting what happened as her well-deserved punishment. In reality, the story is the opposite. Boann dissolves into the waters, meaning that she reintegrates into her state of original purity. The meaning of the text is very clear: *Boann disappears as the White Cow* (Bo-Vinda). All that remains is for her to reappear under a new guise.

She had, in fact, fulfilled her mission, which was to give birth to Oengus, the "Young Son," "the One Choice." He is endowed with eternal youth. He is the image of the Being reborn, reclad in his "habit of light." To reach this point required a kind of sacrificial ritual symbolically described by the incest-adultery of the father and daughter,

---

7. Ibid.

then by Oengus taking possession of the Brugh. Oengus, having been conceived and birthed during the space of one day and one night, representing eternity, acquires possession of the world in the same symbolic space. Time, which is perpetual, is the son of Eternity, just as Being emerges from nonbeing and the finite from the Infinite. The myth of Oengus is constructed on the same outline as the Christian myth; while Dagda represents the unexpressed and unembodied, Mac Oc is expression and incarnation within time as experienced by its duration. This acknowledges Boann's essential role in this matter and subsequently justifies her disappearance in the river waters, a veritable dissolution that confirms her complete "virginity."

But given that the Virgin is immanence, she can and should reincarnate. The mythological tradition of the Gaels therefore shows her reappearing in other guises to fulfill the rest of her mission. Her features can be seen in Etaine, daughter of an Irish king, with whom Mider, the adoptive father of Oengus, is in love. In compliance with custom, it is Oengus who negotiates the "cession" of Etaine by her father to Mider. But this makes Oengus the guarantor and protector of Etaine. It so happens that Mider already has a wife, and she, out of jealousy, arranges through magic to rid herself of the young girl by transforming her into an insect. This insect is rescued by Oengus, who places it in a Chamber of the Sun, "in a room with gleaming windows" filled with "marvelous and aromatic herbs." This Chamber of the Sun, which figures in other Irish texts as well as in the French tale *Folie Tristan* (Tristan's Madness), is a kind of alchemical athanor inside of which the ripening of the Primal Material occurs.

Returned to a primitive state (an insect), the virgin Etaine must go through a series of metamorphoses. She will eventually be absorbed by the king's wife, who will thereby be made pregnant and give birth to a new Etaine, this time human and mortal. It is this second Etaine who will wed the king of Ireland, Eochaid, but who will be recaptured, at the end of a subtle game, by Mider, who will reintegrate her into his own divine and fairylike world. The circumstances are rather odd. Mider plays chess with King Eochaid. He begins by losing two matches and is forced to pay some painful stakes. He wins the third match after having duped his opponent as to the nature of the true stakes. In fact, he was demanding Etaine. Of course, Eochaid attempts to oppose this claim, but he no longer has any recourse, and Mider drags Etaine into the Other World in a veritable "assumption" that exempts her from having to pass through the stage of death.[8]

These events are characteristic of a sociocultural system that was far removed from the Christian mentality, which is why the manuscript transcribers deemed it wise to modify some of the assumptions in the final stories. The mythological scheme remains identical; the characters are the same; but the face of the Virgin is profoundly altered. Boann-Brigit would take on the name Eithne. She still belongs to the band of the Tuatha de Danaan—that is to say, the host of the gods—but she will escape from them. In the curious story entitled "The Food of the House of the Two Goblets,"[9] Christianity is at work in the background. Eithne is the daughter of the steward of Brugh and no longer a princess. She is still, however, the adoptive daughter of Oengus, who therefore finds himself again holding the mission he held in the pagan version, that of protecting the Virgin. Now, this Eithne was insulted by one of Oengus's brothers during one of his visits to the *sidh*, and since that time she had taken no food, contenting herself with drinking only the milk of a brown cow that came from elsewhere (and did not belong to the world of the Tuatha de Danaan).

The insult to Eithne had created a rift between her and her native race. She could no longer digest the food of the gods because she no longer belonged to their world. One day, after bathing with the women of the *sidh* in the waters of the Boyne, she discovered she

---

8. See the summary of this tale in Jean Markale, *Epics of Celtic Ireland* (Rochester, Vt.: Inner Traditions, 2001), 35–40. Translations of different versions of this legend can be found in Guyonvarc'h *Textes mythologiques irlandais,* 241–81.

9. Guyonvarc'h, *Textes mythologiques irlandais,* 257–66.

could no longer see the people of her race—although they could see her—but conversely she could see the hermitage of a Christian priest. This disciple of Saint Patrick instructed her in the faith of Christ. Oengus left no stone unturned in his efforts to bring back his adoptive daughter into the *sidh*. He did not succeed, even with the aid of the wise king Mananann (who plays the role of Mider here). Finally, Oengus engages in a magic duel with Saint Patrick, but the Christian's magic is stronger. Eithne becomes a Christian and receives baptism. It is the victory of the doctrine of Christ over that of the Druids.

Saint Patrick, the great evangelist of the Irish, was a native of the Isle of Britain. During his youth, he had been captured by the Gaels and became the slave of a Druid from whom, it seems, he learned the doctrine and magical practices. Having become a Christian determined to convert the Gaels, he was compelled to baptize and ordain priests from the leaders and the *fili,* who were the Druids of that time. His legend recounts amazing feats, notably his ability to convince most pagans to convert by engaging in magic combats with representatives of the Druidic class, from which he emerged victorious, thereby proving that the "magic" of Christ was superior to the magic of the Tuatha de Danaan. An example of this concerns Eithne, whom the Mac Oc could not dislodge from her Christian destiny although he used all his power as a magician. Taking into account the fact that Eithne is Boann, meaning Brigit, it is Patrick who wrests the Virgin from paganism. The two most honored saints in Ireland are Patrick and Brigitte of Kildare. Patrick is basically a former Druid turned Christian bishop, and Brigitte of Kildare is nothing other than the Christianized appearance of the ancient goddess. Everything falls into place as if a substitution had been made. The pagan Virgin became the Christian Virgin, but smoothly and causing no actual rupture; the continuity is absolute.

This maturation of the mythological legend and its end result in the framework of Christianity, even if it belongs to Irish tradition, is very revealing of the transformations that must have been at work in Gallic society. It provides a fairly good explanation for the transition from Druidism to Christianity in a Gaul that, although subject to Roman order, remained heir to the Celtic mentality. This is not a claim that the Virgin of Chartres is Boann, but that Brigit and Eithne are different guises of the same figure, the Divine Mother, she whom the people of all ages and religions have always viewed as the dispenser of life, hope, knowledge, and the universal love of beings and things, in some way the great Reconciler through whom the redemption of humanity will take place in a rediscovered unity.

It is futile to conduct an all-out search for the features the *statues* have in common. The worth of the image of Our Lady of Under Ground as described by the seventeenth-century historians can be measured only by what it expresses. Our Lady of the Pillar dates from the sixteenth century, but that is unimportant. She embodies the concrete appearance that the people of that time sought to give her. But through this concrete appearance, which undeniably bears the imprint of its time, she expresses a higher reality that is exactly as it was during the time of the Druids. Wouldn't the Virgin in the Window of the Blue Virgin (Notre-Dame de la Belle Verrière), which sits on the south side of the cathedral in a dazzling display of light, be another face of the Virgin that the Irish stories depict inside the Chamber of the Sun where Oengus placed Etaine, in her insect form, among the most aromatic flowers of the world? The symbolic images are only supports. The beauty of these supports is in no way harmful—quite the contrary, as beauty is the expression of the Divine. In one of the pagan versions of the Irish legend, Brigit-Etaine is granted the nickname Be Finn, meaning "beautiful woman." The Virgin of Chartres is incontestably the preeminent Beautiful Woman, and that has caused no complaints. Why wouldn't the Druids have rendered their own homage to the Beautiful Woman of times past, present, and future?

Though emphasizing the beauty of this Virgin of the origins, the Druids did not fail to join with it the idea of maternity. The child of the Virgin is handsome because he has been contained in beauty. A mysterious alchemy connects the "contained" to the "container." This is the theme of the Grail, a vessel more precious and beautiful than any other, which contains only that which is most precious and beautiful and from which a light emanates that is equally ineffable and ungraspable. In the Christian viewpoint, the Virgin Mary must be beautiful and precious because "the fruit of her womb is blessed." It is unimaginable even for a moment that Jesus, God made man, was born of a woman who was not beautiful. Boann, the mother of the Young Son, could be beautiful only because the Mac Oc—who is also, let me repeat, the "One Choice"—was a young god resplendent in all his beauty. And what does this "One Choice" mean? Is it not the implicit recognition that the incarnation of God into history is a *unique* fact, but, in addition, that it was voluntarily consented to by the Virgin—both pagan and Christian? "I am the Lord's servant," Mary answered Archangel Gabriel. Boann said the same thing to Dagda in the Irish story. So where is the difference? There is an amazing concordance between the Christian tradition and Celtic mythology. The Virgin of the Druids does not just foreshadow the Virgin of the Christians: They are one and the same.

A traditional Welsh tale, which is fairly late but little influenced by Christianity, goes even farther in this direction. It is a simple episode, inevitably truncated and mistreated, that was inserted into the older literary narrative concerning the fabled king Arthur, a text known under the title *Culhwch and Olwen,* which appears in a twelfth-century manuscript but displays archaic features that push its time of composition back to the seventh century, based on mythological outlines of a much earlier time.[10] The main figure of this episode is a certain Mabon, who is the so-called son of Modron. The name Mabon had appeared before on Gallo-Roman inscriptions in the Gallic form, Maponos. Meanwhile, Modron is the Welsh form of the Gallic Matrona (shared by Celts and Italians), which is in fact the name of the Marne River.

---

10. *Les Mabinogion*, trans. Joseph Loth (Paris: Les Presses d'Aujour'hui, 1979), 99–145.

To be sure, every time a Virgin is involved, there is water in close proximity, whether it is a spring, a fountain, a well, or a river. Boann dissolved into the Boyne. Eithne abandoned her "pagan" carapace in the same Boyne River. Our Lady of Under Ground is enthroned near the Well of the Saints-Forts, whose waters are miraculous. Our Lady of Lourdes appeared in a cave not far from the Gave, and a spring of healing waters gushes from the ground of that cave. Vivian, the last literary incarnation of Boann-Brigit, is a deity of fresh water and allegedly lives in a castle at the bottom of a lake, hence her name Lady of the Lake. Melusine, another face of this same divine entity, was encountered by Raimondin at the edge of a fountain; once a week, she goes into a cave by herself in her form as a "snake" to bathe in the purifying waters that emerge from the depths.

That said, the name Mabon means "son" and Modron, "mother." The episode in question says nothing about Modron. All we learn is that "Mabon, son of Modron, was stolen from his mother on the third night after his birth."[11] But the important thing in the context of this story is that the hero Culhwch, to succeed at his undertaking, which is to win the daughter of a dreadful giant-king, must obtain the assistance of Mabon. In the company of Arthur's knights, the hero therefore conducts an inquest to learn where Mabon might be found.

Here the tone ceases to be epic and becomes openly mythological, with archaic elements that denote a pre-Celtic origin. Thanks to one of Arthur's loyal retainers who knows all languages, even those of the animals (a detail indicating a shamanic influence), they successively question a blackbird, a stag, an owl, and an eagle (the obvious survival of some totemic structure). The eagle reveals that the only one who knows Mabon's location is a salmon. They interrogate the salmon (the very ancient Celtic theme of the Salmon of Knowledge), who offers to guide them, *underwater,* to a prison located beneath the town of Caer Lloyw (Gloucester), whose name

---

11. Ibid., 1977.

means City of Light. Mounted "on the shoulders of the salmon," two of Arthur's warriors then leave to free Mabon so that he can help the hero achieve his destiny. And the aid that Mabon could lend was not to be sneered at. He was the only person capable of taking possession of a wonderful object (in this instance, a comb) on the head of the ruinous wild boar Twrch Trwyth, an obvious symbol of the forces of darkness and destruction that Christian tradition crystallized under the name Satan.

So Mabon, the "Son" of the "Mother," has a prominent role to play: fight against darkness, chaos, and evil. The analogy with the Christian function of redemption is not at all dubious. A foreshadowing of Christ? Surely not, but it can be said that Mabon is the image of the young god who seeks to restore the balance of the world that has been temporarily disrupted and without which no universal harmony can exist. After all, this was the function of Attis in the matriarchal myth. But in these circumstances, Modron is comparable with Cybele; and her distinctive maternal function, which is so clearly emphasized by her name, makes her akin, whether one likes it or not, to the Virgin Mary.

In any event, this episode from the Welsh story, which is obscure and probably considerably abbreviated, can be illuminated by comparison with the original version of the legend of Lancelot of the Lake. This is the German version of *Lanzelat* by the Swiss Alemannic Ulrich von Zatzikhoven,[12] a version that owes nothing to Chrétien de Troyes's *Knight of the Cart,* and in which the hero is in no way Queen Guinivere's lover, also perfectly foreign to the Arthurian world. Lancelot, as in the common courtly version, is kid-

---

12. This early Lancelot is quite different from the one popularized by the common version of the legend. The origin of the German version is, by its author's own admission, a "French book," but a number of details proves that this "French book"—which is not the one written by Chrétien de Troyes—is the adaptation of an Armorican Breton folk tale. Furthermore, it is explicitly stated in all the versions that Lancelot is Armorican. I have published a summary of it, with large extracts from this text, in my *Tradition celtique en Bretagne armoricaine* (Paris: Payot, 1975), 22–26.

napped as a young child by a water fairy who drags him to the bottom of a lake and raises him in her marvelous palace. This fairy of the waters is obviously Vivian, the Lady of the Lake, a very romanticized image of the ancient Boann (her name comes from the same words, *bo-vinda*). But when the young boy reaches adulthood, the fairy refuses to tell him his name and origins until he has freed her own son, named Mabuz, held prisoner by the evil spells of a black magician. Of course, following many adventures, Lancelot frees Mabuz, and the Lady of the Lake reveals his name to him.

This story seems to demonstrate, in any event, that a hero cannot assume his true personality (his name)—that is to say, take his place in the social group—until he has achieved sufficient exploits. Among these exploits, the most important appears to have been the liberation of Mabuz, in whom it is obviously not difficult to recognize Mabon. This formally identified the Lady of the Lake with the Welsh Modron, therefore with the Gallic Matrona, the preeminent Mother Goddess, as well as with the White Cow of the Irish myth, in other words the triple Brigit—the Virgin of virgins, mistress of knowledge, poetry, and military triumph.

It would be easy to wax sarcastic about the deliberate intent of the Chartrian clergy, up until the eighteenth century, to push the Marian worship in their city back to the time of the Druids. It could in fact be claimed that these clergy meant to demonstrate the anteriority of their sanctuary and draw from that some very comprehensible advantages. It would be equally easy to be sarcastic about the naïveté of some people who discover a Gallo-Roman statue in a field and are entirely ready to recognize it as a representation of the Virgin Mary with the Infant Jesus. What then should we say about those bronze and gold crosses discovered in Bronze Age tombs that analysis shows were manufactured some two thousand years before the crucifixion?

To push back into the time of the Druids the erection of an image representing the *virgo paritura* is perhaps not entirely exact, but the claim that the Druids worshipped the Virgin about to give birth should not be surprising. The Celtic tradition has a wealth of mythological stories regarding a Virgin (without any physical connotations) who gives birth to a son who is a savior and a balancer. There is no question here of claiming that the Druids would have foreseen the future. They may well have been capable of it, but that is not the question. The presence in Celtic mythology of outlines concerning a privileged woman giving birth to a privileged child in circumstances that are always exceptional and colored by the marvelous necessarily shows that this notion existed long before Christianity in Druidic tradition, just as it existed in the majority of the religious traditions of humanity. There is nothing there that can stain the value of the Christian dogma, quite the contrary. There was a Virgin of the Druids. She was not named Mary, and she corresponded to criteria not shared by Christian society, but she was she in whom hope rested, she who held the divine Light—despite the appearance in Rouillard's *Parthénie* of a group of Druids prostrated before a cave in whose opening stood the *virgo paritura,* on a pedestal pompously named "altar of the Druids," and next to a mysterious well that reveals some yet undisclosed secret.

The cave and the well are connected to the worship of the Virgin. In Ephesus itself, the city where the worship of Artemis was so strong long before a single church was consecrated to Mary, mother of Jesus, a cave was worshipped that was believed to have held her body during her short "dormition" just before her triumphant Assumption. In Bethlehem, the Savior is supposed to have been born in a cave, and in Nazareth it is claimed that Mary received the angel of the Annunciation in a cave. This brings to mind what Saint Jerome wrote: "Bethlehem, that is now ours and the most august place in the world, was once shaded by the sacred grove of Tammuz [Adonis], and in the cave where the Infant Jesus wailed, the lover of Venus was once mourned." We cannot harbor any suspicions that Saint Jerome was nostalgic for paganism.

This means the hypothesis that for millennia Chartres was a cult site for the Virgin Mother is entirely plausible. The tenacious folk tradition that places a cave (or a dolmen) beneath the cathedral, the actual presence of a well once known as the Strong Well, the no less tenacious memory of a Virgin holding a child, and the historically proven fact that the great central sanctuary of Gaul was located in the land of the Carnutes together form an argument that is impossible to ignore, even if it cannot lead to an irrevocable conclusion. Chartres is a very likely site for a *nemeton,* that sacred clearing in the center of the forest of the Carnutes. Nor should it be forgotten that the Carnutes are the People of the Mound, those responsible for watching over the *sidh*—that is to say, over the Other World—symbolically localized in those large megalithic complexes the Celts were very familiar with and made into the dwellings of the gods and heroes of ancient times.

Certainly, all this represents a tradition, with its share of vagaries and doubts. But outside this tradition, Chartres clearly possessed something else: the permanence of the Marian cult, and first and foremost the *materialization* of this cult in a very real and very visible cathedral that defies time and space, with its two uneven towers, its nave curved harmoniously all the better to collect the echo of the songs of praise, and its forest of stone dispersed through the rays of light that spill in floods from the stained glass into the propitious shadow where Our Lady of Under Ground keeps watch. And this cathedral pours out. This *outpouring* is important because it provides the exact measurement of what it expresses.

What needs to be taken into consideration is not the *objects* but *what they represent.* A statue of Our Lady says nothing intrinsically; it is only an art object, or, if one prefers, an object of meditation that serves as a focal point for the fundamental impulses of human beings. This is the only justification for the practice of devotion to images that does not fall into what is commonly known as idolatry. It is therefore absurd to waste time determining whether this or that statue dates from this or that era. This is of some interest to historians or archaeologists, but it will be only a target for believers' scorn unless this image sketches the contours through which they will be able to enter their own appeal, their own quest.

The same is true for the sanctuaries. They are worth only what one cares to grant them—what the builders initially sought to give them, but what *others* have placed there out of their own awareness. It is obvious that the more the sanctuary or image actually attains beauty, the more the individual awareness will emerge magnified from the operation of contemplation, and, in the final analysis, prayer. The outpouring of the cathedral of Chartres, the light that inundates it, the darkness that lingers in its crypt, the form of the images that can be perceived there—all this, of course, was intended. But everything also responds to a demand, which may not be identical for each of those who are both the witnesses to and the actors in the spiritual—and aesthetic—drama that plays there. Perhaps it is this, in the final analysis, that is the sole possible definition of a cult: participation in a dramaturgy.

Now, this dramaturgy can be marked out perfectly not only in what can be called the Christian liturgy, but also in what is known about Druidism, on both the theoretical and the cultural planes. In the spirit that animates the Celts, all the gods are Druids and all the Druids are gods. But what gods? It does not seem that the religion practiced by the Celts was a true polytheism. The mythological narratives certainly recount astonishing stories about the gods; they can be seen taking action, fighting, getting intoxicated, and copulating. They can even be seen dying. But this anthropomorphic image is only a *literary narrative,* unless it still holds some concrete rituals that have been forgotten and preserved only in the oral tradition under an allegorical or symbolic form. According to the famous opinion of the Gaul Brennus, recorded by Diodorus Siculus, concerning the Delphi expedition, one can be sure that the Druids could not accept the representation of the gods in human form, which would have been contrary to their fundamental beliefs. "Brennus began to laugh because they assumed the gods had human form, and had crafted them in wood and stone" (Diodorus Siculus, fragment XXII). This destroys the hypothesis that the

Druids of the Carnute region would have erected a statue of the *virgo paritura* and shows their rejection of anthropomorphic depiction and the impossibility of assuming the gods had a human nature.

Analysis of texts of Celtic origin quickly reveals that the gods are physical representations of the social functions attributed to a single deity. The apparent polytheism of the Celts is in reality a monotheism, which would explain why they converted so easily to Christianity. When Patrick, the apostle to Ireland, came to preach the Gospel, he accompanied his preaching with magic "battles" against the Druids. Patrick, representative of God made into a man, possessed more power than the god or gods of Druidism. The Druids had a god that stood outside this relationship to function, Lugh, the Master of All the Arts. But according to Patrick's teaching, Jesus Christ, God made man, by virtue of this fact and in accordance with the Celtic concept, is the preeminent God Druid because he is finally manifested by his Incarnation, and his only possible action is to replace by himself all the gods, or at least all the divine functions. Celtic mythology highlights the existence of a primordial Druid. God incarnated in Christ, therefore, is this primordial Druid, in a world that, to the Celts, was necessarily commingled with the Druidic institution, as without it a Celtic society was impossible.

And if one concurs that a liturgy of any kind is a dramaturgy intended to attune humans with the Divine during an *action* that has no beginning or end, one can conclude that humans are participants in the divine work. This is what Christianity basically is teaching. It is likely the twenty-year course of study that the Druids imparted to their students in the heart of the forest. And if humans are invited to take part in the cosmic drama by the appropriate liturgies symbolizing the efficient actions each individual should undertake, it is because God, whatever he may be, "has need of men." This brings us to the following assertion: *God is not; God becomes.* But for this becoming to conform to this idea of God, it has to be eternal: hence an extraordinary dynamic inspired by rites and beliefs. Hence the celebration of worship outside in a clearing or on a mound. Nature is never absent from the cosmic drama. It is this dynamic enthusiasm, quite revealing of the Celts' religious thought, that we find exalted to its highest point in the cathedral of Chartres.

For this dynamic enthusiasm to manifest, it is necessary that the whole of creation be engaged in a unique process. If God is becoming, which seems to be the case in Celtic thought, the becoming should be achieved under the best conditions. This is where the Virgin on the threshold of giving birth steps in, because becoming involves *perpetual parturition,* one that matches to a surprising degree the words of Saint Paul on the creation at "work." The image of Our Lady is beautiful, not only for its aesthetic qualities, but primarily for what it means. Just what is the parturition it depicts? Is it the physical birth of a child, even if it is a Child-God? In that case, why would Our Lady of Under Ground have her eyes closed? She should be gazing with tenderness and love at her child, and also displaying her pride at having given birth to God. It involves something else entirely, a theological concept of great refinement: The Virgin is the perpetual parturient of a world in becoming, of a God in becoming, of a humanity in becoming. And humans, through their liturgies, take part in this dramaturgy that calls all into question, explains all, and justifies everything.

This is Chartres's message. It is first and foremost a message of Supreme Knowledge, which alone permits the launch into the future of a generating activity without which nothing can be accomplished. So it was a precise purpose that led the builders of Chartres Cathedral to cast toward the heavens those lines of force that emerge from the darkness of the "cave." The Strong Well connects the surface of the earth to the deepest and most mysterious cellar, that of the primordial waters over which the Spirit of God must breathe. But God can manifest in matter only by utilizing the ways of matter. This is what justifies the Virgin with the closed eyes.

When she finally opens her eyes, the world may well be the one that the prophets and Druids of ancient times discerned in the stars, a world that knows neither violence, nor hate, nor injustice, nor death. This may be the world of the Eternal Return, the one that the Virgin is patiently constructing in the depths of her sacred clearing, in the most secret recess of the Druidic forest, behind her mysterious eyelids, the supreme act that will make what is below as what is above.

"One can say that a performance of Wagner in Bayreuth is nothing much when compared to the celebration of High Mass in Chartres Cathedral." These words were spoken by Marcel Proust. They testify to the grandeur of this site, the absolute center of this world to come. It even tempts one to say that the great prophetic flights of *Parsifal* are nothing in the face of the prodigious outpouring bursting from the depths of the cavern where has lain for millennia the eternally creative image of the Virgin on the threshold of birth.

INDEX

290